DAUGHTERS OF CHIVALRY

DAUGHTERS

OF

CHIVALRY

THE FORGOTTEN PRINCESSES OF
KING EDWARD LONGSHANKS

KELCEY WILSON-LEE

PEGASUS BOOKS
NEW YORK LONDON

Daughters of Chivalry

Pegasus Books Ltd.
148 West 37th Street, 13th Floor
New York, NY 10018

Copyright © 2019 by Kelcey Wilson-Lee

First Pegasus Books hardcover edition October 2019

ISBN: 978-1-64313-194-8

10 9 8 7 6 5 4 3 2 1

Printed in the United States of America
Distributed by W. W. Norton & Company, Inc.

For my parents.

Contents

List of Illustrations

28. Horse-trapper embroidered with the royal arms of England (akg-images / Jean-Claude Varga)
29. Crown of Blanche of Lancaster (© Bayerische Schlösserverwaltung, Ulrich Pfeuffer / Maria Scherf, München)
30. The Bermondsey Mazer (On loan from St Mary Magdalen, Bermondsey © Victoria and Albert Museum, London)
31. Lady's gold seal (© The Trustees of the British Museum. All rights reserved)
32. View of Margaret's castle at Tervuren (By Sailko [CC BY 3.0 (https://creativecommons.org/licenses/by/3.0)], from Wikimedia Commons)
33. Funeral of a king (Ms 197 f.22v Funeral of a king, from Liber Regalis (vellum), English School, (14th century) / Museo de Navarra, Pamplona, Spain / Bridgeman Images)
34. Wedding of Edward II and Isabella of France (British Library, London, UK / © British Library Board. All Rights Reserved / Bridgeman Images)
35. The Nine Worthy Women (Thomas de Salluces, *Le chevalier errant* / Bibliothèque nationale de France)

Family Tree

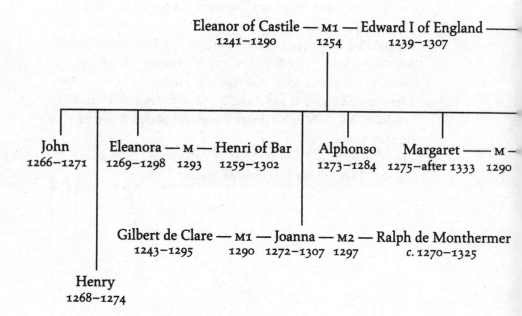

Eleanor of Castile — M1 — Edward I of England
1241–1290   1254   1239–1307

John   Eleanora — M — Henri of Bar   Alphonso   Margaret — M —
1266–1271   1269–1298   1293   1259–1302   1273–1284   1275–after 1333   1290

Gilbert de Clare — M1 — Joanna — M2 — Ralph de Monthermer
1243–1295   1290   1272–1307   1297   c. 1270–1325

Henry
1268–1274

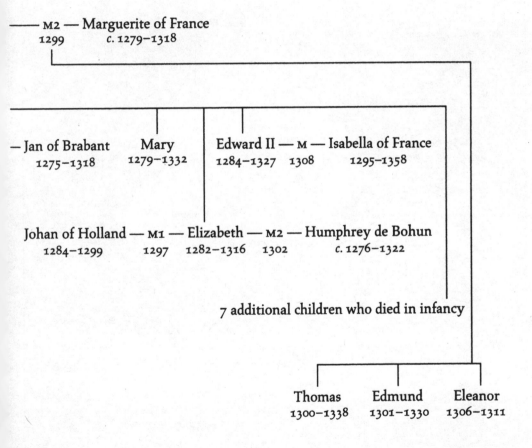

— M2 — Marguerite of France
1299   c. 1279–1318

— Jan of Brabant   Mary   Edward II — M — Isabella of France
   1275–1318   1279–1332   1284–1327   1308   1295–1358

Johan of Holland — M1 — Elizabeth — M2 — Humphrey de Bohun
   1284–1299   1297   1282–1316   1302   c. 1276–1322

7 additional children who died in infancy

Thomas   Edmund   Eleanor
1300–1338   1301–1330   1306–1311

ENGLAND, WALES, AND SCOTLAND, c. 1300

50 miles
80 kilometres

SCOTLAND

North Sea

Stirling
Dunfermline
Linlithgow

Caerlaverock

Tynemouth

Irish Sea

ISLE OF MAN

Knaresborough

ENGLAND

ANGLESEY

Rhuddlan
Caernarfon

Clipstone · Harby

Trent

Walsingham

PRINCIPALITY OF WALES

WELSH MARCHES

Severn

Wye

Tewkesbury
Goodrich
Winchcombe
Woodstock

Northampton

Cambridge · Bury St Edmunds

Clare
Ipswich

Harwich

Pleshey

Langley

Caerphilly

Bristol

Ludgershall
Glastonbury
Amesbury
Winchester

Thames
Windsor

London
Westminster

Guildford

Tonbridge

Dover

Winchelsea

Bristol Channel

ISLE OF WIGHT

English Channel

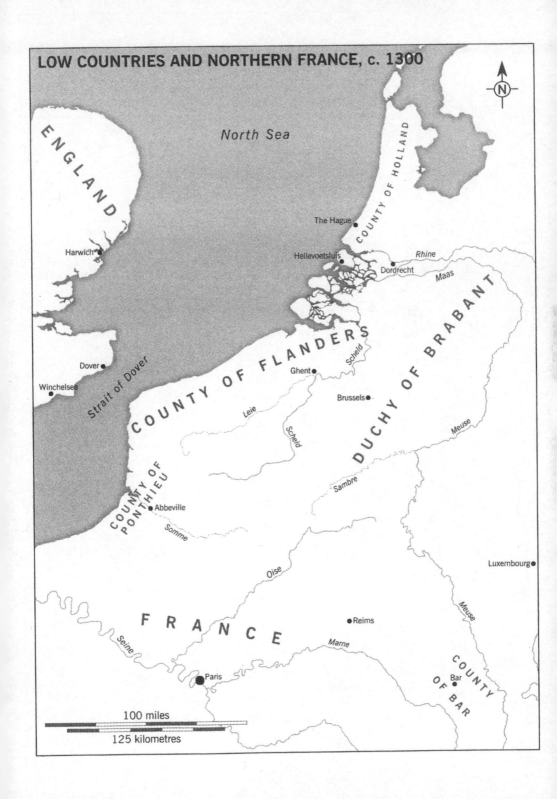

LOW COUNTRIES AND NORTHERN FRANCE, c. 1300

N

North Sea

ENGLAND

COUNTY OF HOLLAND

The Hague

Rhine

Hellevoetsluis

Harwich

Dordrecht

Maas

DUCHY OF BRABANT

Dover

COUNTY OF FLANDERS

Scheld

Winchelsea

Ghent

Strait of Dover

Brussels

Meuse

Leie

Scheld

COUNTY OF PONTHIEU

Sambre

Abbeville

Luxembourg

Somme

Oise

FRANCE

Reims

Seine

Marne

Meuse

COUNTY OF BAR

Bar

Paris

100 miles

125 kilometres

Introduction

Close your eyes and think of a medieval princess. Do you see a woman clothed in vibrant silks and rich velvets, her head, hands, and waist girdled with gleaming gold and sparkling gemstones? Is she sitting at a table creaking under the weight of exotic foods, with precious wines spilling from silver vessels onto fine linens, against a backdrop of tapestries woven with romantic heroes and heroines, or in a painted hall, heraldic banners fluttering behind proclaiming her royal status and connections? Or is she riding a magnificent horse through a forest with a hunt? Or travelling from one luxurious palace to the next in a decorated carriage, stopping to preside over jousting tournaments from raised pavilions or to add lustre to the dais at major feasts and festivals? Despite the richness of her surroundings, in your mind is she ultimately a mere pawn to be traded for the political gain of her father? Are her concerns confined to the beauty of the trinkets that surround her? Is she acquiescent, a person whom the most important things happen to or for, rather than an *actor* in her own right?

There is no doubt that stories of medieval princesses that have built an empire of fairy stories, Hollywood films, theme parks, and cheaply produced ball gowns, all offer a vision of maidenhood focused on passive virtue. Medieval castles promote visits to 'princess towers', reinforcing the link between royal women in history and their powerless fictional counterparts, locked inside or frozen in deathless sleep, condemned simply to wait – their eventual reward, marriage to a male saviour. It is a vision that real medieval princesses would not have recognized in their lives.

Between the end of the Middle Ages (which, depending on whom you ask, occurred in England in the quarter century or so before or after 1500) and the mid-nineteenth century, no one cared much about princesses. History was the preserve of Great Men: kings and bishops, conquerors and tyrants. And even the popular fictional heroines from the dawn of the novel – Fanny Burney's Evelina, Thackeray's Becky Sharp, or Austen's many wonderful women – were isolated from power, confined to the lower rungs of the county gentry or the middle classes. Then, in 1837, an eighteen-year-old girl raised in England became Queen Regnant, the first woman to rule her country since Queen Anne's reign, more than one-hundred-and-twenty years earlier. The countless ways in which Victoria and her long reign shaped Britain, its society, and ultimately its empire have long captured public imagination. How her rule and the lives of her five princess daughters prompted a popular interest in royal women is also of immense significance. The first volume in a pioneering study of medieval women, *Lives of the Queens of England*, was published three years after Victoria came to the throne, written by Agnes Strickland, a poet who undertook research in partnership with her sister, Elizabeth. In the decade that followed, the historian Mary Anne Everett Green published *Letters of Royal and Illustrious Ladies of Great Britain* that for the first time gave a voice to medieval and early modern noblewomen. Her subsequent six-volume masterpiece *Lives of the Princesses of England, from the Norman Conquest* used her command of Latin and medieval French, and her access to original manuscripts, letters, and charters, to construct short biographies of every princess between the reigns of William the Conqueror and Victoria. It remains one of the outstanding achievements of nineteenth-century biography.

Across Europe at this time, as nations emerged from the Industrial Revolution, many of them developed an increasingly romanticized interest in their own histories and native mythologies, seeking connection to a pastoral, pre-industrialized past. In England, this led not only to a widespread interest in the lives of long-dead queens and princesses, but also in other aspects of the Middle Ages. Art and architecture began to feature distinctly medieval elements, such as the Gothic Revival Palace of Westminster and literary works such as Alfred Lord Tennyson's poem *Idylls of the King*, which converted the ancient myth of King Arthur and his court at Camelot into a national epic. And paintings and stained glass panels by the artists known as the Pre-Raphaelite Brotherhood and their followers depicted scenes from medieval romances and folktales – Guinevere and the Lady of the Lake, 'Fair Rosamund', and Isolde – that brought these old stories to new audiences that were hungry to understand what set England apart from other nations.

The romanticizing tendency of – mostly male – Victorian historians made it easy for genuine historical figures such as 'Fair Rosamund' Clifford and the royal women that Strickland and Green wrote about to be melded in popular imagination alongside fictional heroines. Together with the Guineveres and Isoldes of medieval romance, the passive princesses of the fairy tales compiled by the German brothers Jacob and Wilhelm Grimm – whose works were translated into nineteen separate English editions during Victoria's reign – became so well known that they created an expectation that real princesses would conform to these models. It was a pattern perfectly constructed for the burgeoning Victorian middle class, for whom a wife kept at home, safe from the tawdry bustle of the city and the labour market, was a mark of success; they took these newly idealized visions of princesses found in poems and artworks – acquiescent, serene beauties – and held them up as prime examples of womanhood.

In many ways, we have failed to move on from the vision of the medieval past that we inherited from the Victorian era. Most of us, when we hear the word 'princess', still imagine a damsel trapped in a tower like the eponymous heroine of Tennyson's 'Lady of Shalott'. Loosely based on the medieval Arthurian tale of Elaine of Astolat, Tennyson's maiden lives 'full royally apparelled', sleeping on a velvet bed with a garland of pearls encircling her head. Despite the luxury of her chamber, all is not well: she lives alone in a tower encircled by a fence of thorny roses and, though the people passing hear her 'chanting cheerly / Like an angel, singing clearly', they never visit. Inside the tower, the Lady is entranced; forbidden by an unspoken curse from looking directly at the beauty of the world and Camelot, she must instead continually weave a tapestry depicting its glory through the dimmed reflection of a mirror. Finally, one day, Sir Lancelot rides by, his armour and horse trappings glittering in the bright sunlight 'like one burning flame', a 'meteor, trailing light'. Overcome by the sight of his 'coal-black curls', the Lady escapes her tower and sets out in a boat towards Camelot, determined to find her knight. But the nameless curse cannot be evaded, and by the time her boat reaches the city she is no more than a beautiful corpse, which means that her virginity – first signalled by the roses that guarded her bower – has remained intact, despite her evident desire for Lancelot. The lesson is simple: it was the Lady's rejection of the boundaries that had been set for her that spelled her doom. Her action could not go unpunished. Dozens of paintings of the Lady of Shalott (and the inspiration for her, Elaine of Astolat) survive from the late nineteenth century; she represented a perfect tragic heroine for the Victorians. Shades of her story are also present in the fairy tales of princesses that have come down to us from the Brothers Grimm: Rapunzel, trapped in a tower; Snow White, prized for her purity; and Sleeping Beauty, preserved beautifully in sleep.

While Tennyson's Lady was inspired by real medieval romances, his telling of her tale was a very partial vision of the past, selected to suit the tastes of the world that popularized it. Other female icons of the Middle Ages were considerably more active in the ways in which they sought to control their lives, and at the time many were praised for it. There were the virgin-martyrs, many of whom were thought to be scholarly princesses – Agatha, Katherine, Margaret, and Lucy – who fearlessly defied their fathers, and even kings, who sought to control their bodies and minds. Though stories from these saints' lives are largely fictitious, they were held aloft in the medieval period as exemplars for young noblewomen. Highly sympathetic portrayals of secular women living outside the strictures of conventional morality also abounded in romantic fiction and courtly poetry – famous heroines such as Guinevere and Isolde who threw caution to the wind engaging in forbidden affairs, as well as lesser-known maidens and princesses who married virtuous-but-poor knights, enriching and empowering them through their love. For noblewomen, there were also numerous historic examples of powerful queens and formidable and cunning consorts, such as Eleanor of Aquitaine and Blanche of Castile, whose own considerable contributions to medieval culture and history have only recently begun to receive the attention they deserve.

These medieval narratives have largely been forgotten because they did not fit with the values of the intervening age. The women who grew up surrounded by the original narratives were not normally even referred to as 'princesses' until the sixteenth century, but rather 'ladies' or 'daughters of the king' – and they had a much more fluid relationship with power, influence, and action than it suited most Victorian storytellers to recall. Undeniably, their world was brutally patriarchal, and the odds were stacked against any woman who wanted to exercise autonomy, even among the most privileged. Contemporary society divided itself into those who were labourers, priests, and warriors, seemingly leaving noblewomen without any social role to play. It was a world in which the doers were overwhelmingly male. But feudalism – the medieval governing system by which land was ultimately owned by lords, with the use of it offered out for services rendered to them by vassals – necessitated a rigid social hierarchy. For women from the social elite, there was the chance that their status could trump their gender. The most successful among them learned to work within or even use the cultural frameworks of feudalism and chivalry – the social and moral code that governed the behaviour of aristocrats – to achieve considerable influence at the courts of their fathers, brothers, and husbands.

Indeed, it might surprise readers to learn that the medieval princess may have been more than the finely dressed ornament of popular imagination. She might have been a commander of castle garrisons under attack from hostile forces, and a seasoned war traveller. She might have been a diplomat savvy at negotiating international trade agreements, a specialist at using soft power to avert the threat of military confrontation. She may have wielded absolute power over vast estates, scandalized court by secretly marrying an unknown paramour, or disrupted the vows of other unions. Through her patronage of literature and music, her role as a devoted mother and educator to her children, and her own scholarship, she might have helped shape the age in which she lived. And through the cunning manipulation of powerful men and cultural conventions, she may have gained significant power and freedoms to forge her own path in life.

What follows is the story of five medieval princesses, sisters who used their connections and their knowledge of courtly culture to gain and wield considerable power and influence. History has until now utterly overlooked these women and the part they played in shaping England's story. And yet, far from being the passive maidens of fiction, these real-life princesses sought active participation in their own destinies, cultivating authority and deploying financial and political resources to achieve their aims. Occasionally they even defied their father the king, but more commonly they used the power and resources that they were able to muster to promote the interests of England and their family. In so doing, they affirmed their allegiance to their kingly father or brother, whose connection guaranteed their exceptional lives. But through their promotion of English interests, the sisters also stuck a claim that they were playing an important role in the family business, a business to which they would devote their lives, and a role which required them to have privileged access to decision-making. Despite or perhaps because of their wilful personalities and bold actions, they maintained their influence at court for as long as the king held power.

In the middle of November 1272, Henry III, king of England for fifty-six years, died after a long illness. His eldest son, Edward, succeeded him immediately, though he was not crowned until 1274. Two years before his father's death, Edward and his Castilian wife Eleanor had sailed from England to join a united European army led by King Louis IX of France (Edward's uncle), bound on Crusade. Their three small children, four-year-old John, two-year-old Henry, and the infant princess Eleanora, were left back in England. The children lived in a small household, first under the guardianship of their father's respected and powerful uncle, Richard, Earl of Cornwall and, after his death, under the protection of their queenly grandmother, Eleanor of Provence.

Their years abroad did not bring the success Edward had hoped for. Most of the Crusade's leaders, including his kingly French uncle, died before arriving in the Holy Land, and the army was thus too small to stand a chance at re-establishing a Christian kingdom of Jerusalem. Either way, with the responsibility of kingship thrust upon him by his father's death, Edward was forced to return home. However, of their three children, only six-year-old Henry and his five-year-old sister Eleanora awaited their parents on shore when the royal fleet docked at Dover late in the summer of 1274; John, their eldest son and heir, had died two years previously.

The queen had given birth to three more children during their years away, two of whom survived. There was a daughter three years younger than Eleanora: Joanna, called 'of Acre' in recognition of her birth at the port city that was the only surviving vestige of a Christian kingdom in the Holy Land, and also a son, Alphonso, named in honour of his Castilian grandfather. Born in Gascony during the homeward journey, Alphonso was only eight months old when he arrived in England with his parents. His sister Joanna had been left in the care of her maternal grandmother, Jeanne de Dammartin, dowager queen of Castile. Queen Jeanne, who now lived as a widow in the northern French county of Ponthieu, which she held by her own right, persuaded her homeward-bound crusader daughter to leave the toddler princess with her for company. Alone of her siblings, therefore, Joanna's earliest memories were of France rather than England, and her unique early experiences abroad may account for some of the exceptional independence that she would demonstrate in later life.

This is the forgotten story of Eleanora and Joanna, and of their three sisters who would be born after their father became king – Margaret, Mary, and Elizabeth. Thirteen years separated the births of the eldest and youngest royal daughters – an age gap that ensured the women had distinct experiences and that the relationships that forged their adult personalities and priorities were distinct. What they shared with each other and their brothers were the ways in which their childhoods and – to a remarkable extent – their adult lives were shaped by their father's ambition to build an empire. This is a chronicle of the high Middle Ages with a difference: it is the story of what happened just off-centre from the king around whom court coalesced, among his own children; the story of how these royal women lived and learned how to have an impact on their world; the story of five real princesses in the age of chivalry. And, like all chronicles of a reign, it begins with a coronation.[1]

I

Coronation

1274

LONDON, GUILDFORD

The capital was adorned like Camelot, with yards of cloth
billowing down and providing splashes of riotous colour
against the grime of ancient buildings. A fanfare welcomed
Edward I, known as 'Longshanks' for his great height, and his
wife, the Castilian princess Eleanor, as they triumphantly
entered London for their coronation. The date was 18 August
1274. Edward and Eleanor had been abroad on Crusade for four
years, and their arrival in London was the culmination of a
grand, sixteen-day ceremonial progression inland from their
landing site at Dover. According to the chronicler Thomas
Wykes, 'neither tongue nor pen would suffice to describe the
ornament of the city and its citizens, arrayed without regard
for expenditure in honour of the king's majesty'. Through the
tangle of narrow city streets, the king and his entourage wound

slowly westwards, maximizing their visibility to the throngs of Londoners who were seeking a glimpse of their new monarch. The parade ended at the royal palace at Westminster to the west of the city, before the great abbey church, which had been rebuilt at tremendous expense in the fashionable French Gothic style by Edward's father, and where Edward and Eleanor were to be crowned the following day. More than a generation had passed since the last coronation – of Edward's mother Eleanor of Provence, in 1236 – and the crowning of the returning crusader king promised to be a joyous spectacle.[1]

The preparations for the coronation had begun the previous winter. Kitchens had been erected on the outskirts of the sprawling palace to prepare a coronation feast for thousands. Across the country, orders were placed for provisions, with sheriffs from twelve counties charged with supplying extraordinary numbers of animals for the roast meats. Over twenty thousand capons and hens, five hundred oxen and the same number of sheep and swine for roasting on the day were sought from as far away as Somerset and Gloucestershire, while over three hundred bacon pigs had already been required at Windsor by Easter for slaughter and salting. Bishops, abbots, and priors throughout England were required to provide as many swans, peacocks, cranes, rabbits, and kid goats as they could capture from their estates. Immense quantities of fish, including lampreys, eels, pike, and salmon, were also secured: special laws were brought in to keep prices down for the king's buyers by explicitly forbidding fishmongers from buying stock in bulk in an effort to profit from the exceptional demand. Alongside these provisions, new stables and lodges – many of them temporary constructions – were built to house the hundreds of knights who would journey to see their new king crowned.[2]

The pageant reached its climax the following day, the Sunday after the Feast of the Assumption of the Blessed Virgin, when the young royal couple walked from Westminster Palace to the abbey through a newly erected covered walkway that criss-crossed the square separating the two. In London, the conduit at Cheapside, which normally channelled fresh water into the city, ran with wine to slake the thirst of revellers on the hot summer day. Back at Westminster, amid the fluttering heraldic banners and golden robes that glinted in the sun, tensions ran high as leading nobles and churchmen clashed over the rights to perform ceremonial roles in the coronation. The king's own brother Edmund – known as Crouchback, or 'crossed-back', for his participation in the Crusade, an activity already commonly associated with knights wearing cross-embroidered tunics – seems to have either boycotted the ceremony itself or been prohibited from attending, after he was refused the right he claimed to carry *Curtana*, the great sword of state said to have belonged to the legendary hero Tristan. Instead, the sword was carried before the king by one of his most troublesome subjects (and his future son-in-law), Gilbert, the Earl of Gloucester. The Archbishop of York was also aggrieved. His request to preside at the coronation had been denied, as punishment for the indiscretion of publicly carrying his archiepiscopal crozier, or staff of office, outside of his own province – a clear and deliberate attempt to claim precedence over his rival the Archbishop of Canterbury, who conducted the ceremony alone.[3]

Waiting for the new young king inside the abbey were the retinues of the chief lords of his realm, his mother the dowager queen Eleanor of Provence, and his two sisters, Margaret and Beatrice, along with their husbands, the King of Scotland and the Duke of Brittany. Before this assembly, Edward spoke the traditional vows sworn by all English kings and added one of his own: to restore royal authority to what it had been prior to the wars that had blighted his father's reign. His reign would consciously hark back to heroic kings of the past – to Richard the Lionheart, to King Arthur, even to the legendary biblical heroes of the Old Testament – and from its beginning, Edward was intent on projecting greatness. He wore robes of rich silk and, by his side, Eleanor shone with jewels as she was crowned queen. They emerged anointed with chrism – the perfumed holy oil used for consecrating buildings, ordaining priests, and crowning monarchs. During the feast that followed, the King of Scotland and six of the leading English earls presented themselves to Edward on horseback, each with as many as one hundred knights, before each dismounted and set his horse free, a prize for anyone bold enough to catch it. Though this account was likely embellished in the telling, such a flamboyant gesture is illustrative both of the extravagance of the coronation itself and of the important role that chivalric motifs – here, *largesse*, or noble generosity – played in presenting a new king to his subjects.[4]

Three small children were also present at the celebrations, clothed in new robes made especially for the occasion: the new king's eldest children, Henry and Eleanora, and their cousin, John, a younger son of the Duke of Brittany. Nothing is recorded of their experience of this theatre of chivalry. Had they been older, they might have been able to absorb lessons about public display and the performance of regality, but the dizzying spectacle of such an immense gathering and the excitement of close proximity to their usually distant parents must have been overwhelming, and rather exhausting, for children between the ages of five and seven. They were accustomed to living relatively quietly, travelling regularly between royal residences at Guildford, Kempton, and Windsor, with a household consisting of their nurses, some orphaned noble children who lived under the guardianship of the king, and roughly two dozen servants – tailors, cooks, stewards, and pages.

After the coronation, however, they did not remain at court to become better acquainted with their parents, returning instead to live with their grandmother at her dower house that abutted the walls of Guildford Castle. Rebuilt and enlarged following a fire fifteen years before, the complex there was ideally suited to house the royal nursery. Separate chamber blocks had been built off its central aisled hall, not only for the old king and queen but also for Edward and his young bride. This latter suite of rooms – warmed by fireplaces and wainscoting, lit by large glass windows, and painted green and white throughout – probably housed young Henry and Eleanora. Here the royal children were indulged with sweets made from sugars flavoured with rose and violet, with exotic foods such as pomegranates, quinces, prized *cailowe* pears, and almonds – a favourite of Eleanora, for whom they were often specially purchased – and with unusual spices including sandalwood and peony seeds. Regular orders were made for milk, but also for beer and 'new wine', for the children and their nurses to drink, as water was not considered safe for drinking. They were kept warm in winter with furred robes fastened with silver buttons and silken cords, caps trimmed with peacock feathers, and gloves that bore the arms of England sewn into the thumb. But alongside this luxury, the children were also educated in the special perils faced by the rich: a prominent mural in the hall at Guildford illustrated the parable of Dives and Lazarus, in which the wealthy Dives is condemned to hell for refusing to give charity to the poor.[5]

On their return to Guildford after the coronation, the children no doubt expected to fall back into their usual habits, perhaps with the addition of regular visits to their parents in London.

But after only a few weeks, young Henry fell ill. Despite the superior diet that saw the children of the aristocracy grow taller than many of their undernourished base-born contemporaries, medieval medicine offered few proven treatments for acute or recurring illness, and roughly one-third of noble children died before their fifth birthdays. It seems that boys were in slightly more danger than girls (though whether this was because they were more prone to sickness or to injury in the hazard-strewn interiors and landscape of medieval England is unclear). Contemporary belief certainly held that boys were particularly in danger of sickness, as evidenced by the comment attributed to the eleven-year-old Henry III – 'I am a boy and thus easily fall ill'. Edward and Eleanor's first son, John, had died aged five three years earlier, while their parents were still on Crusade. But young girls could also be in danger: his older sisters, Katherine and Joan, had died even younger.[6]

Little Henry seems to have always been sickly. Frequent references in the surviving children's household accounts confirm that medicines (most particularly *diaboriginat*, which was probably a medicinal draught made from the herb borage) were purchased on his behalf, and that the boy was frequently measured so that candles the same height as him could be offered at prominent shrines to win the goodwill of saints and priests who might pray for his good health. The autumn before his parents' return from Crusade, a group of three holy widows had been paid to pray in vigil for the prince; now, as his condition worsened, thirteen such women were retained for the same purpose, while two royal physicians were summoned to treat the sickly child, who died towards the end of October 1274. But, though the king and queen were only a short distance away from their dying son's bedside, they did not travel to Guildford. Perhaps they expected the boy to rally once again, or perhaps they did not wish to disturb the calm intimacy of his final days with the disruption that would unavoidably accompany a royal visit.

Henry's body was transferred to Westminster to be interred alongside his older siblings, but his heart was removed before his body left Guildford and was buried locally in the Franciscan priory that his grieving grandmother had established to house it. This was common practice among the English aristocracy at the time – burying a part of the body at multiple sites ensured that more than one set of clerics would then pray for the deceased's soul. Henry though, was the first of his siblings to be memorialized in this way, which was perhaps evidence of the especially close relationship the dowager queen had developed with her grandchildren. Despite this, Eleanora and her cousin John did not remain at Guildford after Henry's death. Instead, their household was reorganized around her infant brother, Alphonso, not yet a year old and now heir to the English throne.

As a royal daughter in the thirteenth century, Eleanora would not have expected to inherit her father's kingdom; even if Alphonso followed their other siblings to an early grave, there would probably be other brothers. By the time of Edward's accession, the right of primogeniture – the system of inheritance that would govern the descent of noble estates in England until the late twentieth century – was becoming formally established. Under this system, the entirety of a man's estate at his death passed intact to his eldest surviving son without the option to share it between multiple surviving sons. Primogeniture is not the most advantageous system for descendants as a group, since the majority will be utterly excluded from inheritance. It is, however, advantageous to rulers, who can focus their energy on a small number of lords leading great estates rather than on a larger body of lesser nobles that becomes larger and poorer with each successive generation. Primogeniture was not native to England: prior to the Norman Conquest, an estate was commonly divided between the landowner's sons or was held in a form of joint ownership by them, without preference for the eldest. But, in the centuries after the Conquest, feudalism tied land owner- ship ever more closely to military service conducted on behalf of a lord, and partitioning estates became increasingly problem- atic: when a lord died, someone had to take his place within the king's army, requiring an expensive warhorse, armour and weap- onry, and years of training. Should his estate be divided, none of his sons might have the means to afford these knightly trappings. As a result, over time, repeatedly dividing estates would impede the ability of the king to mount an army. The Norman kings of England favoured primogeniture, and they were strong enough rulers to force the practice on their new subjects.

For women, however, the new system was not markedly different from what had come before. Domesday Book makes reference to a small number of women who held land directly from the king, implying limited instances of female landowner- ship under the Anglo-Saxons. But, in practice, women in Anglo-Saxon England inherited only when they had no living brothers. Where women did inherit, estates were commonly divided equally among sisters and – unlike in France, say, where Salic law excluded women from inheriting at all – this continued in Edward's reign, and beyond.

The celebrations that had long accompanied the birth of a male heir were heightened after the adoption of primogeniture, because the arrival of a healthy boy ensured stability for the estate in the next generation. When the citizens of London reconciled with Henry III in July 1266, following their support for Simon de Montfort during the baronial revolt of the preceding years, they marked the occasion by declaring a holiday and organizing a procession in honour of the birth of the king's first grandson and heir: Eleanora's oldest brother, John. Birth notices for first-born sons of the king are common in chronicle sources that often overlooked the arrival of younger princes and princesses. Thus, for example, the Winchester annalist recorded the 1266 birth and 1271 death of Prince John, but was silent on the short lives of the prince's elder sisters or younger brother, whose births did not offer the same promises of stable succession. Messengers bringing news of the successful birth of a son were often better rewarded than those bringing news of the safe delivery of daughters: King Edward, for instance, would later give forty marks to the messenger who brought him the news of a grandson (the son of his daughter Joanna), some eight times the amount he gave the messenger who brought news of a granddaughter. The status of noblewomen was also often elevated by the successful delivery of a healthy boy, as Eleanor of Castile learned following the birth of her second son, when her household was granted the same Christmas robes as her mother-in-law, the queen.[7]

The extra excitement surrounding the births of princes was hardly surprising: the birth of a prince in medieval England was of prime importance not only to his parents, but to the nation. If female heirs were considered problematic under primogeniture – often dividing estates and, almost without exception, transferring lands permanently to another family – then leaving a female heir to a kingdom in the absence of sons could lead to civil war. Only one woman during the medieval period tried to succeed her father to the crown of England: Matilda, widow of the Holy Roman Emperor, wife of the Count of Anjou, and the only surviving child of Henry I. In addition to Matilda, Henry had one legitimate son – the pampered William Adelin – as well as nearly two dozen illegitimate children. But William drowned, along with two of his half-siblings, when the fastest vessel in the king's fleet, the White Ship, foundered after crashing into rocks on the way back to England from Normandy. A possible cause of the accident was that the crew and most of the passengers had been drinking heavily, and pressured the captain to attempt to overtake the king's own ship that had set out from Barfleur hours earlier. In the aftermath of the tragedy, the ageing king married again, to the eighteen-year-old daughter of a Low Countries count, but though the pair were constantly together, no children were forthcoming, and Henry recalled his daughter, Matilda, to England. At Christmas in 1126, the king asked his leading nobles to pledge their support for Matilda's succession. When her cousin Stephen of Blois seized the throne in the immediate aftermath of the king's death, Matilda's adherents declared war. But, even after capturing Stephen, Matilda was never crowned; she was chased away from a planned coronation at Westminster Abbey by a crowd of angry Londoners who were loyal to Stephen. The lengthy power struggle between the rivals is remembered, tellingly, as The Anarchy. Even after Stephen's death Matilda was unable to claim the throne for herself, merely becoming the conduit through which it passed to her son, Henry II.

As the daughter of a king who had been constantly at war, Eleanora would have known intuitively that women who sought to rule were heavily disadvantaged in a society which still required its kings to be warriors, ready to defend their position on the battlefield, clad in heavy chain-mail, and wielding a sword. This was not a hypothetical requirement, but a very practical one. During the baronial revolt of the 1260s, Eleanora's grandfather Henry III had been captured on the field at the Battle of Lewes and forced into a settlement with his enemies that effectively ceded control of the kingdom and offered his heir Prince Edward as a hostage. Edward had fled his jailors in a daring escape – while out hunting under the watch of a guard, he had teasingly tested how fast each horse could ride before mounting the only fresh steed, digging in his heels and absconding into the forest. The prince out-rode his pursuers' tired horses and was soon leading an army that succeeded in defeating – and killing – Simon de Montfort and the other rebel barons, restoring royal power.

Another disadvantage faced by a medieval woman seeking to rule as sovereign queen – a challenge she would have shared with Tudor queens like Elizabeth I – was the common perception that her marriage would automatically make her husband King of England and force a potentially explosive shift in the country's power structures. Married women were legally forbidden to own land: any estates held by an heiress passed to her husband on their marriage and were from then on entirely under his command. Throughout Matilda's bid for the crown, she insisted that she acted as a *feme sole*, a 'woman acting alone', but this did not allay the fear that her husband Geoffrey might seek to exploit his proximity to the throne for the benefit of his own realm, the great county of Anjou, or even to become the true power behind the throne.

Henry III, capitalizing on similar fears that England might be lost to foreign rule, imprisoned his cousin Eleanor of Brittany, his only serious potential rival to the throne, for her entire adult life. Her brother Arthur had almost certainly been murdered by King John, Henry's father, because he and his sister had a stronger claim to the throne, being the children of John's older brother. Eleanor escaped her brother's fate, but could never be free. As a child, she had been betrothed to a French prince, who on marrying her might have claimed the right to rule England.

Instead, she was kept under close guard in apartments at royal castles throughout the country, comfortable but secure from rescue by her loyal supporters or her French fiancé.

Henry's granddaughter Eleanora knew, therefore, that she had little hope of becoming a ruling Queen of England. Her infant brother Alphonso would grow up to be a warrior and she would not; his marriage would bring lands and money into the English royal estate, while hers would take them from it. She might have been her father's eldest child – his *primogenita* – but she was not his heir. She remained, however, heir to Alphonso, the mewling baby who was now the focus of her own household, and she had the strong advantage over him of having already lived through the most dangerous early years of life. In the years that followed, Eleanora spent her time getting to know the parents who had been gone so long, and learning about their plans for her future.

II
Betrothal

1278–82

GLASTONBURY, GUILDFORD

Daylight was fading on the Tuesday following Easter in 1278, while eight-year-old Eleanora, her parents, and a group of monks, looked on as stone slabs were moved aside from the floor of the Lady Chapel in the great abbey church at Glastonbury. Soon the only light was that which flickered from candles, glinting off the gilded moons and sunbursts painted on the chapel walls, casting shadows deep into recesses from where sculpted figures watched silently over the scene. Slowly, two coffins decorated with heraldic images came into view. Once the earth that had covered them had been cleared, the lids of the coffins were pried open, revealing, in one, a crowned skeleton described as 'beautiful' by one of the monks present, the chronicler Adam of Damerham. In the other coffin were the bones of a very tall man, whose death wound on the left side of his skull remained visible, near the crown that had slid off his head after burial. In the dying light, another tall man, who might well have felt a sense of connection to the bones which had been thus disturbed, stood over the coffins: Edward, King of England, was looking at the remains of his greatest predecessor, King Arthur, and his queen, Guinevere.

Eleanora's father was in the middle of his first campaign to conquer Wales, and was beginning to recognize that stories of the fabled king might be used to support his own ambition to rule over all of Britain. Edward's interest in Arthur may have begun while he was away during the Crusades, when he commissioned the romance *Meliadus* about the hero Tristan's father, from Rustichello da Pisa, an Italian writer best known for co-authoring Marco Polo's *Travels*. The Arthurian legend was perfectly constructed for chivalric society, a 'magic mirror' in which the historical past was enriched by sorcery, softened by contemporary religious piety, and populated by virtuous warriors, against a backdrop of imperial majesty. Edward and Queen Eleanor had travelled with their daughter to Glastonbury, a place which blended in the imagination throughout the medieval period with the mysterious Isle of Avalon, where Arthur was conveyed after being mortally wounded in battle. They were there to see the bodies that had been discovered in the churchyard almost a century before, and which had been reburied in the Lady Chapel, the only structure that survived the disastrous fire that swept away the old church and monastic buildings in 1184. By the 1270s, restoration work on the church had progressed to the point where a new vaulted choir in the Gothic style was nearly complete, and, as King Edward gazed on these almost holy relics of British kingship, he determined that they would not simply be reinterred as they had been found. The following day, therefore, with great ceremony, Edward and

Eleanor wrapped the ancient monarchs' bones in precious burial cloths and replaced them inside their coffins, which were sealed with molten lead to protect the bones from grave robbers and reburied before the high altar, the most prestigious burial site in the church and a site usually reserved for the shrines of saints.

The entire sequence was a piece of extraordinary theatricality – from the original 'discovery' of the grave in the churchyard (at a time when the abbey most desperately needed income from a thriving pilgrimage trade) to the carefully concocted heraldic devices that decorated the 'ancient' coffins (even though such devices only came into use in the twelfth century). Someone, almost certainly the monks of Glastonbury Abbey, aimed to provide physical evidence for what had previously only been a local legend, turning the increasingly popular Arthurian stories into a reliable income stream that would support the abbey's rebuilding works. It cannot be known whether Edward and Eleanor, or their daughter Eleanora, were in on the ruse. But the royal couple embraced the opportunity to write themselves into the story of Arthur and his glittering court, and at this and other occasions later that year, their eldest daughter had many opportunities to witness and practise the solemnity with which her parents carried out these ritual performances, thus forging her understanding of the role that majesty and memory might play in legitimizing power.

By the spring of 1278, Eleanora, then eight years old, had left the royal nursery. Her brother Alphonso was four, and he had been joined in the children's household by two younger sisters (Margaret, aged three, and the infant Berengaria, who would die later that spring). Another princess, who was born around the start of that year, did not live long enough for her name to be recorded. But their sister, Joanna of Acre, was still absent from the royal nursery. Joanna was just three years Eleanora's junior, but she had lived at the court of their maternal grandmother in Ponthieu in northern France since their parents' return from the Crusade. As a result, there were no close siblings to accompany Eleanora when she broke away from the nursery to form an independent household. Following the customs of the court, she, too, now perambulated the countryside: seeing, and being seen, by subjects across England at royal estates and religious sites, and frequently visiting her parents or her father's mother, to whom she remained close. Eleanora's new household included over a dozen personal servants – she had a chamberlain, various grooms and cooks, female attendants to keep her company, and many sumpterers whose task it was to transport all the equipment and furnishings necessary for this group from castle to palace to hunting lodge and back, in a never-ending parade.

The books of the Royal Wardrobe that survive from the time detail the entire expenditure of the royal household at this period – including food and clothing, payments to servants, alms offered at shrines, and expenses related to their constant travel. They also tell us that Eleanora joined her parents over Easter and during their stay in Glastonbury. It was an opportune time for the princess to begin wrestling with the frequently contradictory role played by royal women and to learn the art of queenship from her mother. Eleanor, a Castilian princess, had married the heir to the throne of England at the age of twelve; Eleanora, her English daughter, was by this time already betrothed to Alfonso, the heir to Castile's great rival, the kingdom of Aragon.[1]

There was nothing unique about Eleanora's marriage partner being chosen before she could even know what marriage was. From a modern viewpoint, the idea of negotiating the marriage of such young children seems both absurd and cruel, but to think this is to misunderstand both the purpose and process of a dynastic match. Marriages between the children of medieval monarchs rarely had anything to do with romance. The marriage of every royal child – both female and male – was a political opportunity of the highest order, a rare and limited chance to cement an alliance of critical importance by forging a lasting bond of blood. The marriage of daughters, and most particularly daughters such as Eleanora who might one day inherit the throne, was a choice to be made with the utmost consideration, as each marriage would bring a foreign ruler into the very heart of the English royal family. The matches Edward sought for his children conformed to a long-lasting pattern for medieval English royalty, whose spouses most commonly came from the wealthier Iberian kingdoms, the various provinces that make up modern-day France, and the prosperous mercantile counties of the Low Countries, with occasional forays into Germany in the hopes of forging a connection with the Holy Roman Emperor. The fathers of these brides and bridegrooms were those considered by the English king to be his peers, men able to be of use – whether economically or militarily – to England. Any number of dangers, from illness to battle wounds, falls from horses, and house fires, could easily kill a medieval man in his prime, and kings like Edward frequently died long before their children had reached maturity. He had already barely survived an attempted assassination while in the Holy Land, and though the heavily romanticized version of this story in which Queen Eleanor saved her husband by devotedly sucking out the poison from his wound is apocryphal, the tale does highlight the precariousness of life on the throne. Edward's own marriage to Eleanor had been arranged when he was still a child. As his father Henry had explained, 'friendship between princes can be obtained in no more fitting manner than by the link of conjugal troth'. Kings like Edward were therefore keen to make use of the diplomatic opportunities afforded by their children's marriages while they were still alive.[2]

In addition to planning Eleanora's marriage, her parents also initiated plans to wed their younger children to the heirs of rulers with whom England was seeking alliance. Early in 1278, little Margaret was formally betrothed to Jan, the heir of the wealthy Duke of Brabant – a famous jouster whose feats of prowess delighted crowds at tournaments across northern Europe. Although the princess and her fiancé were only three years old at the time, the machinery of their union was already fully developed: the betrothal required written confirmation from Jan's father, mother, and brother, as well as from diverse Brabaçon nobles and the mayors of all the principal cities of the duchy. Equivalent guarantees on the side of the English must also have been sent to Brussels. The terms of the agreement underlined the fact that dynastic marriages such as this were unions of families, not merely of individuals – explicitly stating that, should either child die before the marriage could take place, a younger sibling was to be substituted and the match proceed. The Brabaçon drew up a lengthy summary of the castles, villages, farms, rents, forests, and even windmills at dozens of sites across the duchy that would, decades in the future, be assigned to the duchess Margaret to provide her dower, or widow's portion, after Jan's death (when the bulk of the estate would pass to their heir). The dower estate negotiated for Margaret was estimated to earn an annual income in excess of 3,100 *livres Tournois* (or nearly 800 pounds sterling), enough to provide an income for twenty knightly households at that time. In return for this future security, Edward was required to provide his daughter's dowry. These normally took the form of cash paid in instalments by the bride's family to the groom's, though great heiresses could also bring large estates to their husbands as dowry (as did Eleanor of

Aquitaine, whose immensely wealthy Duchy of Aquitaine tempted not one but two kings to marry her). Margaret's own mother, Eleanor of Castile, brought no dowry, but her marriage had brought assurances from the Castilian court that they would cease to press their claim against England for the Duchy of Gascony, so providing security against a potentially crippling financial risk to the English crown.[3]

The financial burden of dynastic marriages was so substantial that the English monarchs of the twelfth century offloaded the huge cost associated with their daughters' marriages onto their subjects by imposing special taxes that were unpopular enough for Clause 15 of Magna Carta to take specific aim at them:

> We will not concede to anyone to levy aid from his free men, except to ransom himself, to make his eldest son a knight and *to marry his eldest daughter one time,* and for these exceptions the aid must be reasonable.*

Edward was therefore only able to raise a tax to support the dowry of one of his daughters; to secure Margaret's marriage he was forced to either find the dowry of fifty thousand *livres Tournois* himself – or to borrow it from money lenders. The first twenty thousand was payable immediately and three subsequent instalments of ten thousand had to be settled before the marriage took place. It was an immense sum – the equivalent of over six million pounds in today's money; it was also roughly one-third of Edward's annual income, an outlay that even the king would find difficult to fund from his own resources.[4]

The king and queen also made plans for the marriage of their second-eldest daughter Joanna, who remained in the shadows at her grandmother's court in Ponthieu. Probably in

* Italics my own.

deference to Joanna's proximity to the throne of England, the union her parents hoped to arrange was just as grand as that promised to Eleanora – its fulfilment would see Joanna enthroned as queen or even empress. In 1276, an English embassy arrived at the court of Rudolf I, Count of Habsburg in the south-western German Duchy of Swabia. Rudolf had three years earlier been elected King of the Romans by the other German princes, in effect making him heir to the Holy Roman Emperor, and Edward saw the advantage in uniting his daughter with so powerful a prince. The embassy was therefore charged with negotiating a marriage between Joanna and thirteen-year-old Prince Hartman, Rudolf's second son. In addition to agreeing on the matters of dower and dowry, the ambassadors were asked to obtain assurances that, should Rudolf succeed as Holy Roman Emperor, he would nominate Hartman to become King of the Romans – and thus, Joanna might one day be Holy Roman Empress. By May 1278, the formalities were agreed: a dowry of ten thousand marks sterling (or nearly seven thousand pounds) was arranged, while the castles, towns, and valleys that would provide eleven thousand silver marks for Joanna's dower were confirmed by Rudolf, Hartman, and his elder brother Albert. The wedding itself was to take place soon afterwards in England. In June, six-year-old Joanna was recalled from Ponthieu and preparations began to welcome Hartman to London, where he would live while his bride grew to maturity. By November, however, Edward was forced to write again to Rudolf, asking when Hartman would arrive in England. The following spring he learned that unrest within Germany deprived Rudolf of the guard necessary to secure his son's transit to England; Edward accordingly arranged safe conduct and a military escort for his prospective son-in-law through the lands of his ally the Count of Guelders, and provided an English fleet to transport him to England from Dordrecht in Holland, and yet still he did not come.[5]

Though royal children were frequently betrothed during their early childhood, the marriages themselves were usually delayed, and the notion that medieval princesses like Eleanora, Joanna, and Margaret were child-brides can be swiftly discounted. Canon law, which governed marriage, decreed the minimum age at which women and men could be married as twelve and fourteen respectively, and further set down that any underage marriages must be ratified once the children had matured to ensure that their marriage was a free choice. There was no need for *post-facto* ratifications in the cases of Eleanora and her younger sisters, who were, on average, almost eighteen when they first married. And nor were the sisters particularly exceptional in this regard: if their ages at first marriage are compared with those of the royal daughters who came after them, up to and including the sisters of Henry VIII in the early sixteenth century, the average age for first marriage was nearly seventeen. Far from being child-brides, they were, in fact, the same age as young women who can legally marry in Britain today. In fact, only one princess in the medieval period, Blanche of Lancaster, was married below canonical age – in the early fifteenth century, when her father Henry IV was searching desperately for allies to secure his position as a usurper, she was, at the age of ten, married to another German prince with imperial ambitions.[6]

Even when royal women were married young, most such unions would not normally be consummated until several years later. The number of contemporary manuscript copies of *Mirror for Princes* by Thomas Aquinas suggests that the text was in wide circulation during the later medieval period. In this treatise, Aquinas expounds on why women in particular should be safeguarded from premature sexual activity: even where a young woman had reached the age of menarche (her first period), conception at a young age would result in unhealthy or weak offspring and could harm her chances for successful delivery later on. (He also cautioned that early sexual experiences could lead to lechery and lasciviousness in later life.) Therefore, consummation should be delayed until a woman had reached eighteen, and a man twenty-one.

Aquinas's advice was largely heeded by the medieval English aristocracy, and only very rarely were children born to noble-women under the age of fifteen. Mary de Bohun, the wife of Henry IV, bore a stillborn boy at the age of twelve but did not cohabit with her husband for several years afterwards; it was not until she was eighteen that she bore the future Henry V, who was followed in the subsequent eight years by five more healthy children. Margaret Beaufort, the mother of Henry VII, nearly died giving birth to him aged thirteen, and the injuries she sustained during delivery left her unable to have any further children. In both cases, the early consummation of these women's unions ensured that the particularly desirable marriages for their husbands – both women were great heiresses – could not be subsequently revoked. There is some evidence, too, to suggest that Edward I's queen, Eleanor, may have given birth to a prema-ture baby who died immediately, around seven months after their marriage, when she was only thirteen. No further children were born to the couple until she was nineteen, but her aston-ishing childbearing record later in life – she went on to bear fifteen children – indicates that the queen did not struggle with infertility. The pattern, instead, would suggest that the marriage was immediately consummated to ensure that it could not be annulled, and that, though Eleanor fell pregnant at once, the couple did not engage in regular sexual congress until she was eighteen. Her daughters waited even longer – the average age at which they gave birth for the first time was twenty-two, and only one, Joanna, had a baby before she was twenty.[7]

On 15 February 1282, twelve-year-old Eleanora, long accustomed to travelling freely around the countryside, was staying, as she often did, with her grandmother in Guildford – her early childhood home, and the location of the nursery she had shared with her brother Henry and their cousin John of Brittany – when she sat down with a royal scribe to dictate the most important letter of her early life. The girl who described herself as 'Eleanora, eldest daughter of the illustrious King of England' had reached the age of consent to be married. Now she sought publicly to affirm by open letter her willingness to wed Alfonso, Crown Prince of Aragon, 'a man of glory'. In the letter, she gave her own and her parents' consent to two of her father's emissaries to act 'in our place and our name on the matter of the betrothal and marriage', and to agree the terms for dower and dowry. 'As we have no seal of our own', the letter concluded – with the smallest flash of an adolescent's annoyance shining across the centuries – 'we have requested and affixed the seals of the most serene Lady Eleanor, by grace of God, Queen of England, our grandmother, and of the most venerable fathers in Christ, Lords Roger of London and John of Rochester, bishops.'[8]

The letter is unique among the papers pertaining to the marriages of medieval royal daughters – Eleanora's sisters were all silent throughout the process of arranging their matches, and only their brother (their father's eventual heir, Edward II) would issue similar letters when negotiating his own marriage.[9] Eleanora's early independence seems to have engendered a precocious confidence in her. Far from being a passive pawn of her father's diplomatic ambitions, she plainly wished to play an active role in the arrangements for her marriage. She did not merely acquiesce to her father's wishes; she embraced the idea that she might become Queen of Aragon, the embodiment of the link between two nations. This should not surprise us. If the marriages of princesses were normally arranged for them, so were those of princes; like any royal child in the circumstances, Eleanora recognized that the marriage planned for her was prestigious and would place her at the centre of power and influence at a rival court, and that, in turn, would enable her to support the international ambitions of her family. If Eleanora demonstrated a greater propensity than her sisters to be so personally involved in sculpting her future, it may be that her parents encouraged their eldest daughter, who remained second in line to the English throne, to develop a keen interest in international diplomacy as well as a familiarity with statecraft. According to the Italian writer Francesco da Barberino, a contemporary of Eleanora's, noblewomen should be educated because: 'If it happens that she inherits lands she will be better able to rule them'; the king and queen were, it seems, educating their daughter and possible successor about the mechanisms through which she might rule.[10]

Accompanying Eleanora's letter was another from the king, which officially empowered his secretaries to negotiate the terms of his daughter's marriage. A sense of the importance placed upon these negotiations can be gleaned by considering the rank of those assigned to carry out the work: the courtier and the bishop assigned to lead the delegation were accompanied by three other important members of the king's household, including one of his companions on the Crusade and the Constable of the Tower of London. This elite party was expected to be abroad for up to a year, during which they were to display to foreign courts the wealth and cosmopolitan finesse of the English court, and Edward borrowed nearly a thousand pounds from Italian and

English merchants to ensure that they would be able to do so. The embassy was a success, and by late summer in 1282 the terms were agreed. For her dower, Eleanora was granted towns in the Huesca region of Aragon, among them the ancient Frankish capital of Jaca, as well as – extraordinary to the modern reader – 'the Jews and Muslims living within them now and in the future' as her personal possessions; her dowry was agreed at forty thousand *livres Tournois*. At the feast of the Assumption, a member of the English embassy stood in Eleanora's place opposite her young bridegroom Alfonso as proxy, and before two Spanish bishops affirmed by the necessary words the princess's desire to wed the Spanish prince. Eleanora was now officially bound to the Prince of Aragon and destined to become a queen.[11]

The bride herself remained in England. In his preliminary negotiations, her father had requested that, 'if possible', his daughter's arrival in Aragon should be delayed until November 1283, by which time she would be fourteen. If that was not possible, they were to secure at least one year's delay, because 'the queen, her mother, and our dearest mother, will not sustain that she travel before then out of concern for the girl'. Eleanor of Castile and her mother-in-law, Eleanor of Provence, did not always agree, but both women had married and travelled to live in the foreign households of their husbands at young ages, and they were united in seeking to protect Eleanora and her sisters from the same fate. Recognizing, perhaps, the role of mothers in guiding such matters, the Aragonese deployed their own queen (and Alfonso's mother) to plead for a shorter delay, but these pleas were rebuffed. For a time, a diplomatic impasse over the right to rule Sicily also threatened the match. This contention pitted Edward's uncle Charles, King of Sicily, against a movement seeking to place Pedro of Aragon, Eleanora's prospective father-in-law, on the throne. As the crisis progressed, both sides endeavoured to win Edward to their side, and the English king – caught between his allegiance to his uncle and the possibility of extending his son-in-law's kingdom – spent much of the next decade embroiled in efforts to settle the matter. Throughout, Eleanora, though legally bound closer than ever to Alfonso, would remain in England.[12]

Sometime early in 1282, the royal family had learned that Eleanora's sister Joanna would also have no need to travel abroad for a wedding. Her betrothed, Prince Hartman, had drowned in the Rhine at Christmas time the previous year, when a boat in which he was travelling sank. His father wrote to Edward, expressing his sorrow and continued hopes for their alliance, but no suggestion was made that Hartman's brother, Rudolf, might fill his brother's place. The two sisters spent a great deal of time together and with their mother in these years, perfecting their educations and practising to one day become queens.[13]

III
Family

1282–4

RHUDDLAN, CAERNARFON

The king's second eldest daughter, Joanna, was a traveller from birth, born half a world away from England while her parents were on Crusade, and raised at her grandmother's court in Ponthieu. The northern French county was centred around Abbeville, a port city that controlled the ships carrying woad seaward, down the River Somme from Amiens to the Low Countries where the pungent dyestuff would be used to colour that region's famous tapestries a deep blue. While in Ponthieu, Joanna seems to have had early tuition in religion and mathematics from a Spanish cleric within the dowager queen's household, and she also had a native governess, Edeline Papyot, who was responsible for educating her in the arts expected of a thirteenth-century princess – reading and recitation, embroidery and music, riding, falconry, and chess. In 1278, when Joanna's

37

betrothal to Prince Hartman seemed secure, she travelled to England, taking Edeline with her.[1]

On her arrival, aged six, she initially joined her younger siblings Alphonso and Margaret in the royal nursery at Windsor, and in 1279 they were joined by a little sister, Mary. But Joanna was soon travelling around England in the same manner as her older sister Eleanora, attending at her mother's court and going places on her own. In the summer of 1282, aged ten, she travelled with Eleanora and the queen to the frontier of Wales, where her father was engaged in his war against the last independent Welsh princes, the brothers Llywelyn and Dafydd ap Gruffydd. As the English forces marched west across the principality of Gwynedd, the king consolidated his gains through an extraordinarily ambitious and expensive campaign of building works. If power could be made manifest in medieval Europe, it did so in the form of castles. Already an elaborate construction programme had begun across northern Wales and by 1282 there were English castles at Flint, Denbigh, and Rhuddlan, the formidable might of England evident in the thickness of the walls.

With the war far from won, the queen and her daughters took up residence in the frontier castle of Rhuddlan. There, in the barely completed castle – its gardens newly planted to the queen's specifications and its fishpond freshly stocked – Eleanor gave birth to her final daughter, Elizabeth. To celebrate the successful birth, the king summoned dozens of minstrels from across Britain, who travelled to Rhuddlan to entertain the royal family. If Joanna had ever perceived a hint of danger in being so close to an active battlefront, the arrival of scores of musicians singing songs of romance may have allayed her fears. She seems to have enjoyed her time in the dramatic hilly landscape of the north Welsh coastal region, since she returned again to Rhuddlan a year later – in the late summer of 1283, by which time Llywelyn and Dafydd were both dead, the princess and her household were in residence at the castle, requiring a delivery of wheat to make their bread.[2]

The household that accompanied the eleven-year-old Joanna back to Rhuddlan probably included most of those who appear three years later in wardrobe records that list a dozen servants chosen by the queen to look after her daughter. These men and women made up what Joanna called her *familia* (literally, her 'family') – it was an appropriate term for the collection of servants among whom the princess lived her day-to-day life. While we tend to think of families as bound by blood, Joanna's *familia* were an even more constant presence in her life than her sisters or parents; travelling with her everywhere she went, they were witness to and confidant in more of her sorrows, frustrations, and joys than even her own blood relations. Their roles included making her food and clothing, maintaining and transporting the personal furnishings that moved with her, and protecting the household, its people, and goods from banditry, as they all moved slowly and unceasingly across the countryside. Like all noble households in medieval England, Joanna's was overwhelmingly staffed with male servants and, with the exception of Edeline (who would remain with Joanna until her marriage), the princess would have relied on visits to her sisters or mother for most of her interactions with other women.[3]

The most senior members of the princess's household were her private tailor and personal cook (both of whom were named Robert), and, below them, was Reginald, the keeper of Joanna's costly bed and table linens. These fabrics travelled with the princess, furnishing her chamber in castles across the country, and therefore a sumpterer (or transporter) named Hugh was required to pack and move them, as well as an outrider, whose job it was to ride ahead of the main procession and forewarn the permanent staff at each house of the princess's impending arrival, so they could clean and provision the accommodation appropriately. A carter called James was responsible for transporting the heavy goods that made up Joanna's own personal suite of furniture, the wardrobe of silken gowns, gold embroidered robes, and furred capes crafted by the tailor, and the cooking vessels, silver serving dishes, and costly spices like cloves and cumin that equipped her kitchen and table.[4]

The shape of her household roughly mirrored the *familia* of Joanna's sisters Eleanora and Margaret, though the eldest sister always retained more servants and more ladies, whether in deference to her seniority in age or proximity to the throne. Eight-year-old Margaret's nurse Cecily Cleware, who had looked after the princess from soon after her birth and had previously been nurse to Eleanora, remained her principal companion. Peter Burdet, 'squire of the king's daughters', nominally resided with Eleanora and seems to have overseen the older girls' collective expenses, while royal wards, together with the children of their parents' aristocratic servants, kept the princesses company. Alphonso had his own separate household at the age of nine, while four-year-old Mary lived within the royal nursery without the company of her little sister Elizabeth, whom, alone of all her children, the queen had insisted on keeping with her since birth.[5]

In March 1284, Joanna was back in Wales, and further into Gwynedd than had been possible two years earlier. She and her household had travelled once again with Eleanora and their mother, who was heavily pregnant for the sixteenth time but still holding tight to Elizabeth, who was aged almost two. The party moved west along a road that skirted the coast past Conwy, the mist falling down from the hills around Snowdon like a frozen cascade. As the ocean narrowed to a strait, Joanna saw a half-finished castle rise out of the muddy tidal waters before her. The royal party had arrived at Caernarfon, which means 'River Fort' – the most important site in Edward's new Welsh principality, perched at the tip of a peninsula guarding the River Seiont, as it empties into the narrow Menai Strait that separates Wales from the Isle of Anglesey beyond. The castle Edward was building there would become one of the most splendid fortresses to ever adorn the British landscape, the last in a series of lavish, fortified palaces and walled towns that Edward constructed in the heart of the conquered principality.

The king's new castles were placed at sites where they would make an impact: war had barely finished when Conwy Castle began to rise above the demolished remains of Aberconwy Abbey, the traditional burial site of Welsh princes; Harlech Castle soon commandeered a rocky hill that was central to the legend of the Welsh princess Branwen. Caernarfon – first established as a Roman fort and linked by local legend to the Roman Emperor Constantine the Great – had long been associated with the idea of an imperial and unified Britain, and Edward now sought to capitalize on this, by making it the centre of his Welsh dominion. The great Welsh romance cycle *The Mabinogion* includes the story of a dream in which a Roman emperor of Britain foresees a great walled city overlooking a river flowing into the sea opposite an island; alongside the city is a castle with many towers of different colours and a hall with an ivory throne, incised with golden eagles.[6]

At Caernarfon, Edward could recreate this dream in stone and mortar – and, by doing so, firmly link himself to a mythic king who had ruled over the whole of Britain. As part of his subjugation of Wales, Edward also continued to promote his connection to that most famous of legendary rulers, King Arthur: among the royal regalia he captured from the Welsh princes after their defeat was Arthur's reputed crown, an object that conferred the same sacral authority on Welsh princes that

41

the Stone of Scone did on Scottish kings. Now that the silver circlet belonged to Edward, he directed his son Alphonso to present it, along with other gold belonging to the defeated Prince Llywelyn, to the English royal shrine of Edward the Confessor at Westminster Abbey, thereby symbolically crowning his saintly predecessor and namesake with the regalia of Wales.[7]

While castles and crowns played a prominent role in supporting the legitimacy of Edward's claim to Wales, his daughters also played a part in the conquest. The queen's presence in Wales in 1282 and 1284 may be explained by her wish to remain near to her husband, accompanying him on military campaigns as her own mother had done during her father's wars against the Muslim kingdoms of Spain. The presence of Joanna, Eleanora, and Elizabeth, however, requires another explanation. As they grew into maturity, the two eldest daughters increasingly travelled as companions to their mother, intertwining their households with that of the queen. But the presence of the girls at Rhuddlan and Caernarfon also operated as a piece of political theatre to any Welsh loyalists in the vicinity, testament to the royal family's confidence in Edward's military dominance.

By the time Joanna arrived at Caernarfon a month before her twelfth birthday, the principality was effectively conquered, and any risk to her safety was minimal. King Edward had not only defeated the Welsh princes – he also had custody of Llywelyn's only child, a daughter named Gwenllian, born near Bangor only six weeks prior to Elizabeth's birth. Her mother had been Edward's cousin – the daughter of Edward's aunt, a princess who scandalized court by secretly marrying the rebel leader Simon de Montfort – but she had died in childbirth. Nevertheless, although her parents were dead and her uncle was defeated, Welsh hopes for a resurgence may have lain in Gwenllian, and so Edward acted swiftly, sending her as far from Wales as he could, to the Gilbertine convent at Sempringham in Lincolnshire. What Edward's own daughters – who, if their father was deposed might face similar threats – thought about his treatment of their young cousin is unknown. At this stage, they could not know that Gwenllian would subsist at Sempringham for the rest of her fifty-five years, locked away and hidden from Welsh plotters and prospective bridegrooms tempted by the notion of ruling a principality.

With Gwenllian in England in 1284, Wales was without a native prince, but once again the Queen of England was approaching confinement, and the birth of a baby boy in Edward's new administrative capital in Caernarfon would give back to Wales a Welsh-born prince. And thus, though the rest of the castle was still only partially built, the queen and her daughters took up residency at the end of March in the castle's part-completed, unusual polygonal tower – its upper floors unfinished and topped with a temporary roof – known for the centuries since its completion as the Eagle Tower, a reference to the birds that surmounted each of its three turrets. The tower looked directly out to sea and included a water gate that, in the event of a siege, would allow its occupants to take in provisions by boat. Caernarfon's strangely shaped towers, the use of multi-coloured stone banding unique among English-built castles, and even its eagles, were intended to evoke the castle in the *Mabinogion* dream.[8]

The family celebrated Joanna's twelfth birthday in their chamber as the flurry of building work continued in the castle yard. Now of an age to learn about such things, the two older girls were most likely present in the room when the queen gave birth to her fourth son, named for his father and known henceforth as Edward of Caernarfon. A contemporary chronicle recorded how Londoners rejoiced following the news of the prince's birth 'on the feast of St Mark the Evangelist at Caernarfon near Snowdon'.[9]

*

Joanna's parents famously enjoyed a particularly close relationship during their thirty-five-year marriage, and were rarely apart for long. Edward had no bastard children, and there was only ever one brief rumour that questioned his devotion to his wife – this constancy was rare among medieval kings, but consistent with the examples of both his father, Henry III, and his much-admired uncle, Louis IX of France. Together, Edward and Eleanor, along with their retinues of knights, dozens of servants, elaborate wardrobes, and suites of personal furnishings for bedrooms and chapels, travelled in a constantly moving pageant across the country, only stopping for more than a few days for extended stays at Westminster. So elaborate were their usual journeys that often the full suite of the queen's furniture could not be accommodated on her own carts, and extra horses and carriages were hired to follow behind the main train. The royal couple moved ceaselessly. They stopped at royal estates to check on accounts and servants; they visited important shrines, monasteries, and cathedrals, making offerings to local saints and giving alms to feed the poor; they spent feast days hunting in their favourite forests, the king with his prized falcons and the queen with her packs of specially-bred hunting dogs.

Everywhere they went, Edward and Eleanor performed their roles of king and queen before their subjects. Itinerancy was a political necessity for medieval monarchs: townspeople and villagers came to know the royal family, and their feelings of loyalty were engendered and reinforced when they watched the parade of glittering knights and sumptuous carriages that announced the arrival of their king and queen. Through this constant travel, Edward and Eleanor's public selves – actions carefully choreographed, roles cleanly delineated, costumes perfected – were displayed one village at a time to the whole country, all the while highlighting their vast wealth, their power to command large retinues, and the divine right by which they ruled England. This was the court that Joanna and her siblings joined at around the age of eight, and where they learned from their parents how to play their part in the spectacle of kingship. Edward's 'court' was not at all like the great courts anchored to particular palaces that would predominate in later centuries – at sites such as Versailles – but more like a travelling circus of state surrounding the king and queen.[10]

This perpetual travelling prohibited the royal children from attending court until they were old enough to handle its rigours, and also restricted the amount of time their parents could spend in their children's company. However, once they were around seven or eight, the children were considered old enough to ride long hours in the saddle atop a palfrey horse (favoured by ladies of rank for its narrow back and smooth, ambling gait) and to understand their roles in projecting regality. From then on, they frequently joined their parents and, by 1284, the households of Eleanora, Joanna, and sometimes Margaret, were travelling with the court. With her daughters by her side, the queen was able to ensure that in their learning, the royal sisters outstripped almost all their contemporaries, and perhaps in time even their husbands.[11]

Eleanor of Castile was educated to an exceptional degree, even by the standards of Norman England. Noblewomen of the time were taught (like their male counterparts) to read in their native French, as well as basic Latin – at least enough to recite from the psalms and perhaps to understand stories from the lives of saints. Eleanor's brother, Alfonso X 'the Wise' of Castile, in whose court she was raised, believed so strongly that royal daughters should be taught to read, that he included a directive explicitly encouraging this in his code of laws, the Siete Partidas. Once Eleanor became the Queen of England, she established a private scriptorium at Westminster, where two scribes and an illustrator were charged with copying books for her personal use, implying an ability and an appetite for reading that was well above the norm, even for a noblewoman. Eleanor's interests were varied, and offer evidence of what she considered a well-rounded education might entail: among the works copied by her scribes were the *Libro de los Juegos*, or 'Book of Games', a Castilian translation her brother had commissioned from an Arabic chess manual, and the *De re militari* by Vegetius, a Roman text on military tactics that she gave as a gift to her warlike husband. On her marriage, her parents-in-law gave her a copy of the *Life of St Edward the Confessor*, the English royal saint in whose honour Henry had rebuilt Westminster Abbey, a book magnificently illustrated with images of the saintly king and his queen – whose piety, virtue, and beauty showed her to be an ideal courtly lady. We know that Eleanor also read romances: the poet Girart d'Amiens credited the 'beautiful and wise' queen with creating the story for his romance *Escanor*, which features a Northumbrian princess who inspires heroism in Arthur's knights, and she gifted a copy of *Meliadus* (the romance Edward had commissioned) to her brother. She and her daughters would have also had access to the many Arthurian romances owned by her mother-in-law, Eleanor of Provence, who was a dedicated reader of them (although she probably did not write the Provençal romance *Blandin de Cornouailles*, with which some nineteenth-century historians credited her).[12]

Given her evident enjoyment of reading, it is not surprising that the learned queen ensured that her own daughters were educated. Once they had joined court, the sisters and other young female companions, including their cousin Marie of Brittany, were introduced to popular texts via informal reading groups, in which books were read aloud by an accomplished reader, before being discussed within the group. In the king's hall, travelling minstrels might sing to knights of conquest and epic battles, but romances and devotional works were more frequently read in small groups in the upper chambers, and the audiences largely consisted of women. A later Middle English dream poem, *The Parlement of the Three Ages*, records scenes of 'lovely ladies dancing in their chambers, reading glorious romances which tell the true tales of warriors and conquerors and noble kings, how they won worship and wealth in their lives . . .' while knights 'revel in hall singing songs and carols'. Before learning to read on their own, therefore, the princesses would have come to know the most popular tales of the time, stories like Chrétien de Troyes' *Lancelot* and those about the star-crossed lovers Tristan and Isolde. Episodes from these stories, of the struggles between passion and allegiance, likely burned particularly bright in the girls' imaginations, especially as they frequently also appeared on the woollen tapestries and ivory caskets, mirrors, and combs that furnished their chambers. In fact, the stories of noble knights beloved by virtuous princesses were so firmly engrained in the minds of Edward's daughters that (as we shall see later), during a fierce argument with her father as an adult, Joanna reached intuitively for their example. In addition to these secular texts, the sisters would have been familiar, as their mother was, with liturgical texts such as the psalms and stories from the lives of saints, among them the virginal princesses Katherine of Alexandria and Margaret of Antioch – two royal women held up as examples for choosing painful deaths over forced marriages to unbelieving men.[13]

The actual process of learning to read began before the children left their nursery. They were taught using techniques that may even now be familiar to anyone who has taught a child to read: first, they learned the alphabet, before trying to sound out letters and pronounce words aloud. The first words they read were probably in Latin, and they practised using those passages of liturgy that they would have already memorized, with a focus on books with large, clear lettering, such as psalters and books of hours, collections of prayers, and Bible readings intended to be recited throughout the day. To support her children at all ages in their studies, the queen purchased a psalter and seven books of hours on a visit to Cambridge, the fenland university town that was filled with learned copyists who produced manuscripts by the dozen. The princesses may have learned some basic Latin grammar and vocabulary from these (or from specialist textbooks designed for that purpose), but more likely their attention at this stage turned to using the skills they had acquired in lettering and pronunciation to begin reading in Anglo-Norman, a variant of French and their native tongue.[14]

At least one of Eleanor's daughters, Eleanora, had mastered reading well enough by her teens to practise a skill very rare among the medieval aristocracy, and one even her father may have lacked: writing. Though nothing survives written in her own hand (the letter confirming her intention to marry Alfonso of Aragon was, like all public letters, written by a professional scribe), Eleanora's tailor, Peter, purchased some writing tablets and a small leather chest in which to keep them for her, while he was in London to buy silks for her dresses. These tablets were made of wood overlaid with wax and could be written on with a stylus, the primary means of medieval note-taking, as well as practising to write. In subsequent years, further such tablets were purchased for Eleanora, although it is unclear from the records if the princess had taken to making extensive notes or was simply engaged in a prolonged-if-dogged attempt to master the precise penmanship of a medieval scribe – an art form akin to calligraphy. In either case, her purpose in learning to write was likely to enable private correspondence, but she may also have dabbled in composition. Eleanora's younger sister Mary seems also to have inherited their mother's love of books: a chronicle of her family's rule over England, written by the Dominican friar Nicholas Trivet early in the fourteenth century, was dedicated to Mary and was likely commissioned by her. Later, following in the tradition of exceptional female learning, Elizabeth's daughters were known to read Latin and even Greek.[15]

Reading was, however, only one aspect of a princess's formal education, and the queen also ensured that her daughters practised other skills expected of a noblewoman in medieval Europe. These included the art of embroidery, an aspect of their education advocated by their uncle, the King of Castile. Surviving wardrobe accounts provide evidence of frequent purchases of silks in many different colours, and a spindle purchased for Margaret implies that she, at least, also practised weaving. The princesses also rode and hunted; Joanna had three hounds for her own use by 1285, and there are numerous payments made to houndsmen for the maintenance and transportation of animals for the girls' use. They seem to have followed their mother's preference for hunting with specialized hunting dogs such as greyhounds over falcons, and it is probable that the queen herself instructed her daughters in this, her favourite pastime. Music also featured in their education: the princesses lived surrounded by musicians and minstrels and may have had tuition from them – they certainly learned to appreciate listening to it. As an adult, Elizabeth expressed a strong interest in newly fashionable polyphonic choral music – a rainbow of sound compared to the dull monotone of traditional chant. In addition, they likely received tuition in elementary Christian theology, as well as in logic and basic arithmetic from the Dominican canons their mother promoted at court. Eleanora, who expected to become Queen of

Aragon, undoubtedly also took the opportunity to learn Iberian phrases from her Castilian mother, which would help her navigate her early days at the Aragonese court.[16]

The education of princesses was not, however, solely about acquiring the right skills; in order to succeed at sophisticated foreign courts, the sisters also needed to learn how to conduct themselves. From their mother and governesses, and from the cautionary tales of feminine excesses they would have heard and read, Eleanor's daughters learned to present themselves as serious and composed young women, demure yet steadfast, who always employed manners appropriate to their station. In the vernacular of the time, they learned 'courtesy'.

Their broad and immensely privileged education was designed to produce young women who could act as patrons, advisors, and, if necessary, regents, and who would exemplify the height of chivalric sophistication to foreign visitors at court and – after their marriages – to foreign courts, their knowledge and skills reflecting well on the cultural refinement of their native England and their family. As contemporary romantic heroines, such as Felice from the popular thirteenth-century romance *Guy of Warwick*, or as holy virgins such as Katherine of Alexandria demonstrated, with their renowned knowledge of astronomy, arithmetic, and geometry, these elite women were expected to be impressively educated.

Joanna and her sister Eleanora left Caernarfon near the end of summer, with their mother, Elizabeth, and baby brother Edward, heading inland to Chester and then south towards Bristol. Having safely delivered another prince, the queen seems to have turned her mind once again to planning for the future of her eldest, Alphonso. A few months earlier, she had commissioned a psalter to be presented to him on the occasion of his forthcoming marriage to Margaret, the daughter of the Count of Holland. The sumptuously illustrated psalter was too ambitious a project for the queen's own scriptorium and was most likely produced by a specialist London atelier. Its parchment pages were filled with decorations of personal significance to the young prince: surrounding the psalms were vivid drawings of birds and a man on horseback directing a falcon hunt, suggesting that he shared his father's special interest in falconry; images of knights in victory against beasts and giants; and depictions of the heraldic arms of the heir-apparent of England intertwined with those of Holland. Efforts were also made to ensure that the book would appeal to Alphonso's intended wife, including the addition of delicate illustrations in the margins of a woman hunting with hounds and a mermaid breastfeeding her baby. However, work on the manuscript stopped suddenly, with only the first eight folios complete; on 19 August 1284, ten-year-old Alphonso – the first of Edward and Eleanor's sons to survive the dangerous early years of childhood – died suddenly. The Archbishop of Canterbury wrote to the king, not in the usual Latin of clerics but in the more intimate Anglo-Norman that they would have spoken to each other:

> Sire, by the power of reason that God has given you, you understand well that no accident comes about on Earth that does not pass first before the judgment of the Emperor of Heaven and His court. From there are allotted all of the good things and the suffering of all ills, because by these ills He often brings about the good things. And because of this, sire, we are firm in the belief that the terrible accident that came about, which resulted in the death of the child who was a hope to us all, happened so that the malice of the present day did not taint his goodness . . .

The sadness expressed in the archbishop's words to the king – words of comfort that Alphonso had been saved from the evils of this world – shows the compassion he felt for the king's sudden and unexpected loss of his son and heir. The queen was so affected by Alphonso's death that she had his heart removed before he was buried at Westminster, so that it could one day be buried with hers at the London house of the Dominican preachers whom she particularly favoured. Alphonso's younger sisters, Margaret and Mary, must also have been devastated by his death, as they had spent much of their lives with their brother in the royal nursery.[17]

Once again, the heir to the throne of England was a tiny baby boy, and the second-in-line was his eldest sister Eleanora, now fifteen years old and awaiting her father's release to travel to Aragon and finalize her marriage.

IV
Vows

1285–6
AMESBURY

On the feast of the Assumption of the Virgin, in August 1285, Mary of Woodstock, the fourth surviving daughter of the king, knelt before the high altar of the spacious priory church at Amesbury. Surrounded by her parents, her sisters, and thirteen other noble young women, the princess pledged herself to a very different life from that of the chivalric court, and one which placed an emphasis on poverty – a word that her parents and siblings would never be asked to embrace – obedience, and perpetual chastity. Mary was to become a nun; so too were the thirteen companions chosen to share her day and her future.[1]

The young princess played her part in the ceremony well, though her young age – she was only six – might suggest that she did not fully understand the life to which she was signing up, especially given the ostentatious nature that would characterize

53

her as an adult. Her mother, however, understood all too well and was strongly opposed to her daughter's veiling at such an early age. Just as she had campaigned that Eleanora should not be sent off at twelve to get married in Spain, so too she lobbied her husband that their second-youngest daughter, who was still being raised in the royal nursery alongside Elizabeth and Prince Edward, not be asked to give up what she could not yet comprehend: a future husband, children of her own, the freedom to move about in the world – the very things that gave the queen's own life purpose. She was also unconvinced as to the reason Mary was being given up to the nuns. Edward's mother, Eleanor of Provence, now that her life at the apex of power was nearly over, sought to comfort her soul by retiring in exceptional piety. The queen's doubts were well known and, in an effort to assuage them, someone (probably the dowager queen) had arranged for the abbess of the convent's motherhouse to write directly to the queen. In her letter, the abbess appealed both to Eleanor's maternal and her royal instincts, addressing her as 'dearest mother in Christ' and 'most excellent mother', while praising the 'great honour' that would come to the king by placing his daughter in the convent. She concluded by pointing out that the queen's child would be extremely well placed to pray for the souls of her family – a not unimportant consideration in a culture where the prayers of the living were thought to be the soul's speediest route to heaven. The letter did little to convince the queen, and a chronicle later dedicated to Princess Mary recorded that her mother assented to her veiling 'with difficulty'. But the king sided with his mother, and the plans for enclosing little Mary at Amesbury went ahead.[2]

Mary's grandmother had been a widow for more than a dozen years and was now in her seventh decade. The 1270s had been a particularly difficult time for her and, after losing her husband in 1272, she devoted herself to the care of her grandchildren. Two years later, when Henry died, she was so grief-stricken that she established a Franciscan priory at Guildford in his honour, where she hoped to find peace. But within six months there were more deaths in the family. Her second son's wife, the young heiress Aveline de Forz, died in childbirth, along with her twin infants, and her own two daughters (Margaret, Queen of Scotland, and Beatrice, who would have become Countess of Brittany) followed Henry and Aveline to early graves. The chronicler Thomas Wykes wrote that the dowager queen was only comforted in her grief at losing her daughters by the presence of her surviving grandchildren. By the early 1280s, however, she had decided to retire from public life and live out her days as a nun. The English royal family had long patronized the Benedictine abbey of nuns at Fontevrault in Anjou, part of the ancestral English royal lands for the past century; it was an abbey that no less a person than the great Queen Eleanor of Aquitaine, wife of Henry II, had retired to in her own final years.[3]

But Fontevrault was far away, and by the late thirteenth century the English king no longer ruled Anjou; instead of Fontevrault itself, therefore, Eleanor chose an English convent under its rule, the priory at Amesbury, in the rolling hills of Wiltshire. Today Amesbury is best known as the town closest to the ancient pagan site of Stonehenge, known until modern times as the Giant's Circle. The circle, according to Geoffrey of Monmouth and the medieval chroniclers who succeeded him, was formed by the legendary wizard Merlin, who used magic to transport its stones, constructing a lasting monument to those Britons who fell fighting the Saxon invaders. (This Arthurian explanation for Stonehenge may be why Amesbury was later believed to be the convent to which Queen Guinevere retired after Arthur's death.) The priory at Amesbury was also ancient;

formally founded in the tenth century but probably on the site of an earlier monastery, it was established by the Anglo-Saxon queen Ælfthryth (mother of the famously 'Unready', or poorly advised, Æthelred) and remained a rather undistinguished Benedictine house of nuns for two centuries, before being dissolved and refounded in the twelfth century by Henry II as a daughter house of Fontevrault. Now under royal patronage, the next century saw significant expansion in the wealth and size of the priory. By the late thirteenth century, Amesbury was a bustling, prosperous community of more than seventy mostly aristocratic nuns, with two dozen resident men serving as priests or lay brethren who performed Mass, acted as confessors, and provided financial administration for the priory. They lived under the rule of a prioress and a prior, who governed the women and men respectively. In addition to the household domestics who served the community, labourers looked after the two hundred oxen, two dozen horses, and over four thousand sheep that between them provided meat, transportation, and income (from wool) to the priory. Amesbury had also acquired a reputation as a monastery fitting for English royal women: among its recent royal patrons was Eleanor of Brittany, the unfortunate countess who spent her life forcibly enclosed at royal castles throughout the country by King John and Henry III. On her death, not having anything else, she bestowed her body to the convent.[4]

As the dowager queen prepared to take the veil and devote the rest of her life to God at Amesbury, she begged Edward to assign two of her granddaughters to keep her company. She was probably the first to make the argument, later echoed by the Abbess of Fontevrault in her letter to Eleanor of Castile, that she and the children would pray together each day for the souls of the royal family and for the glory of England. It was an argument that Edward – caught as he was between the wishes of his mother and his wife – found compelling; time and again, the king would demonstrate the belief that his daughters had roles to play in the dynasty's larger ambitions, and having a nun in the family could prove useful. Princess Mary – the eldest not already pledged in marriage – and her cousin Eleanor of Brittany therefore entered the convent in the company of other aristocratic daughters, to provide companionship for their grandmother.[5]

Mary's veiling was unique among princesses in the later medieval period – most kings did not have such a surplus of daughters that they could easily afford to throw away the opportunity for a diplomatic marriage. But Edward had five daughters, including Mary's three elder siblings, all of whom were betrothed yet unmarried, and her little sister Elizabeth, who was just three and remained unmatched. It had been over a hundred years since a member of the royal family had become a nun. In the middle of the eleventh century, Cecily, the eldest daughter of William the Conqueror, had joined a community of nuns established by her father at Caen in Normandy, and was much admired for her piety. And in 1160, Mary, the daughter of King Stephen, was serving as Abbess of Romsey when she was 'abducted' (almost certainly she willingly eloped) by a Low Countries nobleman and, her vow of perpetual chastity notwithstanding, much to the shock and horror of Christendom, married him. Their union caused such a scandal that their County of Boulogne was placed under papal interdict, whereby no one living within its borders could receive the vital sacraments of baptism, marriage, or the last rites, which essentially left the souls of every man, woman, and child in the county in moral peril. Despite giving birth to two daughters, Mary could never escape the stigma associated with her marriage, and eventually returned to live in a convent, repenting the abandonment of her religious vows and pledging once again to live a chaste life. If, a century later, young Mary of Woodstock knew of these unfortunate tales, she must have hoped that hers would be a more successful monastic career.

Mary's entry into Amesbury was also exceptional in other respects: young women were meant to be sixteen before they took vows, and normally only entered convents as novices a year or two before this. Although some authorities argued that girls could be professed at twelve (the same age they were deemed mature enough to be married), the entry and veiling of children much younger than this age was rare, and seems only to have occurred among the highest aristocracy. Given that she was only six, Mary could not have expected to be professed as a full nun, and it was a further six years before she made her formal vows in 1291, when she had reached the age of twelve. In addition, in contrast to most nuns, Mary did not pay the usual dowry, or entry fee, on joining Amesbury; rather, the princess represented potential future windfalls, such as when, in 1289, 'for the love which the king bears to his daughter', her father waived, forever, the annual allowance for the nearby manor of Melksham due from the convent to the Exchequer, saving the priory in excess of twenty-seven pounds each year. This amount represented pure profit for Amesbury, as the princess was also provided with a generous annual allowance of one hundred pounds to cover the upkeep of her private chamber, to be paid in two instalments each year, throughout her life. Her income was more than double that needed to provide two full knightly households, but in this case its sole purpose was to furnish Mary's chamber (in which she dined, read, and possibly slept) and to procure special food-stuffs for her table. As a nun, her clothing was expected to be simple, unlike the extravagant furs, jewels, and other fineries worn by her worldly sisters. Mary was also granted an annual provision of wood (forty oaks, taken from royal forests near

Amesbury) to burn in her chamber fireplace, as well as twenty tuns of wine from the Bordeaux claret merchants which docked at the nearest port of Southampton. In accepting the six-year-old princess into their official membership, the financial and social position of Amesbury Priory was significantly strengthened, which undoubtedly eased any anxieties the community felt about the propriety and wisdom of veiling a nun so young.[6]

Throughout the autumn of 1285, Mary and her noble companions settled into their new lives in the priory. As students and novices, the girls spent their days in a kind of convent school, learning to read and to recite the psalms and the responses to verses they would need to know for their roles in a monastic community. The heart of the convent, long since worn to ruin, consisted of a cloister lined with stone seats, where the community could gather during clement weather. A large dining hall, or *frater*; a communal dormitory two hundred feet long, where most of the nuns slept; a chapter house that served as the community's official meeting room; a large kitchen; and a hall all came off the square cloisters. Beyond were separate buildings that included the buttery, pantry, and the prioress's lodgings, as well as a number of other discrete suites, one of which was set aside to accommodate the Abbess of Fontevrault or her representative, and another of which was likely the suite of rooms that Eleanor of Provence began building in the early 1280s to house herself and her granddaughters in appropriate style. Further out from the central spaces inhabited by the nuns and novices were lodgings for the male clerics resident at Amesbury, an infirmary, a hay barn, and stables, all enclosed by a gatehouse and set within a park that included herb and vegetable gardens, orchards, and fishponds nestled in bends along the River Avon at the southern edge of Salisbury Plain.[7]

The princess's day-to-day routine may have shifted slowly

into the normal daily pattern of a novice: a steady but demanding schedule of communal prayer and private reading punctuated by three meals and eight hours of sleep. The primacy of the Divine Offices in monastic life – matins and lauds spoken in the middle of the night, followed by prime, tierce, sext, none, vespers, and compline throughout the day – almost certainly mean that Mary was learning to participate in these ceremonies immediately or soon after arriving at Amesbury, quickly deploying the knowledge she gained to sing hymns and recite key passages of scripture from memory. The diminutive six-year-old must have appeared desperately out of place as she stood in the nuns' choir stalls among the mostly adult community. She would have gone to confession frequently, received communion at least once a month, and listened to sermons extolling the virtues of purity and humility at Mass in the priory's church twice each day. It was a rigorous routine for a young child, and she must especially have struggled with the broken sleep patterns required to fulfil her duty as a bride of Christ.

Every waking moment of Mary's day would have been dominated by communal prayer or quiet reflection – silence was observed for much of the day, and no time was set aside for play. Nevertheless, it is hard to imagine that she did not manage to find a way to have fun with the other noble novices or the secular children boarding within the convent. At Christmas time, she may have been entertained by minstrels or musicians – they were ostensibly forbidden within convents, but were so frequently lamented by church authorities that their presence must have been common – or perhaps even performed the part of Girl Abbess, a customary game in which, during the Feast of St Nicholas, the patron saint of children, the youngest novice or nun would lead the community in dancing and revelry. Mary's diversions from the strict daily observations and practices would more usually have included tuition in reading, most likely initially with psalters and over time with broader devotional material, such as collections of saints' lives borrowed from the priory library or from fellow nuns. She would also have had access to chivalric romances borrowed from fellow nuns or from her grandmother's collection, tales that would have resonated with her own experiences at court. Even after her installation at Amesbury, Mary continued to preside alongside her family members at special events; for example, soon after she entered the priory in the autumn of 1285, she attended the Winchester tournament where her father, concerned that the number of knights was falling precipitously and desperate to preserve his fighting force, compelled forty-four wealthy men to become knights.

Amesbury was home to a community of monks – men like the Brother Richard who looked after the princess's finances – as well as a variety of servants of both genders. Male and female visitors were also in frequent attendance, including Mary's parents and siblings, who spent a week at Amesbury in early 1286. The king and queen were at the time travelling back towards London from Exeter, where they had spent Christmas with Eleanora, Joanna, and Margaret. The princesses had been on pilgrimage together, first to Glastonbury and then westward via minor shrines – practising the public piety expected of royal women – before joining their parents. They arrived at Amesbury en route from the village of Dinton in Cranborne Chase, Dorset, to Upavon near the North Wessex Downs, resplendent in newly embellished gowns of vibrant silks and linen, embroidered with gold and sprinkled with ornaments, including the six dozen silver buttons that Eleanora's personal tailor had sewn onto her dresses in the weeks leading up to the holiday. These sumptuous robes would have contrasted sharply with the simple black gown intended to be worn by a nun like Mary, but the declarations against nuns wearing brightly coloured, silken or bejewelled clothing and ornaments, which were repeated throughout the later Middle Ages, suggest that luxurious, worldly clothing made at least occasional appearances within the cloister, and it is easy to imagine the young novice's gaze lingering longingly on the forbidden beautiful dresses of her elder sisters. Eleanora had fallen ill on the way back from Exeter, and her servants were sent to procure lemons, spices, almonds, figs, and raisins and bring them to Amesbury – perhaps her mother felt the bright flavours of her youth in Spain might help to rally her daughter's spirits. The rest of the family feasted with Mary, spending over thirty pounds during a single week, a significant increase on their usual weekly expenses.[8]

Mary seemed to be struggling to adjust to life at Amesbury – she was terribly homesick and spent much of the spring of 1286 ensconced within the bosom of her family, away from the priory to which she was pledged. This was unusual. Nuns of the Fontevrault Order were meant to be strictly enclosed – unable in normal circumstances to venture outside the walls of their convent, and explicitly forbidden from spending excessive periods away from the monastic precinct or dining in the company of secular men and women. At the time that Mary joined Amesbury, the Archbishop of Canterbury was engaged in a decades-long battle to enforce the rules of enclosure, particularly for nuns. He issued a set of rules, including the instruction that:

> For the purpose of obtaining a surer witness to chastity, we ordain that nuns shall not leave the precincts of the monastery, save for necessary business which cannot be performed by other persons. Hence we condemn for ever, by these present letters those sojourns which were wont to be made in the houses of friends, for the sake of pleasure and of escaping from discipline.

Without doubt, Mary's position secured her a much greater freedom of movement throughout her life than most nuns would have enjoyed; favouritism was officially prohibited, but none dared to challenge the king or queen on the propriety of their child visiting her family. Therefore, in March she visited court at Winchester and, later that month, her father and Eleanora were back at Amesbury once more, where Eleanora purchased a new horse she named Rougement, after the castle in Exeter where they had spent Christmas. In May, Mary left the enclosure of the priory once again to travel with the whole royal family to Dover, where they welcomed home her grandmother Eleanor of Provence, who had returned from a tour of continental relatives as she prepared for her own veiling ceremony. Mary remained at court for nearly a month, probably both to become better acquainted with the dowager queen whose principal companion she would soon become, and to say goodbye to her parents, as they prepared to travel to Gascony to mediate between rival kings for the throne of Sicily. Before they departed, the queen arranged for Mary to have an additional fifty marks each year to supplement her income, most likely to reassure herself that her daughter would be well provided for while she and Edward were far away.[9]

Mary's extraordinary income meant she would always live apart from her peers – her private chamber was much more luxuriously furnished than the convent dormitory in which most of her fellow novices and nuns slept, and her separate dining table was more sumptuously laid. Her connections, too, marked her out even among the other, largely aristocratic, nuns. When she was finally professed at the age of twelve, the ceremony was overseen by three English bishops appointed to the task by the Archbishop of Canterbury. At the ceremony's conclusion, Mary stood with her peers, as gold rings set with sapphires were placed on their fingers. The rings, gifts from the king, were emblems of the girls' roles as brides of Christ – the deep blue of the stones symbolized the girls' purity and recalled the celestial robes in which the Blessed Virgin was clothed on her assumption.[10]

Even after she was professed, Mary continued to visit her parents, during which she eschewed the daily routine of prayer and quiet contemplation at Amesbury, for the rather more colourful delights of court and the exceptional freedoms that only she, among her peers, enjoyed. She may also have come to associate the emotional comfort of being surrounded by family *at* court with the material comforts *of* court. From a very young age, therefore, Mary grew up understanding that, as a princess, she could take greater licence than her peers, and that she had both the motive and the means to exert her desires.

However, alongside the special freedoms and privileges that accompanied her position came exceptional responsibilities. Later, during her adolescence, Mary was enlisted on more than one occasion to represent the Abbess of Fontevrault in negotiations with her father. The abbess was clearly seeking to maximize her direct link with royal authority through Mary, but this forced the princess into a difficult position. Aged fourteen, she travelled to court to argue before the king on behalf of the abbess and *against the nuns of Amesbury*; the abbess believed that her rights had been ignored when the Amesbury nuns had elected their own prioress, rather than deferring to the abbess's authority to appoint one. The king ultimately sided with the position his daughter advanced, and issued a ruling that guaranteed the abbess her right to appoint a new prioress. It cannot have been easy for Mary when she returned to the convent, having helped deprive her fellow nuns of their autonomy. The abbess was clearly pleased though and, seeing the influence the young royal

nun could wield, enlisted Mary among her regular legal representatives in England. At other times, the Amesbury community
deployed the princess for their own gain, such as when Mary
wrote to her father imploring his support against encroachments
on the priory's estate. This was effective, for while many landowners might have dared to challenge a convent of nuns ruled
by a distant superior living in France, none would have considered making moves against the king's daughter, and especially
not while he was watching. And so, in this way, the nun-princess
was, from an early age, deploying her access to royal decision-
making for the gain of associates.[11]

This kind of intercession was perhaps the central political and
ceremonial role for royal women in medieval England. Once her
grandmother joined the community in July 1286, on the anniversary of the reburial of St Thomas Becket – a saint to whom
the royal family pledged special allegiance – at Westminster,
Mary would have had ample opportunity to learn from her. She
would also have read about the art of intercession through texts
available to her at Amesbury – for example, the popular *Chasteau
d'Amours*, written earlier in the century by Robert Grosseteste,
Bishop of Lincoln. This Norman-French allegorical poem would
have been particularly meaningful to women living under a vow
of chastity since it described the Virgin Mary as the 'castle of
love' in which God dwells on earth, her strong walls the virginity
that guards what is precious within from evil. But another allegorical story within the *Chasteau d'Amours* might have felt
even more directly relevant to the young Mary; it describes
earth as a chivalric kingdom ruled by God as a just and powerful
king whose four daughters – Mercy, Truth, Justice, and Peace
– help him to rule. As the fourth daughter of a king, Mary could
hardly have failed to relate the tale to herself and her sisters.
The story continues with Adam, God's servant, cast into prison

for disloyalty to the king, while each of the daughters makes a plea to their father regarding Adam's fate: Mercy asks for forgiveness, Truth and Justice both require his punishment, and Peace cannot abide in the country until her sisters are united again. Ultimately, their brother Christ sacrifices himself to appease Truth and Justice while embracing Mercy, and to cause Peace to return to the kingdom. The story at the heart of the *Chasteau d'Amours* uses simple allegory to answer the question of why God sacrificed his son, but it also illustrates the common understanding of the role of royal women, including both the practice of intercession and the profound impact that such intercession can have. Mary, like the allegorical daughters of God, became adept at practising intercession in her early years at Amesbury. She would struggle more with fulfilling those other expectations of nuns throughout her life – her vows of poverty, obedience, and chastity.[12]

V
Growing Up

1286–9
LANGLEY

In the middle of May 1286, the king and queen, their households, and a large group of courtiers sailed from Dover to
Wissant, just south of Calais. Edward and Eleanor expected to
be away from their kingdom and their children for about a year,
but the various matters on the continent demanding their attention were more complex than they had bargained for, and they
would, in fact, not return to English soil for over three years.
This time away from their parents' influence meant different
things for each of their children.

For Eleanora, now seventeen, the separation from her parents
must have been difficult. Since being reunited with them
following their return from the Crusades twelve years before,
she had spent a considerable amount of time with them and had
grown close to both. Indeed, her presence seems to have been

most acutely missed by the king and queen, since her name was most frequently attached to gifts sent home from abroad. Eleanora was also the child with the most direct stake in her father's activities in Europe: chief among Edward's reasons for travelling abroad was his attempt to negotiate peace between his French relatives and Eleanora's prospective Aragonese in-laws. The war between these two kingdoms was a matter of acute personal anxiety for the king, who had spent years trying to avoid getting involved. On one side was his uncle, a French count; on the other was Eleanora's prospective father-in-law. By 1283, the situation had grown so desperate that the parties agreed to solve the matter by single combat at Bordeaux – a one-on-one duel between the competing kings, placing the lives of both monarchs in extreme peril – and Edward was asked to act as arbiter; but still he refused to be dragged in. In the years that followed, the competing forces engaged in pitched battles at sites across the Mediterranean. Matters worsened when the Pope sided with the French and, to prevent the powerful union of English and Aragonese interests, expressly forbade any of Edward's children from marrying any of the sons, daughters, nieces, or nephews of the King of Aragon. The consummation of Eleanora's marriage – the act that would convert her 'proxy' marriage of 1282 into a fully binding one, and the princess into a queen – could not proceed in these circumstances, but nor was she free to marry elsewhere. The only option that would have freed her from her contract with Alfonso would have been becoming a nun, which she presumably did not wish to do. Even worse for her father, the French king became personally involved in the war, threatening to call Edward's knightly service that he owed for holding the fief of Gascony – refusing this would have been impossible for Edward if he wished to retain his continental holdings.[1]

Meanwhile, the war also stood in the way of Edward's greatest personal ambition: to return to the Holy Land on another Crusade that would succeed where his earlier one had not, in claiming once more a Kingdom of Jerusalem for Christianity. In order to achieve his aim, Edward needed a pan-European effort, but this was out of the question while two of Western Europe's greatest powers were spending money and sacrificing the lives of their men in wars with each other. In 1286 Edward decided to step in and negotiate a settlement that would not only make his crusading dreams possible but would also pave the way for Eleanora to finally travel to Aragon and consummate her marriage to Alfonso, who had become king on his father's death in 1285.

Aged fourteen, Joanna had also been close to her mother for many years, though she too showed her self-reliance – perhaps a product of her early years in Ponthieu – by striking out from court on journeys with her household, such as that which had taken her to Rhuddlan in 1283. For her, the departure of her parents meant the end of opportunities for Eleanor or Edward to shape her character, for she married and left court soon after their return. At the age of eleven, Margaret had only travelled beyond her nursery for a few years when it once again became the centre of her existence, and her parents' departure meant she missed out on much of the learning that her older sisters had enjoyed in the company of the queen. Instead, Margaret's character was shaped by the governesses and aristocratic ladies who frequented the sisters in their parents' absence, teaching them the skills expected of noblewomen, and offering advice and companionship to their charges. She would mature into the most conventional of the sisters, a fitting match for her betrothed, Jan. Heir to the famous chivalric Duke of Brabant, and Margaret's contemporary, Jan had arrived in England in 1284 to complete his education at Edward's court, but seems to have focused more on courtly pursuits than learning about statecraft.

Their parents' trip to Gascony was least destabilizing for the youngest siblings at home, four-year-old Elizabeth and two-year-old Edward, as the house they had lived in since the death of their brother Alphonso two years earlier became the nucleus around which the older royal children circulated for the three years their parents were away. Located at Langley in Hertfordshire (known since the fifteenth century as King's Langley), their mother's new palace was set in rolling parkland filled with deer for hunting, and surrounded by a moat. Langley was well equipped with a sizable kitchen and pantry, and included a cloistered court paved in green and white tiles, with a large central hall that, in the following decade, was extensively refurbished and decorated with fifty-two painted heraldic shields and a scene of knights on their way to a tournament, against a background of vivid yellow and vermillion. Separate lodgings for the king and queen, and their children, offered the luxury of privacy, while a chapel, extensive stables that housed a camel as well as horses, gardens, and a vineyard completed the site.[2]

One of the king's crusading companions was assigned to lead the household, which functioned as a kind of court in miniature formed around the tiny prince, his sisters, and their noble companions, who were mostly the wards of their parents and children of their parents' closest friends and servants. During the years in which the king and queen were in Gascony, the palace at Langley served as their official state residence, remaining open to receive visitors. A sizable military guard was housed at or near to the palace, comprising of seven knights, nine serjeants-at-arms, and various other armed men – a small army to protect the royal children from anyone who might seek to take advantage of the king's absence and overthrow his rule or kidnap or harm his heirs. The expense of maintaining this force was immense – over four thousand pounds were spent each year the king was away on feeding, clothing, and paying the wages for all servants and guards of the children – and yet its strength must have been a great comfort to the king and queen, so far removed from their children and unable to come easily to their assistance.[3]

While Mary remained at Amesbury with her grandmother, the rest of the siblings spent Christmas in 1286, the first year their parents were abroad, at Langley. Eleanora, Joanna, and Margaret's companions were also present: the Ponthevin governess Edeline Papyot, Matilda de Haversham (a ward of the queen and a minor heiress), and three other ladies. Their cousin John of Brittany – who had been close to Eleanora since her nursery days – was frequently present, as was his sister Marie, who spent her adolescence as a companion to Eleanora. Margaret's fiancé, Jan of Brabant, was also in attendance with his men, including a knight, a horsemaster, a tailor, a falconer, and a lute player – all the assistants a cosmopolitan young man of the thirteenth century needed to cultivate his chivalry. A messenger from Gascony brought the king and queen's Christmas tidings to their children, while shipments of luxury foods and clothing were brought in to the royal household. In preparation for the cold winter wind, Langley was provided with furs imported by merchants from Lucca and Turin, and from the royal storehouses in London came deliveries of spices and ginger, almonds, fruits including figs, dates, and raisins, and loaves of sugar to prepare the traditional holiday confections. These included sweetmeats such as gingerbread men, spiced with saffron and decorated with raisins and orange peel; *frumenty*, a boiled milk dish made with honey and spices; and *posset*, a thick, eggy drink, laced with nutmeg. Gomage, Prince Edward's butler, was responsible for procuring the wine necessary for the whole princely *familia* – the wine cellar at Langley during the 1280s must have been insufficient, since nearly seventy pounds was spent in 1291 building a new *cave*, more than seventy feet long – and the household clerks sourced the additional candles needed to provide light for feasts that lasted long into the dark winter nights.[4]

The royal children would have had new robes made from many-coloured cloths and skins – the older of them wore silken gowns encircled at the waist by pelt girdles (Eleanora's most likely covered in silver buttons, as was clearly a favourite style of hers), under a heavy silk or velvet mantle fastened by a jewelled clasp, and topped with gold headdresses or feather caps. That Christmas, Jan ordered new white tournament saddles and several new pairs of golden spurs for himself and one of his knights. The food served at the palace would have included seasonal favourites such as venison, or delicacies such as suckling pig or swan, bones of both of which have been found discarded among contemporaneous debris at the palace.[5]

Amid the splendour of Christmas at Langley, Eleanora may have worn the coronet her father had sent from Paris earlier that year. This gold circlet, a gift from the king of France, was set with sapphires, emeralds, rubies, and pearls; it was a crown fit for a queen but, rather than bestow it on his own wife, Edward passed it to the daughter whose status remained intangible due to the ongoing contention between Aragon and France. It is easy to imagine that a man as conscious of the role of symbolism as Edward, might have seen some justice in giving his daughter a crown from the same man who was denying her her place as Queen of Aragon.

Ever her parents' daughter, Eleanora spent the early years at Langley perfecting the art of queenship. Above all, she practised intercession on behalf of her loyal servants and friends. One touching example concerned a household knight named Sir Eustace de Hache who was in danger of losing his estate, because he insisted on remaining with the household guard even when his feudal lord required his military service elsewhere – as well as feeling loyal to the royal children, Sir Eustace was likely worried about losing his annuity of twelve pounds in fees and livery. He appealed to Eleanora for assistance, and found her to be a strident supporter. She wrote to the cousin her father had appointed regent, praising Sir Eustace's loyal service and asking for royal release from his feudal obligations. While Eleanora's letter did not, on that occasion, win the requested release for the knight, his subsequent summons to Parliament and elevation to a baronial title in the early fourteenth century indicates that his devotion to the royal household was ultimately rewarded.[6]

Perhaps the most fascinating instances of Eleanora's intercession were on behalf of subjects of the Crown who appealed to her for assistance while her parents were in Gascony. On one such occasion, she was approached by Eleanor of Saint Paul, a London heiress or widow who – perhaps exhausted by the persecution she suffered or sensing there would be worse to come – had recently converted from Judaism to Christianity. Like most converts at the time, she learned soon after her conversion that her whole estate, including her goods, chattels, and properties, as well as all debts that had been owing to her, would now be confiscated by the king's men, who sheltered disingenuously behind the claim that they merely wished to protect the reborn soul of a Christian from the taint of association with usury. Somehow, Eleanor of Saint Paul managed to appeal to the princess and she found a willing lobbyist in Eleanora. Among the king's first notices relating to his children after returning from Gascony was an order to restore Eleanor of Saint Paul's property to its rightful mistress, noting that 'the king has given them to her at the instance of Eleanora, his daughter'. Tempting as it is to see this act of intercession as condemnation by Eleanora of her father's appalling treatment of the Jewish population, whom he had already expelled from Gascony and would soon expel from England, there is not enough evidence to support this. She may have argued against the wisdom of punishing those who converted to Christianity, or perhaps she especially took to Eleanor of Saint Paul as an individual. What is clear is that Eleanora perceived an injustice in the case and wanted to use her influence to put it right.[7]

Like her sisters, Eleanora learned to deploy her connections on behalf of faithful servants, subjects, and causes from her mother and grandmother, but in practising intercession she was also modelling herself on the behaviour of another important queen: the Blessed Virgin Mary. From the thirteenth century, throughout Western Europe, a growing cult positioned Mary, the mother of God, as the ultimate intercessor – the crowned queen who sat enthroned next to her son, ever-ready to offer counsel as he governed the Kingdom of Heaven. Hers was considered the voice that might most readily influence his judgments. The Virgin was the woman on whom all Christian women sought to model themselves – as practically impossible as it was for mere humans to emulate a virgin mother – but, as Queen of Heaven, she was an especially important role model for women like Eleanora. The royal daughters almost certainly heard poems from the *Cantigas de Santa Maria,* a collection composed (or at least guided in their composition) by their maternal uncle, the king of Castile, sung by minstrels visiting the English court from Castile. This extraordinary cycle of poems describing miracles attributed to the Virgin comprises more than four hundred songs that tell apocryphal stories from the life of Mary. The *Cantigas* would have been appropriate poems for the nieces of the Castilian king because they offered clear moral patterns for medieval women, while also highlighting the importance of intercession as a means for royal women to make an impact in the world. The piety they promoted included the forms of ritualized piety and the performance of good works practised by Eleanora and her sisters throughout their lives, parading before their father's subjects on pilgrimage to shrines across the country – a simultaneous act of both genuine devotion and display, one of the public roles that royal women were expected to play.

In April of the second year of her parents' absence, a glimmer of hope shone on Eleanora's prospects as queen-in-waiting of Aragon: the pro-French Pope who had issued the proclamation forbidding her marriage to Alfonso died, and there were hopes in England and Aragon that his successor might come from outside the French king's orbit of influence. Later that year, in the small town of Oloron-Sainte-Marie, situated between Gascony and Aragon, Edward's party met Alfonso's and, amid feasts and jousting, devised a treaty to settle the question of who, between his cousins in the House of Anjou and King Alfonso, his prospective son-in-law, was the rightful King of Sicily. At the same time, the terms of dower and dowry for Eleanora's marriage were confirmed by both parties, and Edward declared that, as soon as a new pope was chosen, he would send an embassy to procure 'diligently . . . without fraud or other machinations' a licence to contract the marriage between Alfonso and Eleanora, 'our dearest first-born'. He promised that, within three months of securing this licence, he would send Eleanora to Aragon so the marriage might be consummated. How invigorating this news must have been to the princess who, after so many years of delay, might now have been within reach of marriage and the queenship she had long been practising.[8]

But in the months that followed, the treaty agreed at Oloron foundered. Edward redoubled his efforts to settle the Sicilian succession, finally securing a workable treaty between the two families late in 1288. However, by this point the new Pope – the one who it was hoped would grant Eleanora's marriage – was in post, and he immediately cancelled Edward's treaty, arguing that it failed to protect papal interests. Furthermore, he then disastrously excommunicated Alfonso and, from that point on, although Edward and Alfonso remained in frequent contact over the continuing Sicilian crisis, nothing further is mentioned of Eleanora and Alfonso's marriage. There was no way an English princess could wed a man who had been excommunicated, and nor was she free to make another match, since her 'proxy' marriage was legally binding. By late 1288, aged nineteen, dutiful Eleanora was still frozen in marital limbo.

By contrast, plans for Joanna's marriage progressed steadily throughout the late 1280s. After the death of Hartman, the German prince to whom Joanna had been betrothed as a child, discussions began to wed her to one of her father's wealthiest – and most problematic – magnates. Gilbert de Clare (known as 'the Red' because of his hair, though it also described his temperament), was Earl of Gloucester and Hertford, and one of the greatest of the famed Marcher lords of Wales, who were granted almost absolute power over the estates along England's borders, providing a buffer to the wilder lands beyond. Gilbert had a complicated history with the royal family. Succeeding his father at the age of eighteen in 1263, when the barons of England were surging towards rebellion, Gilbert initially aligned himself with rebel leader Simon de Montfort against King Henry but then, during the course of the civil war, switched sides no less than five times, ultimately proving a crucial ally of the royal family and one whose military support was critical in defeating the rebels. Despite this, his reconciliation with Edward was strained, and their personal relationship remained uneasy. By the 1280s, however, the men once again shared an adversary, in the form of Llywelyn ap Gruffydd, the Welsh prince whose power stretched from Glamorgan in the south to Snowdonia in the north. Gilbert's great wealth and ability to draw significant military forces from England and across Glamorgan meant that he could be a powerful ally in the war to conquer Wales. His relative independence from the Crown as one of the greatest Marcher lords also meant Edward would always struggle to keep him in line. Therefore, the king's view that a marital alliance making Gilbert his own son might help control him was clearly insightful (and Gilbert, for his part, clearly saw the personal advantage in building a closer relationship to the king), and Joanna was available.

In 1283 her marriage to Gilbert was agreed. She was eleven, while he was forty. But, before the earl could wed the king's daughter, he needed to divorce his first wife. Back when he was only nine years old, Gilbert's father had arranged for him to marry six-year-old Alice de Lusignan, daughter of King Henry III's half-brother, in the hope that a close connection to the royal family might strengthen the Clare family's position in England. Their two daughters were born to the couple just over a decade later, but by 1267, Alice and Gilbert were estranged, and in 1271 they formally separated. The cause of the dissolution of their marriage is unrecorded in formal documents, but rumours circulated that, while being held captive during the civil war, the countess had engaged in an adulterous affair with her cousin, Prince Edward. More than a dozen years later, when he became engaged to Joanna, Gilbert appealed to be released from his marriage, and in June 1285, he finally secured a settlement which granted Alice ample lands and manors, and set him free to marry again. During the years that Edward was in Gascony, Gilbert dutifully supported the royal cause, serving as captain on an expedition to put down a rebellion in Wales over the summer of 1287. Despite this service, he remained unable to restrain his aggressive impulses, at one point invading neighbouring Brecon estates belonging to the Earl of Hereford, a competing Marcher lord, with a small army. Gilbert also sent his messengers to Rome to request the dispensation he would need to marry Joanna (because she was a cousin of his first wife). Perhaps surprisingly, given that the match between the young princess and the magnate old enough to be her father was undoubtedly driven by political opportunism on both sides, Gilbert also played the romantic suitor, showering Joanna with silk tunics and a set of matching dresses made of the finest deep blue cloth imported from Tarsus in Turkey, for his bride-to-be and her two closest sisters, Eleanora and Margaret.[9]

Joanna awaited the freedom her marriage would bring with some impatience. Having exhibited an independence of spirit from an early age, she had grown into a fiercely proud and stubborn young woman, and was known for her bold behaviour. In one instance, the princess quarrelled with Giles de Audenarde, the steward who governed the children's household, and refused thereafter to deal with him; rather than receiving money from him to pay for her purchases, she instead ran up a long series of petty debts to various merchants. Concerned that Audenarde might complain of her behaviour to her father, Joanna sent two knights to Gascony to deliver her version of the story to Edward, along with a letter in which she beseeched 'dear sire, we beg you . . . to believe the things which they shall tell you by word of mouth from me.' Joanna and Audenarde never reconciled but, from the description of the quarrel merely as 'some contention' between Joanna and Audenarde in the queen's wardrobe book, Joanna's parents seem to have shrugged off the teenager's dramatic gesture, with the queen paying off her daughter's debts upon their return home.[10]

Joanna was clearly not afraid to challenge authority, even when it represented her own father, as Audenarde did in his role as steward of the children's household. This trait became increasingly apparent as she grew to adulthood, and might be considered her defining characteristic. Perhaps surprisingly to some modern readers, young aristocratic women in the thirteenth century like Joanna were allowed – and even encouraged – to practise fierce defiance. Popular stories from the lives of the holy virgin martyrs made a virtue of their refusal to back down against powerful men who aimed to compel them into marriage or to renounce their beliefs. This acceptable defiance was, however, always closely circumscribed: the disobedience of the virgin saints only ever sought to protect their chastity and to defend their devotion to Christ. Yet it is hard to disentangle the women praised as saints from the theme of resistance, and Joanna may have found models for defiant womanhood in these popular devotional stories that emboldened her own actions and encouraged her feeling that she was in charge of her own destiny. She stood firm against those whom she should by all contemporary conventions have obeyed, confident that her position as daughter of the king granted her exceptional licence.[11]

Margaret, meanwhile, was growing into a wholly different young woman from her older sisters. Instead of Eleanora's active embrace of her royal duty or Joanna's rebellious streak, she was engaged in perfecting the art of female nobility, perhaps encouraged by the example of Edeline Papyot or the other aristocratic women who frequented Langley in the years her parents were away. Margaret spent her adolescence modelling herself on the idealized image of a fashionable courtly lady, highly accomplished in embroidery, weaving, and hunting. Wardrobe accounts record that spindles, silks of many colours and thicknesses, and gold thread were constantly being procured for her use – in one case, her squire Thomas was sent to purchase two hundred ounces of gold thread 'for the making of garlands and treasures'. Margaret also, along with all her siblings, was a keen hunter – the king's huntsman Philip spent a month just before Christmas in 1286 at Langley, bringing twenty hounds with him. He was often back again during the following years, each time bringing with him packs of dogs, including *berceletts*, small hunting dogs like modern beagles, that belonged to Queen Eleanor. As Prince Edward was only a toddler, he was not Philip's primary pupil; rather his teenage sisters would have gone on most of the hunts he organized. The queen evidently wished, despite her absence, to ensure her daughters continued developing their skills and a love of hunting with hounds that she shared – and they seem to have embraced the tradition.[12]

As Margaret was consciously cultivating a courtly identity, her young fiancé was developing his chivalric persona. Jan spent his years in England nurturing his skills in tournament arts such as jousting, in hunting with falcons, in entertaining parties of important noblemen, giving them expensive gifts and gambling with dice, and in patronizing music. His desire to become a model knight was undoubtedly influenced by his father, who was perhaps the most famous jouster of his generation across Northern Europe, but it may also have been inspired by the clear efforts his fiancée was making to project ideal medieval womanhood. His devotion to the art of the hunt was remarkable even for the age. The earliest seal that survives for Jan shows that his public identity was synonymous with the sophisticated pastime of hunting: he is depicted as a young man on horseback, with a hooded falcon perched on his hand and another flying next to the horse, while a dog runs alongside. Margaret, meanwhile, focused not only on being beautifully dressed and skilled with a needle, but also on cultivating the 'feminine virtues' of Courtesy – evidently lacking in her sister Joanna – and Meekness – not necessarily compatible with Eleanora's active diplomatic interventions and manoeuvring on behalf of friends. If she could perfect these virtues and project an aura of ideal womanhood, Margaret could grow to wield significant cultural influence in Brabant, but, as she entered adolescence, the pressure to mature into the ideal woman must have felt acute.[13]

For Elizabeth, the years her parents were away would have nearly erased them entirely from her memory. She, alone of all the royal children, had lived in her parents' itinerant household for her first two-and-a-half years, and she was closer as a young child to her parents than any of their other children. Later, the warmth and strength of love that the adult Elizabeth showed her father suggests that some sliver of memory of an early parental bond remained. Before the king and queen left England, perhaps in consideration that travel was risky, they arranged her marriage to the son of the Count of Holland. Elizabeth was not yet three when the embassy finalized the agreement. The betrothal was another echo of the tragedy of Alphonso's death: Elizabeth's young fiancé, even younger than her, was the baby brother of Margaret, the intended bride of Prince Alphonso, for whom the glorious, unfinished psalter had been commissioned.[14]

When king and queen finally arrived back at Dover in the autumn of 1289, the seven-year-old Elizabeth, who grew up knowing she would be Countess of Holland and a stand-in for the alliance that her dead brother was meant to secure, must have been unrecognizable to her parents. More used to nurse-maids and servants, she and her five-year-old brother Edward may have lingered shyly on the fringes of the party, but Eleanora, by this time twenty years old, Joanna, seventeen, and Margaret, fourteen, would have waited eagerly for the sight of their parents. Ten-year-old Mary remained at Amesbury in the company of their grandmother, but the five children who made up the welcoming party travelled to the coast for a fortnight, in a carriage fitted out with new scarlet silk mattresses and golden cushions trimmed in green silk to dampen the jostling. No records survive to attest the family members' feelings on their reunion, but given that all six of their children were alive, healthy, and rapidly blossoming, Edward and Eleanor must have been greatly relieved. This homecoming was certainly in stark contrast to their arrival home twelve years earlier, when they returned after the Crusade to a dead father, with one son also dead, and another one dying.[15]

VI
Union

In the royal apartments at Winchester Castle on 20 April, ten days before her wedding to Gilbert and three days shy of her eighteenth birthday, Joanna counted the number of servants in her household, as well as in the households of her two sisters, Eleanora and Margaret. To her fury, she realized that they both had larger households than she did and, by extension, the appearance of superior influence or closer association with their royal parents. The teenager did not contain her displeasure; rather, she immediately demanded additional yeomen, so that her household would appear every bit as prestigious as those of her sisters. Eager to appease his hot-tempered daughter, and perhaps conscious that meeting her demands would soon be another man's problem, her father acquiesced, promptly hiring two pages to join Joanna's household for a fixed term of nine days, with their employment ceasing the day she married.[1]

In the whirlwind leading up to Joanna's wedding, it is not clear how she first noticed the discrepancy between the size of her retinue and those of her sisters, but, as she prepared to wed a noble Englishman rather than a foreign ruler like her younger sister Margaret, she may have been primed to perceive slights. The papal permission that enabled Joanna's marriage to Earl Gilbert came through near the end of 1289, not long after her parents had arrived back in England from Gascony. Soon after their return it had become apparent that the queen was steadily declining in health: while on the continent in 1287, she had contracted 'quartan fever', a variant of malaria in which fever appeared intermittently, lasting three days and then disappearing. This pattern of ill health would recur periodically over the next few years, gradually weakening a body that had given birth to sixteen children. Eleanor's condition had sufficiently deteriorated by early 1290 that she was preparing a chapel for the burial of her heart at the Dominican priory in London and had taken steps towards commissioning a tomb. Presumably wishing to see her children as settled as possible while she was alive, she and Edward decided to expedite Joanna's wedding to Gilbert, as well as Margaret's to Jan of Brabant.[2]

Throughout the late winter and early spring of 1290, the final legal guarantees were put in place to provide for Joanna and any future children she might bear, while also instituting safeguards to secure the first and second places in the line of succession for little Prince Edward and the still-unmarried Eleanora. (Under primogeniture, the estate of a lord who died without sons was divided equally between his daughters; the king was therefore seeking to prevent his estate – and the kingdom – from fracturing.) Gilbert surrendered the entirety of his family's estates in

England, Wales, and Ireland to the king, who re-granted those in Ireland to him alone. The estates in England and Wales were instead settled jointly on Gilbert and Joanna, and *her* heirs, even if by a subsequent husband. This was an extraordinary gesture of faith by Gilbert – effectively disinheriting his two daughters in the hope of producing a son by Joanna. But it was not the only test of loyalty that Edward demanded of his prospective son-in-law: on 17 April Gilbert travelled to Amesbury. The king and queen, and their five children who were still residing within the royal household, were at the priory visiting Mary and the dowager queen – one of several visits they made to Amesbury after their arrival back in England. The Archbishop of Canterbury, five other bishops, and eight noblemen, had also travelled to Amesbury to witness Gilbert's pledge to honour the king's chosen path for the succession of the English crown. Before this august assembly, Gilbert swore an oath to support the rule of Prince Edward (now six years old) and his heirs, or, if the prince should die without heirs, to support Eleanora as rightful Queen of England. This pledge was the final guarantee Edward required of his most powerful and least predictable magnate before sanctioning the marriage that would place him, in right of his wife, third in line to the throne of England. On the same day, perhaps in some way to confirm her proximity to the throne, Eleanora received from her mother a gold headdress and *zone*, a girdle that encircled the hips over a gown, made by the queen's goldsmith.[3]

The party, including Mary, then travelled on to Winchester, where they were joined by Margaret's fiancé Jan for a tournament in celebration of the two forthcoming royal weddings. The following morning, amid the row between Joanna and her parents over her number of pages, the family visited the cathedral, where they made offerings at several shrines before crowds. Later in the day, the tournament took place in a field just outside the city; competitors included both bridegrooms-to-be – Jan, whose expenses for the event were paid for by King Edward, and Gilbert, who paid his own way – as well as other young noblemen including John of Brittany, Eleanora's childhood companion at Guildford and Langley. The event culminated in a feast, during which the king unveiled the enormous round table, eighteen feet in diameter, that still hangs today on the wall of Winchester Castle's great hall. No detailed record of the feast survives, though it is likely to have included a set piece of Arthurian-inspired drama acted out around the round table by the noblemen at the feast – a Brabaçon verse chronicle of loosely fictionalized, romantic episodes from King Edward's life includes a description of Edward hosting a wedding feast around a round table, and ends with the king's exhortation to the wedding guests to conduct their lives according to the chivalric model of Arthur's court. Since the occasion was in celebration of their forthcoming weddings, we can expect that Joanna and Gilbert, and Margaret and Jan, presided over the festivities, and that they were perhaps among the twenty-odd people seated at the round table itself. For the brides-to-be and their elder sister Eleanora, the tournament at Winchester may have seemed especially sumptuous, but for Mary – only one year away from taking her final vow of poverty – the stark difference between court and her daily life of contemplation and prayer at Amesbury would have been hugely amplified during these festivities. It is hard not to wonder whether she jealously eyed her sisters or wondered why her destiny had not included being the focal point around which lavish international feasts might convene.[4]

The king heartily embraced the opportunity provided by his daughters' weddings to promote once again his association with

King Arthur. He could not have chosen a better backdrop than Winchester Castle: it was a perfect place in which to unveil a real-life round table and to conjure the spirit of chivalric romance. Since Geoffrey of Monmouth, Winchester had been associated with the stories of King Arthur, and during Edward's reign it was believed that the king had held court in the city. In reality, the castle was built after the Norman Conquest, and was heavily refurbished and extended by Edward's father, Henry III, who had been born there. It was he who had built the great hall, one of the most beautiful surviving examples of the age: more than one hundred feet long, the hall remains well-lit, with large windows, gracefully divided by two rows of dark stone columns that are speckled with tiny fossilized shells that were quarried at the Isle of Purbeck in nearby Dorset. The interior was white-washed, and a large mural at each end would have drawn in the viewer's attention. Above the king's high table was a depiction of the Wheel of Fortune, recalling the fickle nature of worldly glory, and at the other end a *mappa mundi* showed the known world, with England in the far west (at the bottom) and the Garden of Eden in the far east (at the top). On the occasion of Edward's round table tournament, four long cloths-of-gold were purchased to drape along the lower wall below the murals, which would have shimmered in the candlelight after sunset. For the teenage princesses about to be married, the tournament and feast may have been the first time they were at the centre of their father's myth-making, and the first sign that their roles within the royal family would be elevated by marriage, when they would no longer just be the king's children but also links to important political and diplomatic connections.

The feast at Winchester must have been an exceptionally lavish event, given the tens of thousands of gallons of wine that were consumed during the day and evening. The next day, the royal family began making their way back to Westminster, where Joanna was to be married the following week. Amid all the complex final negotiations surrounding the succession and the preparations for the lavish tournament, there had not been sufficient time to assemble the usual elaborate bridal trousseau for Joanna. Her parents had seven new dresses made to accompany her to her new home, as well as twenty-five pairs of soft leather shoes (footwear seems never to have lasted for long on the muddy pathways and cold stone floors of medieval England, and dozens of new pairs were being constantly purchased for the royal family), and fifteen pairs of gloves, but no new wedding gown. Instead, the bride and her two eldest sisters had fashionable *quintises*, or silk super-tunics that were designed to be worn over a close-fitting gown, reworked for the occasion.

Though she was denied a new gown to wear at the wedding, Joanna was at least gifted extraordinary jewels that would have outshone her sisters on the occasion. While in Paris, Adam, the queen's goldsmith, had procured a golden headdress set with rubies and emeralds, and a matching solid-gold *zone* encrusted with dozens more precious gems. Joanna's youngest sister Elizabeth was not left out; her mother gave the seven-year-old girl a small crown of her own to wear on the day.

On the morning of the wedding, on 30 April 1290, the princess-bride and her sisters donned their gowns and jewels and walked across the yard from the Palace of Westminster to the great abbey church. The bride's attendants at the private ceremony included her parents, her sisters and little brother, and many of the royal wards with whom she had been raised. It was intimate in scale for a royal wedding, but it was still the first royal marriage to take place inside the vast Gothic abbey since it had been rebuilt by her grandfather. Once inside, Joanna and Gilbert prostrated themselves before the altar at which her parents had been crowned sixteen years before. Mass was performed by the king's chaplain and when the wedding ring was lifted from the missal book, Joanna spoke the simple words, 'I take you to be my husband', that bound her to Gilbert, body and soul. The chaplain then blessed the couple with prayers reiterating their newfound partnership, the husband's duty to protect, and the wife's obligation to be loveable, wise, and faithful. He left out, however, a clause comparing the indissolubility of marriage to the covenant between Christ and the Church, given that this was excluded from second marriage ceremonies.[5]

When they emerged from the church, the earl and his new countess walked with their guests to a temporary hall that had been constructed within the palace grounds. The walls were lined with cloths covering the hall's skeletal construction, and the decorations would have included painted shields and heraldic banners displaying the red chevrons and gold of the House of Clare, intertwined with red and gold royal arms. Inside, a feast was laid out on trestle tables covered in fine linens. The festivities must have been merry: among several minstrels recorded entertaining at the event was Poveret, minstrel to the Marshal of Champagne. Wine clearly flowed freely since, at some point during the feast, the Sheriff of London, a prosperous cloth merchant named Fulk St Edmund, fell into a table and did such damage that it required subsequent repair.[6]

If, ten days before, Joanna had worried about her perceived status in comparison to her sisters', she was now a countess and joint landholder of one of the largest estates in England – and, what is more, she held a tighter grip on the Clare lands than her husband, since they would descend to her children, whether or not they were his. Now that she was married and fully of age, Joanna was freed from her parents' commands as well as from the influence of her long-serving governess, Lady Edeline.

In the days immediately following her wedding, however, she was still acting as a royal daughter, offering gifts to poor widows, along with her sisters Eleanora and Margaret, and receiving wedding presents from her parents, including a new carriage drawn by five horses. The king and queen clearly expected their second daughter to remain within their orbit for at least a short while, anticipating that she would stay at court until Margaret's wedding, planned for July. But only a week into married life, Joanna and her husband abruptly left court with their household of nearly two hundred servants and retainers, and travelled to the Clare family estates in Glamorgan. Their departure was probably the result of a dispute between the king and Gilbert, who through his lordship of Glamorgan claimed an income from the vacant bishopric of Llandaff, north of Cardiff. As a Welsh Marcher lord, Gilbert claimed greater autonomy over his Glamorgan estate than over his English lands, with the right to build castles and wage wars, appoint sheriffs and preside over courts, and to establish boroughs, markets, and forests. Within Glamorgan, he was almost a king – his predecessor had in 1247 been referred to as 'dominus et quasi rex', and Gilbert was even more king-like: when Edward visited Glamorgan after defeating the Welsh princes in 1284, Gilbert escorted him throughout the province like an equal. He felt his claim to the income from Llandaff was legitimate within the traditions of the March, but after his defeat of the Welsh princes in the north of the country, Edward had begun trying to rein in the autonomy of the Marcher lords further south and resisted Gilbert's claim. When Gilbert and his new wife left London, the king and queen were furious, but they were also newly powerless to compel their now-married daughter to remain at court. Their only way to punish Joanna was to impound and reclaim the small trousseau that had been prepared for her – they instead gifted the seven new gowns to

Margaret and a *zone* of pearls to Eleanora, along with a note explaining that the gowns had been reclaimed in punishment because Joanna had left court before Margaret's wedding. Weeks later, they would hear the news that their new son-in-law had launched a raid into Brecon against a rival Marcher lord, in strict defiance of the king's orders.[7]

Joanna had been given to Gilbert by her father in an effort to rein in the tempestuous earl, and her body came to symbolize, in a very literal sense, the link between the two men. It is clear that, in the time leading up to her marriage, she was used for the purposes of both her father and her husband-to-be. Gilbert sought Joanna's hand because it represented his own elevation in status – through her he would achieve even greater proximity to royal authority and the power and influence that came with it; Edward agreed to the marriage in the hope of taming Gilbert. Neither would have thought to wonder what the teenager who was the focus of their negotiations wanted. At first glance, the eighteen-year-old princess seems like little more than a pawn for her father to marry her off however he chose. But that is to mistake the role of the bride, who was required not just to acquiesce to her father's wishes, but to be an active participant in the ceremony, appearing before the crowds as the incarnation of regal poise and publicly proclaiming her desire to forge a union. Dynastic marriage undoubtedly included an element of exchange (although the normal custom of matching husband and wife who were roughly the same age meant that boys were as frequently the objects of this exchange as girls), but it did not necessarily disempower its female participants.

In key ways, the ritual was not unlike the pledge of homage at the very heart of medieval society by a vassal to his feudal lord, in which service was sworn for the promise of reward and protection. Like the vassal, the bride pledged herself to her lord because she expected to gain from the relationship. Joanna – never shy about expressing her dissatisfaction – professed her desire to be wed to a husband thirty years her senior because she stood to benefit from becoming the wife of one of the most powerful and independent lords in her father's realm. When she left court before Margaret's wedding, she was expressing her new freedom. But she also agreed to the marriage because she recognized that whatever helped her father, also helped her. Joanna's position, like that of her sisters, was special *because* of her relation to the king, a connection that was key to every advantage she held. The link was so inextricable that any fluctuation in her father's power would directly impact her own influence. Her fate, in other words, was intimately tied to that of her family – and her interests were bound indissolubly to those of her father and her family.[8]

Two months after Joanna was married, she returned to court to collect the trousseau (without the impounded dresses) that her parents had not had time to prepare before her wedding. On 2 July, her father instructed the keeper of the London Exchange to release three hundred marks' worth of the finest refined silver (imported from Ghent) for vessels and utensils to furnish her table. The silver was melted down and moulded to form the most-prized pieces among a collection of more than one hundred silver dishes and bowls, innumerable spoons and small dishes to hold spices and salt, vessels for wine and water, and a chapel set with a censer and an alms dish made in the shape of a ship. There was also gold: small pitchers to hold Eucharist wine, dozens of gold drinking cups, and a large bowl that alone cost almost nineteen pounds, around half the yearly income of a knightly household. She was given four large canopied beds for herself and her chief servants – enormous wooden-framed pieces that dominated medieval bedchambers and were normally the largest and costliest items of furniture, including not only the frame itself but also heavy feather mattresses, cushions, and layers of velvet and imported silk curtains that enclosed the air to keep occupants warm throughout winter. While the decorations of Joanna's bedclothes are unrecorded, they would have rivalled the richest of her gowns in their embroidery and the use of gold and silver thread: those which accompanied other English princesses to their marital homes included motifs of fighting dragons, stag hunts, and intertwined heraldic shields. Baskets and chests filled with table and bed linens, cushions, and her new carriage completed her household furnishings. Consumable goods also appear in the list of the king's gifts to his daughter on her marriage: pantry goods, silk belts with silver embroidery that could be given out as gifts to Joanna's new household servants and friends, and enough candles to fill a cart. Six carts were required to transport the complete trousseau assembled at the Tower of London to Clerkenwell north of the city, where the bride was in residence with her husband.[9]

Meanwhile, back at Westminster, the final preparations were underway for fifteen-year-old Margaret's marriage to Jan of Brabant, her fiancé since infancy and a fixture at court for five years. In contrast to Joanna's wedding, the ceremony on 8 July was full of dizzying pageantry designed to showcase the wealth and cosmopolitan finesse of Edward's court to the groom's father, the visiting Duke of Brabant, and his entourage. In the days leading up to the ceremony, the queen was in almost constant contact with her goldsmith, who had been charged with gathering the bridal jewels that would accompany Margaret as she began life as the consort of a foreign court. These included a silver nuptial crown for the wedding ceremony itself, another gold crown studded with three hundred emeralds, and a golden *chaplet* – a circular band worn around the head, covered in rubies and pearls, with the heraldic leopard of England picked out in sapphires. Each time Margaret wore this chaplet in her new duchy, it would explicitly recall to all who saw it her connection, and by extension Jan's, to the English king. The day before the wedding, the final touches were put in place, as table linens and tapestries to furnish the feast that would follow the ceremony were transported from the Tower of London up the Thames to the palace at Westminster.[10]

Eleanora was twenty-one by this point, and no closer to marrying her own fiancé, the King of Aragon, unless his excommunication could be lifted. She might easily have felt aggrieved and wondered when it would finally be her turn as she walked across the yard from the palace to the abbey church, for the second time that year, to watch her younger sister get married. If so, her parents sought to distract her from this sensitivity. For the ceremony, the eldest princess wore a new gown that sparkled with more than six hundred of her favourite silver buttons, the effect of which would have given her dress a dazzling appearance in the bright summer sun. For Eleanora's only remaining companion, her youngest sister Elizabeth, not yet eight, the event was a taste of her own future; just as Margaret was to become Duchess of Brabant, Elizabeth would one day be countess of nearby Holland. Their paths would in 1290 have felt clearly aligned, and this knowledge must have been at the front of Elizabeth's mind as she took in the vibrant sights and sounds.

The young bridal couple at the centre of the festivities were intent on developing chivalric reputations, and the glittering spectacle of assembled nobles and entertainers from across Europe must have pleased them very much. Yet they must also have realized that, while the programme officially celebrated their personal union, its truer intent was to cement the diplomatic alliance which their wedding represented. Jan might easily have felt outshone by his celebrated father, who arrived at the head of a delegation of one hundred and forty Low Country noblemen and -women. He was recognized as one of the great chivalric princes of his generation, a gifted warrior and tournament favourite, and newly enriched following his great military triumph two years before at Worringen, one of the decisive battles of the age. Clearly, he was everything his son and heir hoped to emulate, and he did not disappoint at the wedding, arriving dressed in a fashionable cape made of *vair* (a popular black fur, with rows of regular white triangles pointing downward) over a tunic, which he changed no less than three times throughout the day, presumably in part because he must have been sweating profusely in the July heat.

Following the ceremony, a sumptuous feast took place in Westminster Palace. According to a contemporary chronicler, the feast was attended by thousands of well-wishers. In addition to the large party who had travelled from abroad, the bride's brother, six-year-old future king Edward of Caernarfon, was said to have led a train of eighty knights dressed in armour; Margaret's uncle, the Earl of Cornwall, was accompanied by a hundred knights, and sixty ladies. Another one hundred and three knights and sixty ladies were said to have accompanied Joanna's husband, Earl Gilbert. The countess herself was not far away, in residence at Clerkenwell, but her presence at Margaret's wedding is unrecorded. If Bartholomew can be trusted, Joanna was one of the few aristocrats in England to miss the event – in addition to the hundreds listed above, dozens of knights each accompanied the leading earls, while over seven hundred other knights and ladies, and more than a thousand Londoners, all dressed in their richest attire, were said to have made up the party.[11]

There were so many revellers that the party spilled out from the royal palace, dancing and carousing in the surrounding streets. The guests were entertained by hundreds of performers who had travelled from across Europe, such as Calot Jean, a Sicilian dwarf who was regularly employed as the fool of the Count of Artois – he arrived with the Brabaçon delegation and earned forty shillings as a payment from the king. In all, 426 minstrels and musicians – including harpers, trumpeters, lutenists, and fiddlers – performed for a share of one hundred pounds, provided by the bridegroom and distributed the morning after the wedding by the king's harper. To judge by the fourteen days it took four young pages to collect the candles required for the event, the festivities must have continued well into the early hours. Unsurprisingly given their scale, the celebrations grew raucous – the king himself, perhaps recalling the table damaged by the Sheriff of London at Joanna's wedding feast, became so incensed with the unruly behaviour of a young squire, that he beat him with a stick.[12]

The splendour and pomp surrounding this dynastic union formed an occasion people would remember, an event that would be talked about across Europe. It was staged to impress the aristocracy of England on whose loyalty King Edward depended, the Brabaçon nobility into which his daughter was marrying, and the wider group of European rulers whose emissaries would have borne witness to the magnificence on display. This was the reason behind the jewels and glittering robes, the feast that fed thousands, and the hundreds of assembled knights: to declare Edward's wealth and England's sophistication to his subjects and princely peers. The family of the bridegroom, too, needed to present themselves splendidly to avoid seeming unrefined by comparison – which accounts for the vast number of entertainers they hired, the huge delegation that would have cost a fortune to transport, and the stylish-but-impractical furs in July. Weddings like Margaret's represented investments in the expansion of English economic and political influence, as well as opportunities for European nobles to come together and perform their shared culture. In doing so, they played an important role in promoting English cultural hegemony and maintaining peace between neighbouring nations.

Rumours of the wedding's magnificence spread throughout England and were considered sufficiently fascinating by a monk from the cathedral priory at Norwich that he devoted a lengthy section of his chronicle to describing the wedding. Bartholomew had not been as enthralled with Joanna's smaller wedding two months before, which is recorded very plainly, noting only that 'the Earl of Gloucester took Lady Joanna, daughter of the king, as his wife, and the wedding was celebrated near parliament in London after Easter'.[13]

Joanna's absence from all the splendour is surprising. Her reason for missing her sister's wedding can only be surmised, but as she was staying nearby in Clerkenwell, and as her husband participated in the event with such a large retinue, she could not claim the excuse of being too far away to travel. Recalling how recently she had thrown a tantrum on realizing that Margaret's household had two more pages than her own, it is difficult to avoid the impression that the courtly magnificence of her younger sister's wedding, compared to the relative quiet of her own, might have chafed at the new countess, forcing her to realize her little sister now outranked her, and leaving her unable to bear taking part in the celebrations.

VII
Three Deaths

1290–1

CLIPSTONE, AMESBURY

In late summer 1290, the newly married Margaret, together with her husband, her parents, and her sister Eleanora, left London and headed north-east through Hertfordshire, Buckinghamshire, Northamptonshire, and into Lincolnshire. While on her travels Margaret seems to have embraced the same new-found freedoms and independence from her parents that Joanna had enjoyed shortly after her marriage. Like many fifteen-year-olds, Margaret struggled to get out of bed early – and, for her, freedom meant skipping morning Masses, much to the horror of her father. By 8 September, the party had travelled as far as the manor of Torpel, south of Stamford, where Margaret and Jan issued their first charter as a married couple, assigning the men who would look after her dower estate. Jan's seal is affixed to the letter, but Margaret seems not yet to have had a seal of her own and instead used her mother's. Soon after they sealed the charter, Jan departed for an extended visit back to Brabant, where he was to learn about statecraft from his father, their names appearing side-by-side on papers granting particular privileges to communities within their duchy.[1]

Meanwhile, Margaret and Eleanora continued onwards with their parents, travelling in a pattern that would have felt very familiar from their many years of itinerant courtly living. From Torpel they headed west towards Nottingham and then north to Clipstone. The residence there was a favourite of the royal family in the thirteenth century; it was a sprawling palace in the middle of a deer park dotted with immense oaks near the centre of Sherwood Forest, where ancient laws reserved 'beasts of the chase' for pursuit by the king. The palace had been predominantly built in the late twelfth century by Henry II; inside a gate were a collection of chapels, halls, and kitchens, with separate chambers for the king and queen, as well as lodgings for the many retainers who shared the English royal family's thirst for the hunt. In 1282, Edward had added an immense stable block capable of housing two hundred horses, probably to accommodate a breeding programme for hunters – the hardy-yet-agile horses used in stag and fox hunting.[2]

The family arrived at Clipstone in mid-September, whereupon the king sent a message to London, summoning his men northwards to Clipstone for the annual Parliament at the end of October. Near the end of September, the royal party were off again, looping into Derbyshire and Cheshire as far as Macclesfield then back along the southern perimeter of the Peak over the course of about three weeks. Along the way, they checked on the queen's properties, and hunted stags in the Peak Forest. It is possible that the king and queen had planned to travel to Scotland to meet Prince Edward's newly betrothed, Margaret, the 'Maid of Norway', a princess who, at seven years old, was also the rightful Queen of Scotland through her mother's line. However, a close examination of the distances travelled each day throughout the autumn reveals a steady decline in their daily progress and this, together with the king's decision to call Parliament to Clipstone, suggests that Eleanor's worsening health may have halted their travel. The queen had throughout her life coped robustly with constant long journeys, but she was now rapidly declining and Edward may have realized he could neither continue onward nor make it back to Westminster without leaving Eleanor behind. Unwilling to leave his wife in the circumstances, the king instead summoned his men to him.[3]

The Parliament at Clipstone was the first since Edward had expelled the Jewish population of England during the previous July. This expulsion had been years in the making, with the king taxing the Jewish population of the country so heavily and regularly (they were exempt from the protections of Magna Carta) that, by 1290, there was little left to tax. The king confiscated and sold their properties (realizing more than two thousand pounds of profit), claimed the right to collect all debts owing to them (minus interest, to avoid charges of usury), and issued a proclamation ordering the whole Jewish population to leave the country. In addition to the economic benefit he gained from confiscating Jewish property, Edward probably knew the gesture would prove popular, since almost everyone owed money to Jewish lenders, who were the only people able to lend, and all interest was wiped clean. By late October, the mood among the nobles and leading churchmen had turned from celebration to religious duty, and the king once again entertained talks of joining an expedition to bolster the city of Acre from an invading Muslim army from Egypt.[4]

The royal households were at that time jostling for space at

Clipstone with the parliamentary representatives who had travelled north and were accommodated wherever rooms might be found in the villages around the king's house, their humble cart horses and sumpter mules crammed into the stables of the royal stud. And not far behind them came Joanna, the Countess of Gloucester and Hertford, accompanied by a single groom. Her journey from Clerkenwell could not have been pleasant. She travelled through the wet and cold English late autumn on horseback, on roads even more worn than was usual for that time of year by the recent tread of horses carrying the parliamentary knights. Joanna's fatigue and discomfort at confronting the elements, along with the frequent jolts of travelling on horseback, would have exacerbated any sickness she felt from being nearly two months pregnant. Still, she may have reasoned that the proposed journey – even at an inhospitable time of year – was unlikely to be as dramatic as the crusade to save Acre that she and her husband had briefly pledged to make back in the summer. Nor would it be as uncomfortable as those journeys undertaken by her own mother, who had travelled on her own crusade across Europe to the Holy Land and back, and through battle-scarred landscapes during her many pregnancies. In any event, she had been summoned to Clipstone, and it was not a request she could fail to answer.[5]

Trailing the main royal party northward was the nursery household of Elizabeth and Edward, brought from Langley. Their grandmother had written from Amesbury to express her unease with the idea of the young children travelling north so late in the year: 'When we were there, we could not avoid being ill, on account of the bad climate. We pray you therefore, deign to provide some place in the south, where [they] can have a good and temperate climate, and dwell there while you visit the north.' Her anxiety went unheeded, and the children's household was already at Clipstone when Joanna arrived. Only Mary's presence is unrecorded; perhaps her grandmother's concerns about children travelling during poor weather were allowed in the case of the young nun to overrule her mother's desire to see the child. On arrival at Clipstone, Joanna found most members of her immediate family, as well as an enormous assembly of knights and magnates.[6]

The Queen's Chamber at Clipstone looked out on the deer park through delicately arched windows, but the view was normally blocked from the inside, with the light and cold kept at bay. Eleanor always installed heavy tapestries in her rooms, similar to those that had lined the walls and the floors of the Spanish palaces of her childhood – this small concession to the comforts of home marked her out as foreign to the English observers like the chronicler Matthew Paris, who could not fathom the absurdity of putting a carpet *on the floor*. As she became increasingly weak, she called her children to her so that she could give them some of her favourite personal effects to remember her by; among them was a great crown studded with rubies, emeralds, and pearls that she bequeathed to Elizabeth, who all her life would remember her mother in association with this fabulous gift.[7]

Prince Edward was only six and, as her health failed, Eleanor must have worried that he would share the fate of his brothers John, Henry, and Alphonso, and end his life in an early grave rather than on the throne. She may have wondered whether one of his elder sisters would wear the crown instead: Eleanora, the prince's heir, now in her third decade and still husbandless, or the tempestuous Countess Joanna, who was possibly even then carrying a future king inside her belly. Margaret's path seemed to mirror her own most closely – both women married princes who were destined to rule, both had known their spouses from early adolescence, and both pairs of married couples were close in age, unlike the nearly thirty years that separated Joanna and her husband – and this knowledge may have brought comfort to a mother hoping her daughter might enjoy as happy a union as she had. Very little can be said of Eleanor's relationship with Elizabeth, given the extremely limited time they spent together after Elizabeth's first years, but Eleanor's gift-giving suggests a desire to instil in her youngest daughter a sense of the role she would be expected to play in the pageantry of courtly culture.

The family remained together until Parliament dispersed on 13 November. The next day, the youngest children left Clipstone and began the return trip to Langley, while Joanna most likely headed back to Clerkenwell. Their parents, probably accompanied by Eleanora and Margaret, made for Lincoln. It was a journey that under normal travelling conditions could be easily accomplished in one day. But the queen never made it that far; her health finally failed on the journey from Clipstone, and she came to a stop in the small village of Harby, just five miles short of Lincoln. Medicines were frantically procured, but nothing seemed to slow the queen's decline. On the evening of 28 November, in a manor house owned by a relative of one of her courtiers, Eleanor of Castile died at the age of forty-nine, her husband of nearly four decades by her side, with two of their five daughters present or close by. The disarray within the royal household was so great that, for several days before and several days after the queen's death, it ceased to function as a machine of statecraft – letters were sent without being copied into official registers, and the king refused to deal with the usual daily paperwork of governing. For Eleanora and Margaret, the grief at their mother's death can only have been compounded by witnessing their all-powerful father struggling to cope with the enormity of his loss.

*

The programme of commemoration that Edward put in place following Eleanor's death is among the most extraordinary in European history, and illustrates both medieval attitudes to death and memory, and also the important political role that royal women could play even after their deaths. The manner and aftermath of the queen's passing would have instructed her daughters about the roles they were expected to embody. Immediately following her death, the queen's body completed the remaining five miles of its journey to Lincoln, where it was embalmed. The inner organs were removed and the body was wrapped in linen and preserved against rapid decay with the help of sweet-smelling spices, herbs, and precious resins imported from the east. This process, which is now more commonly associated with ancient Egypt than with medieval England, was fairly common among the aristocracy, before Pope Boniface VIII issued a declaration against the practice in 1299. By removing the inner organs from the body, they might be buried in a separate place from the body, thus increasing the number of prayers that could be elicited from priests and the faithful viewing a tomb. As with the separate burial of little Henry's heart at the Franciscan friary in Guildford, the extra prayers were thought to speed the journey of the soul through the sufferings of purgatory to the bliss of heaven. This practice of bodily division and separate burial also enabled high status individuals like Eleanor of Castile to make personal choices about their ultimate resting place while also fulfilling their dynastic responsibilities.[8]

After Eleanor's internal organs, except her heart, were buried in the Lady Chapel at Lincoln Cathedral, her body and heart were then taken south. The funeral cortege was led by the king, but probably also included Eleanora and Margaret. It proceeded at a stately pace along a somewhat circuitous route seemingly designed to take in sites associated with the queen, making twelve overnight stops – at Grantham, Stamford, Geddington, Hardingstone, Stony Stratford, Woburn, Dunstable, St Albans, Waltham, Westcheap, and Charing – on the way to Westminster Abbey. The journey provided ample opportunities for members of the public to witness the astonishing majesty of the regal party, which may have been joined by Elizabeth and Prince Edward at St Albans, close to Langley, and by Joanna at Westcheap (now Cheapside, in London). After nearly two weeks, the mourners' parade arrived at Westminster where, on 17 December, in a magnificent funeral ceremony at which her husband, children, and most of the nobility of England were present, the queen's body was solemnly laid to rest in a temporary grave near the high altar. A separate ceremony followed in which her heart – now joined with that of her beloved son Alphonso – was interred in the now-lost priory church of the Dominicans near modern-day Blackfriars Station in London. These ceremonies inaugurated a programme of remembrance that lasted years and took in locations across England: within six months of her death, more than forty-seven thousand Masses had been sung for the queen's soul, episcopal indulgences (or exemptions from penance) and special alms were promised to those who prayed for her; at Bath, Coventry, and St Albans, priests were employed to pray continuously on her behalf.

At each of the three burial sites, sumptuous monuments were constructed in the years immediately following Eleanor's death. Only one, at Westminster, survives intact: the gilded bronze life-size effigy of the queen, posed as she appeared on her seal, sculpted by the London goldsmith William Torel and placed atop a polished marble tomb chest. The depiction of Eleanor grants her all the graces of idealized medieval beauty – a high forehead, a long neck, and delicate features – but these details would not have been readily visible from ground level by the scores of pilgrims who filed around the tomb as they circled close to the nearby shrine of the greatest English royal saint, Edward the Confessor. Above all else, Eleanor's Westminster monument projected the idea of wealth and powerful connection: the copious deployment of images of castles and lions reminded viewers of the queen's association with the royal Spanish houses of Castile and Leon; the French inscription recalled her descent from a king and a countess; the golden effigy required the purchase and melting down of 476 gold florins, the solid gold coins minted in Florence that served as a nearly universal high-level currency in the later medieval period. A copy of this memorial was installed at Lincoln, exporting the grandeur of its metropolitan craftsman-ship to audiences far from London – its success as a symbol of royal power may be inferred from its destruction by Oliver Cromwell's men following the Siege of Lincoln over three centu-ries later. The final memorial, at Blackfriars, was lost when the priory church was dismantled following the Dissolution of the Monasteries in the mid-sixteenth century; there, accessible only to members of the Dominican order, the double heart burial of Eleanor and Alphonso was commemorated by a memorial featuring devotional paintings and the figure of an angel, wholly different to the representation of royalty in the public cathedrals at Westminster and Lincoln.

These elaborate and costly memorials were merely the begin-ning of a unique commemorative programme that Edward constructed following Eleanor's death at Harby. In the years that followed, he installed a prominent public monument to her memory at each of the sites her body had rested overnight on the journey from Lincoln to Westminster: the dozen so-called Eleanor Crosses are among the best-known examples of medieval commemoration, and are often pointed to as evidence of the king's great love for his wife. Each of the twelve monuments was distinct, the work of a number of craftsmen from London and local workshops, but all took the form of tall, lavishly decorated stone pillars featuring life-size statues of the queen gazing serenely out over crossroads and market squares, under ornate Gothic canopies topped with the eponymous crosses. Her posture evoked contemporary representations of the Virgin Mary as Queen of Heaven (the ultimate intercessor), while heraldic shields recalled her connection to Castile, and some of the monuments also included carved depictions of books – an appropriate memorial to a well-educated woman. This series of monuments, only three of which survive today, is unique in the history of England; its commissioner, King Edward, was inspired by a tribute constructed following the death of his uncle Louis IX of France, remembered as St Louis. Like the monuments that covered her body, viscera, and heart, these memorials were intended to prompt viewers to pray for the queen's soul, but they also demonstrated Edward's wealth, glorified his reign, and commemorated his connection through Eleanor to powerful continental courts.[9]

Their daughters may never have seen many of the twelve Eleanor Crosses that recalled their mother's memory at the crossroads and market sites between Clipstone and Lincoln, though Elizabeth, living at Langley, would regularly have gazed into the eyes of the mother she barely knew while passing the statue in nearby St Albans. Their eyes would also have fallen on her gilded monument at Westminster during the annual celebrations on the anniversary of her death and on other important occasions, given the tomb's position immediately adjacent to the central shrine in the royal abbey. These representations of their mother emphasized Eleanor's role as a conduit of royal power, dignity, and prestige even beyond her death, celebrating her as an everlasting princess-queen and embodying the connection between England and Castile. By placing her tomb alongside that of Henry III and the shrine of Edward the Confessor, Edward aligned the memory of his beloved wife with English royal authority and even sanctity, the prestige of which, in turn, reflected positively on Eleanor. The monument is therefore not only a manifestation in marble and gold of the role that princesses were expected to play, but also of the way that their individual interests were inextricably aligned with those of the dynasties from which they sprang. The prestige that Eleanor's Castilian royal connections brought to her husband's court enhanced his cultural authority both at home in England and also within a continental context. At the same time, her own influence was strengthened by any improvement in Edward's position. She was not simply a pawn, but a partner in the project of Castilian and English kingship. This was a lesson not lost on her daughters.

Just over two months after Eleanor died, Edward travelled to Amesbury to visit Mary and his mother. He undoubtedly shared the details surrounding the queen's death with them – Mary, after all, was the only child who had not travelled to say goodbye at Clipstone, and it would have been natural for her to seek reassurance that her mother had thought of her during her final weeks. The king likely brought Mary a remembrance her mother had set aside for her when she was sharing her personal effects among her children. At Amesbury, Edward would have found his second-youngest daughter rapidly entering adolescence. She was nearly twelve – the age Queen Eleanor had been when Edward met and married her. For Mary, the end of her youth meant not marriage, of course, but that she was nearly old enough to graduate from her lengthy novitiate and become a fully professed nun, as her elder cousin Eleanor of Brittany had done the previous year. The ceremony which accompanied her final vows of poverty, obedience, and chastity would be the most significant moment of Mary's life, and a critically important step, if she was to be elected abbess of the order's motherhouse at Fontevrault, as befitted a princess of her status. Her cousin Eleanor, only four years Mary's senior and living with her and their grandmother at Amesbury since 1285, had transferred to Fontevrault in the preceding year at the request of her own father, the Duke of Brittany. Mary was only kept at Amesbury to provide company for their grandmother, and the princess may have discussed both the ceremony of her final vows planned for that autumn and longer-term plans for her transfer to Fontevrault with her father.

The latter topic must have seemed highly relevant by the winter of 1291, as the king would have found his mother, the dowager queen Eleanor of Provence, at the very advanced age of sixty-eight and clearly weakening. In addition to deriving what comfort he could from his mother in his time of grief, Edward most likely discussed with her the expectations surrounding Mary's planned move to Fontevrault, as well as his plans for the goldsmith William Torel to craft matching, side-by-side effigies to commemorate his father and his own wife at Westminster – plans that, in practice, excluded the dowager queen from being buried alongside her husband in the great church he had rebuilt at Westminster. Edward might, too, have spoken to his mother about the developing crisis relating to the Scottish succession – she would have taken a personal interest, since her own daughter Margaret had been the grandmother (and namesake) of young Margaret of Norway, the tiny Queen of Scotland who had died tragically at Orkney the previous autumn, having fallen ill on her way to marry Prince Edward. For the dowager queen, the death of her young great-granddaughter – the last of her five direct descendants among the Scottish royal family – must have been a bitter blow. Edward would probably have shared his plans to travel north and arbitrate, as feudal overlord of Scotland, between the competing claims of Robert Bruce and John Balliol for the Scottish crown.

Three months later, the king was at Norham near the east coast on the River Tweed considering these competing proposals, when a messenger arrived from the Cotswold town of Winchcombe. The messenger had not come primarily in search of King Edward but of his son-in-law, Gilbert, who was also in attendance. The news was joyous: on around 10 May, the Countess Joanna had successfully delivered her first child, a healthy baby boy, whom the countess named Gilbert, for his father. The king's pleasure at learning of the safe birth of his first grandchild – fourth-in-line to the throne, and a healthy male – is apparent in the gift of one hundred pounds he made to the messenger. The chronicler Thomas Wykes described Gilbert's joy as 'inestimable'; he was probably also very relieved that his gamble in disinheriting his daughters to marry the princess had paid off with the birth of a longed-for male heir for the Clare fortune. Joanna seems to have felt some trepidation as her delivery approached – the fact that the news came from Winchcombe suggests she had taken up residence at Hailes Abbey, an immense Cistercian monastery and one of the most important pilgrimage sites in the country: at that abbey, she would have felt protected by the presence of one of England's most precious relics, a phial of the Holy Blood, reportedly collected from the wound in Christ's side as he was dying on the cross. Safely delivered, the baby's birth was enthusiastically greeted across the country and is recorded in several chronicles, the commentators perhaps considering that he might one day become king.[10]

One month later, another messenger arrived from the south with less welcome news for the king. His mother had died at Amesbury, on the feast of the Nativity of St John the Baptist.

Mary's time as companion to her grandmother had come to an end, and she was now free to move to Fontevrault. Back at Amesbury, the nuns had the body of the deceased queen embalmed, since there was initial confusion over where she would be buried and any funeral would need to wait until the royal party had returned south. The dowager was not laid to rest in the priory church until September, in a funeral presided over by her son and the principal magnates and prelates of the country. The occasion likely also brought Mary's sisters and brother together at Amesbury, probably for the first time since the tournament at Winchester the previous year. So much had happened during the previous fifteen months: two sisters had been married, one had become a mother, and another was on the verge of taking her final vows as a nun. Their mother and doting grandmother – the two queens who provided the princesses with distinct models for how to live, reflect well on the English royal line, and achieve influence as a royal woman – were both dead.

The deaths of the queen and the queen mother in such quick succession would have had a greater impact on Eleanora than on anyone else, except perhaps her father. The eldest princess had remained close to her grandmother, visiting her regularly even after she entered the priory. She had also been close to her mother – from the age of eight, Eleanora was an almost constant figure at court, frequently travelling around the country in the company of the queen and her ladies. These two women were not just family for Eleanora – they were the most direct and accessible role models she had in trying to understand her own future path and to craft her own royal female persona. For more than a decade, the princess watched and learned to emulate their behaviours, though she would have found their styles of queenship different, and even opposing, in many respects, and this too would have shaped her understanding of the possibilities open to her. Now they were dead, and for Eleanora, both everything and nothing had changed.

At twenty-two, she remained in the same limbo she had inhabited for the past decade, irreversibly attached to a king she was forbidden to marry. How many times must she have regretted the caution her mother and grandmother had exercised in persuading her father not to send her to Aragon at the age of twelve. Then, suddenly, her situation changed irrevocably. Alfonso, King of Aragon, sometime ally of Edward, and Eleanora's proxy husband whom she had never met, died after a short illness, less than one week before her grandmother's death. And so she was forced to confront simultaneously the loss of the grandmother who had been the single constant throughout her life – who had nursed her dying siblings during their parents' lengthy journeys abroad – and the knowledge that she would now never be Queen of Aragon. She might have cast her mind back to lessons with her mother on the different dialects and foreign customs of Spain, wondering what to do with the accumulated knowledge of a woman who had spent a decade preparing to take on a role that she was now denied. In the months that followed, as a new hierarchy formed at court, with Eleanora taking on an enhanced role as the senior royal woman, she may have wondered whom she would marry, freed as she was from her bond to Aragon.

For her sisters Joanna, Margaret, and Elizabeth, life continued as it had before the upheavals caused by the deaths of the two queens: Joanna was pregnant again by the end of the year, with a daughter she would name Eleanor for her mother, grandmother and sister; Margaret remained at court, joined again by her young husband after he returned to complete his education under his father-in-law. Elizabeth remained at Langley with her brother, waiting to take her own place beside the heir to the County of Holland.

For Mary, this period marked a significant turning point in life. That autumn she took her final vows, kneeling before three bishops in the priory church where her grandmother's body had only just been laid to rest. This profession bound Mary ever more tightly to the order of Fontevrault, of which she was now a full member. The death of her grandmother, however, also released the young nun from her ties to Amesbury – since before she entered six years earlier, her parents had agreed that Mary would transfer to the motherhouse in Anjou after the death of the dowager queen. The abbess of Fontevrault was unlikely to overlook so rich a prize for her house as the daughter of a king, and accordingly travelled to England in early December to collect Mary. She would have found London filled with solemn pageantry, as all the assembled aristocracy of England had been summoned to Westminster Abbey to participate in the decorous proceedings that marked the first anniversary of Queen Eleanor's death, as well as the burial of the queen mother's heart at Greyfriars, the church of the London Franciscans.

However, things did not go according to plan for the abbess, for at some point during her week-long stay, she was informed that Mary would not be joining her on the return to Anjou after all, but would instead remain at Amesbury. Whether Mary refused to go or her father, having lost his wife and mother in quick succession, determined not to give up his child, Mary's path no longer took her out of England, outside the kingdom her father ruled, and where her own influence – since she could never marry a foreign ruler – might be greatest. Like her sister Joanna, who was married to an English nobleman, Mary remained a princess at home.

VIII

Alliance

1293–5

BRISTOL, BAR, WESTMINSTER

On 30 August 1293, King Edward commanded Reginald de Grey, Chief Justice of Chester, to summon the principal knights of Cheshire to Bristol on the Sunday after the feast of the Holy Rood. Notices to the same effect were sent to the Sheriffs of Cornwall, Cumberland, Derbyshire, Essex, Hertford, Lancashire, Northampton, Nottinghamshire, Surrey, and Sussex, each detailing a list of local aristocrats who were expected to join the royal household for the long-awaited wedding feast of the king's eldest daughter Eleanora. Finally, twelve years after her proxy marriage to Alfonso of Aragon, at the age of twenty-four, she was to be married, though not to a king – rather, her fiancé was a mere count, the ruler of Bar, a small province sandwiched between the French county of Champagne and the German Duchy of Lorraine.[1]

Near the start of that year, a delegation from Bar had arrived at King Edward's court. At this time, the king's household usually included Eleanora, Margaret and Jan. They spent most of Lent in the flat Norfolk countryside that year, and the proximity of the king during the season of penitence was of interest to the Norwich monk and chronicler Bartholomew Cotton. He recorded that the royal household was quiet, with only a small number of its usual noble attendants present, but that Henri III, the recently elevated Count of Bar, arrived with his priestly brother Theobald and some of his knights and spent the greater part of the season with the king in East Anglia. Though the cause of his visit to England is unrecorded, Henri had most likely come to discuss a political and military alliance against the French crown: nearly a decade earlier, the Countess of Champagne, his nearest rival, had married the heir to the French throne, and his own lands now seemed in danger of being subsumed by French expansionism.[2]

The Lenten visit to Norfolk could hardly have given Henri the same display of the cultural sophistication of England that Edward was normally so determined to present to the ruling families of northern Europe – of the chivalric finesse projected at Margaret's wedding, for example, or of the round table tournaments at Winchester. Nevertheless, Henri, whose personal ambition of travel in the Holy Land had only been curtailed by his elevation to ruler of Bar following the death of his own father, would certainly have admired Edward, the famous crusader king who continually professed his ambition for peace in Europe so he might retake the Cross and reconquer Jerusalem for Christianity. Even if the stay in Norfolk did not showcase England's wealth and cultural refinement at its best, the young count was probably afforded greater access to the king than he might have enjoyed in the bustle of a full court at Westminster.

The men seem to have made a favourable impression on each other – throughout that spring and summer, Henri remained by the king's side as he resumed his unceasing progress throughout England. Travelling with the royal party, he would have frequently interacted with Eleanora, whose elevated status since her mother's death was signalled by a personal household that had grown to include such specialized administrators as a clerk of the stables and a keeper of her wines, in addition to a chaplain, sumpterers and chariot runners, ladies and pages.[3]

Within a few months – and seemingly agreed in conversation by the parties involved rather than by the usual teams of diplomats (whose negotiations would have been better recorded) – the Count of Bar was betrothed to marry the eldest English princess. Aged thirty-four and still unwed, Henri had stumbled on extraordinary fortune: such a minor prince could hardly have anticipated that the great English king would bless Henri's marriage to his first-born child, who was second-in-line to the English crown. That this agreement was reached suggests a strong personal connection between Henri and Edward, and possibly a personal connection between Henri and his future bride. The somewhat one-sided nature of the marriage between the minor count and the daughter of a king is made clear in comparing the dowry and dower agreed for this match with that of Margaret, who married the heir to the comparatively wealthy Duchy of Brabant. Eleanora's dowry was set at ten thousand marks, or seven thousand pounds, while Margaret's had been nearly double that amount. The dower estate that Eleanora stood to receive on Henri's death, however, was worth nearly five times as much as that promised to her younger sister – an astonishing fifteen thousand *livres Tournois* per year, or nearly four thousand pounds. To achieve this immense value, Henri agreed to place in his bride's hands an estate that included many of the principal towns in his province, as well as the home castle at Bar itself. This was the price that a minor count might expect to pay for marrying the daughter of a king, and Henri acceded unhesitatingly to the expectations of the English negotiators.[4]

For Eleanora, the match with the count may have felt like more of a mixed blessing. She undoubtedly understood the importance of wifehood and motherhood to her own success as a royal woman – she could hardly have failed to internalize these messages, omnipresent in medieval culture, from the direct example of her own mother, prodigiously fertile and beloved by the king. Turning twenty-four that summer, she may have considered that her childbearing years were dwindling – this might be her last opportunity to succeed as a fertile consort. Count Henri must also have been sufficiently amiable during the months he was resident at court for her to pledge her life to him. He was, however, only a count, and a minor one at that; the small and rather unremarkable county of Bar was no replacement for Aragon, the rich and exotic kingdom that Eleanora had been promised for so many years. Barring the death of her brother Edward, she would never be a queen if she married Henri, and even her younger sister Margaret would, as Duchess of Brabant, outrank her. Surely there might yet be opportunities to make a union more worthy of her own position?

If these doubts ever crept into her mind, they were quickly cast aside, and the marriage plans progressed with such rapidity that Eleanora must have been enthusiastic about keeping the matter moving. Ultimately, Edward's most dutiful daughter may have embraced a marriage that had somewhat anticlimactic personal resonance because the link she would forge with Henri was of unambiguous benefit to England, to her father, and to her family's position in Western Europe. For the same fears about France's imperial expansionist ambitions that brought Henri first to England were also increasingly concerning Edward. His trusted counsellor the Bishop of Durham Anthony Bek, who had led the original delegation to Aragon to negotiate Eleanora's betrothal to Alfonso, had cautioned Edward of the need to shore up alliances across the Low Countries and Germany, and this was undoubtedly on the king's mind during the months that he entertained the young count whose lands bordered the ever-growing French empire. Eleanora, the daughter who had from early adolescence shown a keen interest in statecraft and the role her marriage might play in securing England's border regions now embraced the potential to unite with a man willing to put his military might in service to the English cause. She would become the Countess of Bar and build there a lasting ally for England. And as Henri and his subjects spoke French, she would have no need to learn another tongue.

As England's aristocracy were being summoned to Bristol for the wedding in the early weeks of September, the bride's youngest siblings Elizabeth, now aged eleven, and Edward, aged nine, headed west from their summer tour of the royal palaces surrounding London. Eleven days before the wedding, they called in at Amesbury to collect Mary, before travelling onwards to Bristol to reconvene with their father, Eleanora, Margaret and Jan. The children were frequently in each other's company during this period: in January, Joanna had visited Elizabeth and Edward at Langley – her home during the years their parents were in Gascony; after a year in the Welsh Marches, the visit must have felt comfortingly familiar to Joanna, since she and her travelling entourage came back again in May to meet up with her siblings at Mortlake, doubling the household's usual consumption of wine. One weekend in June, Mary and a large suite of her attendants from Amesbury had visited Elizabeth and Edward while they were in residence at Kennington Palace, just south of London; the following week, Jan arrived with thirty horses and twenty-four grooms on the way to a tournament in Fulham and stayed for nearly a week, to the exasperation of the children's accountant, who was forced to secure food and wages for the many grooms, and fodder for their horses. Arriving at Bristol for Eleanora's wedding, Mary took the opportunity to complain to her father that her allowance of one hundred pounds a year to furnish her chamber and table was insufficient. The fourteen-year-old nun was accustomed to living richly – despite the seeming incongruity between such luxury and her religious habit – and she was feeling the pinch after her grandmother's death meant that the dowager's income was no longer subsidizing her own. The king, when his daughters complained about something that could be fixed by throwing money at the problem, seems readily to have acceded: he issued a decree to double the income of his 'dearest daughter' from the treasury to two hundred pounds each year, 'to sustain her chamber'.[5]

Once again, only Joanna missed her sister's wedding. For more than a year, the countess had been resident just across the Bristol Channel at the castle of Caerphilly in Glamorgan, the Clares' most spectacular Welsh residence. Her two-year-old son Gilbert seems still to have been living with his mother at this time; they were joined by a baby sister named Eleanor in November 1292. One of the children was sick that autumn, and after returning from attending the king at Berwick to see Robert Bruce resign his claim to the Scottish throne, their father was either worried about his child's ill-health or used the excuse to put off returning to London. The child recovered, and by the following year, little Gilbert and his younger sister were established within a separate children's household in residence at Usk Castle, twenty miles north-east of Caerphilly.[6]

By the late summer of 1293, Joanna was pregnant again, though her condition would not have kept her from attending the wedding of her closest sister. What did intervene, however, was a rebellion that broke out on some of the Clare estates around Kilkenny in Ireland: her husband was determined to assemble a force of knights to sail west and take back control. The earl was once again in the king's good graces, following his arrest and the temporary confiscation of Glamorgan the year before, when he had refused Edward's command to cease his ongoing private war with the Earl of Hereford, lord of neighbouring Brecon. The king issued Gilbert with an exorbitant fine of ten thousand marks, but it was never paid, and within months Glamorgan was back in Gilbert's control. Edward had been pressured to forgive his son-in-law by other magnates, who argued that Gilbert had only been exercising those freedoms traditionally associated with Marcher lordship, but he also softened his stance in recognition that he would in effect be depriving his daughter and grandson of their inheritance; even at the point of confiscating Glamorgan, the charter clarifies that Joanna, 'daughter of the king', is not to be disinherited, and that the judgment was only to be in effect for the term of Gilbert's life.[7]

If Joanna's own feelings about the dispute between her husband and father were in doubt, they were clarified when she opted to join Gilbert on his campaign in Ireland, despite the dangers inherent in travelling and the fact that she would need to leave her young children in England. She was, after all, the daughter of Eleanor of Castile, who had twice left her small children at home to accompany her husband overseas. Her mother's example could not have been far from her mind as, together with her principal ladies, as well as chaplains and harpists, she accompanied the earl and his knights and sailed in June, intending to stay three years, and missing her sister's wedding.[8]

The wedding and feast they missed must have been sumptuous: the king ordered his Keeper of the Forest of Dean (just north of the River Severn) to provide thirty bucks – non-native fallow deer, introduced to England by the Romans and again later by the Normans for hunting – as well as four harts, fully mature males from the larger red deer species. There was some debate about which prelate should perform the ceremony: Archbishop Peckham of Canterbury had died in the previous spring, and his successor was away in Rome being confirmed by the Pope; meanwhile the Archbishop of York was in disgrace with King Edward, for having excommunicated a court favourite. Ultimately, the Archbishop of Dublin was prevailed upon to travel across the Irish Sea and solemnize the marriage at St Augustine's Abbey, preserved today as Bristol Cathedral, on 20 September.[9]

In the months that followed their wedding, Henri went back to his province, while Eleanora prepared to leave England and join him. Her father assembled a magnificent retinue to accompany her on her journey, led by the Bishop of London, the Earl of Hereford and Essex, the Dean of St Paul's Cathedral, and more than a dozen knights, including Sir Eustace de Hache (whose loyalty to Eleanora had been proven almost a decade before, when he refused to leave his post protecting her, even though it cost him part of his estate). Sir Eustace was one of four knights specially appointed to ensure that the lands assigned to the new countess's dower produced the extraordinary sum promised by the count – a reminder of the rushed nature of the wedding the previous autumn. On 17 March

1294, Edward presented a vacant benefice to Henri's brother Theobald, who had remained in England, a testimony to the king's high regard for his new son-in-law. One week later, however, sickness assailed the family, striking down both the nine-year-old Prince Edward and his visiting nineteen-year-old sister Margaret with fever, just after the feast of the Annunciation of the Virgin. For more than two weeks, the pair languished; this was surely a torturous time for the king, as he was forced to confront once again the memory of Alphonso's death a decade before, at nearly the same age as Prince Edward was then. Finally, their fevers broke – a surviving letter from a member of the royal household conveys what must have been extraordinary relief: 'thank God', the children were recovering. Given the seriousness of their sickness, the delay in Eleanora's departure from Dover may have been caused by the threat of her brother dying. If Prince Edward had followed his elder brothers to an early grave, Eleanora would instantly have risen to become heir to the throne – and the baby growing inside her might have become a future king of England.[10]

Once Prince Edward and Margaret were convalescing, the king accompanied Eleanora to Dover, where she had previously seen him off on and welcomed him home from his continental voyages. Now it was her turn to undertake a journey. The dangers of childbirth also awaited her in the months to come, and though Eleanora was young and Edward was still fit and robust at fifty-three, father and daughter may have wondered if this would be their final goodbye. On 14 April, Eleanora and her companions set sail. After two weeks they reached the city of Bar, nestled among high, steep gorges overlooking the quiet Ornain River, where Henri had arranged a tournament in her honour. Arriving in the small city, the English party paraded through the gates in the city walls and across an ancient wooden bridge (which

would be replaced seventeen years later by the picturesque stone
Pont Notre-Dame that stands today). Many of Eleanora's attendants may have lodged in the great Benedictine priory, the massive
Romanesque church that dominated the lower part of the city
and which had recently been enhanced with an intricate new
Gothic choir. If the eyes of the citizens of Bar were focused on
their new, pregnant countess as she paraded past, hers would
have remained fixed on the great towers of the medieval castle,
perched atop a promontory which overlooked the narrow valley.
It is easy to wonder whether, at the first sight of her new home,
Eleanora recalled that the castle was a key part of her dower
estate – this was to be *her* castle.

The welcome tournament took place on 3 May, probably on
the high, flat ground behind the castle. Among those who
answered the invitation to participate was a familiar face: the
Duke of Brabant, Margaret's father-in-law, whose dashing figure
Eleanora would have remembered from her sister's wedding
festivities four years before. The duke, in his early forties, was
in prime health, a famed warrior after his astonishing victory
at the Battle of Worringen six years earlier, and a jousting hero,
who was said to have triumphed at more than seventy tournaments across northern Europe. According to the chronicler Jean
de Thielrode, the duke arrived in Bar with a retinue of one
hundred and ten knights. At the hour of vespers, the evening
prayer shortly before sunset, the duke was persuaded to enter
the lists, don his armour, and mount his horse. In the fading
spring light, his horse twice thundered past that of a French
knight named Pierre de Bausner, but on the third pass, their
lances hit one another with such force, that both men were
thrown to the ground. The duke suffered a grave injury to his
arm and was taken from the field, having summoned the strength
to pardon Pierre, who had offered his own life in forfeit. Within

hours, the duke was dead, presumably having bled to death from the wound. For the spectators at the tournament, the gruesome death of the renowned warrior – a man whom the chroniclers called the 'flower of chivalry, the ornament of the universe, the joy of the world' – must have been an upsetting and abrupt end to the glorious pageantry of the day. For a pregnant Eleanora, watching the tragic unfolding of festivities that were intended to inaugurate her life in Bar from the stands, it would have been gut-wrenching.[11]

Back in England, the news of the old duke's death came with a summons for his son and heir, Jan II, to return to Brabant. Margaret was by this time nineteen years old and, having been married for four years, was well into what should have been her prime childbearing years. She was also, after Eleanora had departed for Bar, the only royal woman normally resident at court, though her eleven-year-old sister Elizabeth, who normally lived in the household of her brother Edward, visited occasionally. Now that Jan had succeeded as duke, the pressure on Margaret to produce an heir to secure the duchy's future was amplified, and there was no obvious argument for her to remain in England rather than to take up residence with her husband in Bar. In Canterbury that autumn, her robes were mended by her long-serving tailor Roger, and orders were placed with a London saddler for a new saddle and saddle-cloth. The king's goldsmith, Adam, was paid three hundred pounds to make new pieces of jewellery for the duchess, which must have been intended to form part of her trousseau and, by November, ships were being prepared at Dover to transport her to Brabant. Jan's departure was delayed by an outbreak of rebellion in Wales – he and his men had joined the king on campaign – and by the preparations for a joint military venture that would see Brabant and England united against France, but in June 1295 he sailed from Harwich in three ships provisioned for 'the dearest son of the king' by his father-in-law. Curiously, Margaret remained at home. A delay may have been intended to allow Jan to settle back in Brabant before he welcomed his wife; furthermore, Margaret's trousseau – which lacked a natural champion after her mother's death – may not have been fully compiled. However, as the months after Jan's departure turned into years and still Margaret resolutely remained in England with little further evidence to suggest she was preparing to move to Brabant, it is clear that her resistance must have had a broader cause. She had no reason to doubt the status of her marriage: her match was prestigious – the most prestigious achieved by any of her sisters. She also knew her husband well; this was not a case of a princess fearing to fall into the clutches of an unknown man.[12]

Like all daughters of kings, Margaret could hardly have been ignorant of the expectations placed on her role in a dynastic marriage, which included for many princesses the challenge of leaving home to spend the rest of one's life in a foreign land. These women had been raised to follow in their mothers' footsteps as diplomatic brides – it was a commonly understood aspect of their position. Perhaps the most popular chivalric romance of the age was a story whose central plot focused on a young princess travelling across the sea to marry a king; in *Tristan and Isolde*, the Cornish knight Tristan and Irish princess Isolde mistakenly drink a love potion and fall helplessly in love while he is escorting her to marry his uncle, King Mark of Cornwall. The romance was ubiquitous in the late thirteenth century, with its scenes depicted on countless tapestries, ivory caskets, and combs, such as those that would have furnished Margaret's chambers – and its central morals about duty and loyalty would have been familiar to Margaret. She would have recognized the expectation encapsulated in Tristan's words to Isolde, as she sails away from Ireland and all she has ever known, to marry a foreign king,

> You must take heart! You had much rather be a great Queen in a strange land than humble and obscure at home. Honour and ease abroad, and shame in your father's kingdom have a very different flavour!

Margaret's reasons for refusing to accompany Jan to Brabant are unrecorded, but if Tristan's words represent a common fear among princesses travelling abroad for marriage, they also hint at what may have been behind Margaret's reluctance. Brabant was a 'strange land' to the English princess, so much stranger than even Bar must have seemed to Eleanora, because Brabant was Dutch-speaking.[13]

The Brabaçon court poet dedicated a verse chronicle of the old duke's famous victory at the Battle of Worringen to Margaret in 1294, shortly before the tragic tournament. The dedication of literary works aimed at teaching recently married princesses about the glorious history of their new countries was not uncommon in the later Middle Ages. When Margaret's mother, Eleanor of Castile, had arrived as a young bride in England, she received an illustrated copy of an Anglo-Norman *Life of Saint Edward the Confessor* from her father-in-law, the original text of which had been presented to her mother-in-law in the early years of her own queenship. The manuscript, which survives in the collection of the University of Cambridge, expounds the life of the pious king in whose honour Eleanor's husband had been named, undoubtedly intending to impress the Spanish princess and fill her with pride in her husband's saintly royal predecessor. The Dutch chronicle, presented to Margaret forty years later, similarly sought to excite pride and admiration in the young princess for the illustrious life of her husband's father, and to reinforce the honour inherent in her association with the House of Brabant. Its opening, however, also shows how intimidating it might have been for a young woman to move to a country whose language she did not speak. Addressing itself to 'Lady Margaret of England', the poet offers that 'since she cannot understand Dutch, therefore I send her the gift of a Dutch poem, by which she may learn the language.' The copy of the manuscript given to Margaret has been lost, and if she pored over it, practising the Dutch language by repeatedly reciting the elegiac descriptions of her father-in-law's famous victory, or sought out tuition in the language of her future subjects, any such efforts are hidden from history.[14]

Margaret most likely did not make a strenuous effort to learn Dutch, at least not while she remained in England. The example of her mother, fluent in the Castilian of her brother's court and also in the French of her own mother's province of Ponthieu, shows that consorts of ruling men need not necessarily learn to speak the language used by the majority of the population. In Eleanor's case, her Ponthevin French would have served perfectly when she arrived at the English court, which was still dominated in the middle of the thirteenth century by the Anglo-Norman dialect that William the Conqueror had brought over two centuries earlier. More than two decades after she arrived, Eleanor either still did not speak English or did not feel confident at using it: when the townspeople of St Albans sought her intercession in a disagreement with the local abbot in 1275, they aimed to complain directly to the queen and chased down her carriage (despite the best efforts of the abbot to steer it away from the crowd); they gained an audience with her, but their chosen (native English) spokeswoman was unable to make their case – instead, the petitioners were forced to make a written appeal in French. Margaret's husband had been living at the

English court since the age of ten, and would undoubtedly have achieved full fluency in Anglo-Norman, which explains why language had not been a barrier in her relationship with him.[15]

Beyond her relationship with her husband, however, Margaret was strongly incentivized to learn Dutch. Brabant was a province at the centre of several linguistic traditions, with French and even a dialect of German spoken in parts, but Dutch was the predominant tongue throughout the province. Linguistic variation, moreover, could lead to the formation of political factions. Early in her own marriage, Margaret's mother had proved her usefulness as a diplomatic bride, by obtaining favourable trading conditions in England for merchants from her home country. If Margaret hoped to emulate her mother, she would need to navigate the language-based factions in Brabant by speaking directly to magnates from each language group, and respond to their attempts to make connections through her. The role of duchess-princess promised Margaret extraordinary opportunities to act as intercessor between Brabant and England, particularly in matters pertaining to trade and international politics, but she could easily fall victim to factionalism if she was unable to navigate the politics at court in Brussels.

On a more personal level, Margaret may have been reluctant to give up her household and the relationships she had developed with long-standing servants and companions. The king's wardrobe accounts demonstrate a startling stability in the membership of the households of his daughters: in 1295, Margaret was still being served by a number of the same people who had been in her household a decade earlier. These men and women had been part of Margaret's life since her childhood – they were with her during the years her parents were in Gascony, they travelled with her when she moved between her father and her brother, and they remained part of her household, or 'family', when her other sisters moved away. But Margaret's retinue in Brabant would necessarily consist of local servants and aristocrats, so her own household would be disbanded. Nor could she keep forever her English ladies – women like Alice de Neutembre, Margaret's 'damsel', who was sufficiently important to her in June 1294 that she begged her father to assign Alice lands to supplement her income. Even if, as a contemporary Brabaçon romance suggests, many aristocratic youths may have been familiar with French by this date, Margaret would need to start afresh in building relationships at court in Brussels. When she finally did travel to Brabant in 1297, only two ladies were in the large train of English noblemen who accompanied the young duchess, and at least one of them was recalled to England within six months of leaving. For someone like Margaret, who had spent her life surrounded by the same faces each day, the sudden feeling of being alone and not knowing whom to trust must have been incredibly intimidating.[16]

The undeniable impression remains that Margaret avoided joining Jan in Brabant for as long as she possibly could. For his part, Jan does not seem to have minded that his wife stayed away – heavy pressure from her husband's court would have been hard for the duchess to resist. Rather than any dramatic refusal to travel, the records simply suggest that no one – neither the duchess nor her father or estranged husband – did anything to disturb the status quo, in which she remained attached to her father's household. Whatever other reasons may have kept the young couple apart, they clearly were not desperate to be together; in all likelihood, they were not so lucky as her parents had been in finding true companionship within their dynastic marriage. A lack of connection is not surprising among couples whose unions were founded on international diplomacy, trade, and family aggrandizement. It is difficult to say whether young women like Margaret felt disappointed or aggrieved in the knowledge that they would never experience the passion and romance of the stories so richly embroidered throughout chivalric society. Most members of the medieval elite, men and women, would not have expected to find romantic love within their marriages – but Margaret's perspective would certainly have been affected by her own parents' exceptionally close relationship.

She may also have felt acutely the limitations on female power in medieval society, particularly when a woman was married. In a world in which the chief public role of royal women was the performance of intercession, her ability to sway her husband's judgment in favour of those she wished to promote was paramount. Margaret would only have autonomy over any estate in Brabant if Jan predeceased her, when she would gain access to her dower lands; as long as Jan lived, it would be Margaret's ability to influence his behaviour that would determine her political and cultural contributions. By contrast, in England, surrounded by her long-serving household and with the assurance provided by her role as daughter of the king, Margaret was in a position to make things happen on her own: grants made to those in her service during the years after her marriage while she remained in England ('at the instance of the king's daughter Margaret, consort of Jan of Brabant' or 'for his service to Margaret, Duchess of Brabant, the king's daughter') show that she was able to exercise power at her father's court. She was also able to win privileges for Brabaçon merchants trading in England, just as her mother had done for the merchants of Castile after her own marriage. By 1295, she had known Jan for nearly a decade. If after that, and five years of marriage, she either still did not feel close to him or worried that their relationship would not allow her a power base that would guarantee the same degree of comfort, freedoms, and influence she enjoyed as a daughter of the king, Margaret may have resisted giving up her position in England. Her reality was a far cry from the 'humble and obscure' position that Tristan warned Isolde not to cling to, and she appears to have been reluctant to trade it for an uncertain future in Brabant.[17]

Even as Margaret delayed her departure from England, the time was fast approaching for her youngest sister, Elizabeth, to follow in the duchess's footsteps. She had been betrothed as long as she could remember, the daughter who, through her marriage, would secure the alliance her father had previously attempted to make with Holland when he betrothed Prince Alphonso to the daughter of Floris V. Elizabeth's match shared remarkable parallels with that of Margaret: her fiancé Johan of Holland, another Dutch-speaking boy, was an exact contemporary of her brother Edward and slightly her junior, and after their betrothal was agreed, he was sent over to England to be raised alongside his future bride in the hope that this would bind the cloth-making heartland of Holland to wool-exporting England. Johan arrived in England soon after Elizabeth's parents had returned from Gascony and lived with a small household of his own between court and the children's establishment that travelled in summer and spent the winter months at Langley. For Elizabeth, his visits would have felt little different from the constant stream of high-born visitors who frequented the household she shared with her brother Edward – young knights, distant cousins, and the children of great lords all stopped by the miniature court on their way somewhere, hoping to eat well for a couple of days at the king's expense and to strengthen their relationship with the future sovereign, Prince Edward.

Elizabeth's adolescence differed from those of her elder sisters in ways that seem to have had a lasting influence on her as an adult. Her mother's death meant she lacked a strong female figure to model herself on. The passionate devotion that she showed to her female companions as an adult suggests that her early life was devoid of familial warmth and rather lonely, with her brother the only constant, and he increasingly separated from her as the pair grew up. As well as missing out a close relationship with their mother, the youngest royal children were also deprived of her tuition. Elizabeth was most likely taught to read by Sir Guy Ferre, *magister*, or tutor, to Prince Edward, but there is no evidence that she attained skills in writing as her sister Eleanora had, and nor is it clear whether the children had regular access to many books. Sir Guy also taught the children to ride – a herald's celebratory poem written in 1300 praises the young prince who 'managed his steed wonderfully well', and his sister will have had plenty of opportunities to achieve this same proficiency. As young adults, Elizabeth and Prince Edward also shared a love of polyphonic music, suggesting that this fashionable art form newly radiating outward from the churches of Paris may have featured in their upbringing. Little else, however, is known about Elizabeth's formal education. In the year before her marriage, she seems to have spent a great deal of time with Margaret, who probably sought to help Elizabeth develop her courtly skills and prepare for life as a consort in the Low Countries. However, these visits could not replace what she had lost when her mother died; now that she was approaching the age of marriage, this loss must have been felt especially acutely.[18]

IX
Ladies of War

1294–7

CAERPHILLY, BAR

The Countess of Gloucester's chamber on the upper floor of her castle at Caerphilly had two windows: one, large and glazed, outlined by delicately shaped stonework, looked down over the castle's busy inner courtyard; the other was smaller and round and looked south, out over the great mere that provided the fortress's principal protection, past the small village, and to the hills beyond. In October 1294, Joanna's view was filled with flames, and the sound of daily life that reverberated within the castle walls was pierced with screams; rebellion had erupted across Wales, and the insurgents had come to attack the Clare stronghold, deep in the heart of Glamorgan.

Just weeks before, as the harvest approached, men had been on the move in enormous numbers, heading south and east to Portsmouth, under the order of the king. They were expected there by the end of September, to support King Edward in his effort to relieve the English-held lands in Gascony, which had been invaded by the French the previous spring. But before the vast army of thousands of men and more than fifteen hundred horses could set sail, terrible news arrived from Caernarfon, where the king's men were still at work completing his fortress. The castle had been captured, and its constable had been killed. With the defensive might of the king's prized stronghold in the hands of an occupying enemy, rebels were proclaiming loyalty to Madog ap Llewellyn (a distant cousin of the last native prince defeated a decade before by Edward), who now claimed the Welsh principality. The smouldering embers of Welsh independence that remained after Edward's initial conquest had been fanned by a heavy and unpopular tax levied by the English king, as well as by his demand that Welshmen fight for England in Gascony. Within a month, four of Edward's other Welsh castles had been overcome, and those still under the king's control were garrisoned with scores of knights and archers. The provisions intended for the Gascony campaign were instead sent to Worcester, from where the king and his principal magnates were assembling to quash the rebellion.[1]

Far to the south, Joanna and Gilbert may have considered the uprising unlikely to spread into their lands – Glamorgan was under the tight grip of Gilbert and his men, and there had been no flickers of insurgence during the decades in which he and his father had consolidated their authority over the Marcher lordship. But the rebellion came, led by Morgan ap Maredudd, the son of a landowner dispossessed by the Clares in the uplands to the north of Glamorgan. And, unlike Madog in the north, who fought in the name of an independent Wales and sought to drive out the English conquerors, Morgan's grievances were decidedly personal, as he publicly declared himself in opposition to Gilbert rather than to the king. He and his supporters attacked and captured Gilbert's castle in Morlais, on the border with Brecon. Morgan then moved south, burning the Clare castles of Kenfig and Llangynwyd. Joanna had returned to Caerphilly with Gilbert six months earlier, unaware that a country seemingly ever on the brink of violent war was about to explode once more. But, one autumn day in October 1294, the rebels attacked the castle and the adjacent town; eighty houses were destroyed by fire.[2]

In the medieval English imagination, the Welsh Marches were a lawless area – a land in which the king's laws did not prevail, and where the local Marcher lord had the final say in all matters of law, property, and life. Adding to these anxieties, the March was a borderland in terms of culture, inhabited by Welshmen who spoke a strange language and had bizarre customs. Joanna had, it seems, always been attracted to the frontier, demonstrated by her childhood ventures into the northern part of Wales, her professed zeal for the ill-fated Crusade of 1290, and her enthusiasm in joining the campaign to Ireland. She was in this regard well suited to her married life, much of which was spent in the Marcher estates that she held jointly with Gilbert: in the lordships of Glamorgan, Newport, Caerleon and Usk, which were together worth roughly 2,500 pounds each year, nearly half the total income of the Clare estates. It was a society built around war: in England, military prowess was a chivalric ideal to which noblemen might aspire; in the Welsh Marches, it was a necessity for any lord who wished to maintain control of his lands. The great historian of the Marcher lords, Rees Davies, called them 'lords of war', and Joanna's husband was perhaps the most powerful of all. Like many of their peers in the March, Joanna and Gilbert also held large estates in England, spread over nineteen counties, including Clare in Suffolk and Tewkesbury in

Gloucestershire. That they spent so much time in the March can probably be attributed to the relative freedom they held within these estates to rule as they pleased, away from Gilbert's often-fraught relationship with the king. In Glamorgan, the Clare lord was 'like a king', and his wife, the English princess, seems to have relished the independence that she had in the province.[3]

By the 1290s Glamorgan had twenty-three castles, many of which had been either built or substantially rebuilt by Gilbert or his father during the decades that they secured their authority over their March estates. When the rebellion broke out, Joanna would have been glad for the safety of strongholds like Caerphilly Castle, the most luxuriously appointed of the Clare homes in Glamorgan. The castle had been built rapidly in the later 1260s, at a time when Gilbert was still battling for control of the Glamorgan uplands, and was a physical manifestation of his authority along the frontier. Its structure provided in the 1280s a model for the castles Edward built in the north of Wales to secure his own conquest, and by the time Joanna was living there in the 1290s, the castle functioned as an administrative centre for the whole Clare estate within the March. It was well placed geographically, more or less in the centre of the family's Welsh lands, which stretched from Monmouth, near the English border, to Neath, adjacent to the Gower Peninsula. The castle's immense towers, walls, and gates were heavily restored in the twentieth century, and today provide a sense of the power that Gilbert and Joanna held within Glamorgan. The castle was surrounded by two tall stone walls, set with towers on an artificial island that could only be accessed by three separate drawbridges and through colossal gatehouses, each shielded by heavy iron portcullises. Inside these defences, a double-height great hall was warmed by a central fire. At one end of the hall was the service wing, with pantry and buttery, and above it a small chapel; at the other was the suite of spacious private apartments in which Joanna and Gilbert lived with their children, including fireplaces and a large window framed by delicate tracery, which overlooked the courtyard below.

Caerphilly Castle was built to project the Clare family's wealth and power on the surrounding countryside and to impress their peers with its magnificence and modern comforts. It was also a virtually impregnable fortress, designed to withstand the onslaught of an army. Its model was probably Kenilworth Castle, where during the baronial wars of the 1260s, Gilbert had seen first-hand how a lake-like moat called a mere might allow a stronghold to stand firm for six months against continuous attack. The mere at Caerphilly was broad and surrounded the castle on all sides, preventing siege engines like catapults, trebuchets and battering rams from gaining the close proximity necessary to reach the castle walls. Its towers were strong and its bridges could be raised. In 1294, the castle withstood Morgan ap Maredudd's loosely organized band of rebels, but Gilbert was unable to crush the rebellion outright. The Dunstable chronicle records that the earl, Joanna, and their men were pushed out of Wales, 'so that he barely escaped alive'. The couple fled to safety in England with their three tiny children: little Gilbert, aged three, Eleanor, who was two, and a second daughter named Margaret for her mother's second sister, who was about a year old. Joanna was forced to suffer the anxiety and indignity of being forcibly expelled from her estates by violent insurgents. She was twenty-two and pregnant with her fourth child – proof that, at least in one respect, her ageing husband remained vigorous, even as he struggled to regain control of his Welsh lands.[4]

Throughout the ensuing winter, news of the king's forces fighting in the north of Wales, with many of the principal Marcher lords leading armies across the region against the insurgency, filtered

back to Joanna. She knew the place names well from her childhood travels along the north Welsh coast. In early 1295, her
father was besieged at Conwy Castle and had to be relieved by
a naval rescue, but by spring the tide had turned against the
rebellion and, after a decisive English victory early in March,
the king's forces rapidly recaptured Anglesey. In the south the
following month, Gilbert initiated a fresh expedition; Joanna
would have been assured to learn that he had soon recaptured
Cardiff, but despite this, he was unable to consolidate his victory
against Morgan. When the king's forces finally arrived in the
south, however, the rebels put up no resistance, and Morgan
submitted himself directly to the king, reiterating that his grievances were only against Gilbert. The earl demanded the
punishment of the rebels, but to his fury the king received the
insurgents into the royal peace, pardoning Morgan and eventually employing him on commissions. Most gallingly, the king
once again confiscated the province from his son-in-law, instead
placing it under the control of a custodian appointed from among
his men. For the second time in three years, Joanna faced the
prospect of her income being halved overnight, as the prosperous
sheep farms of Glamorgan, the salmon fisheries of Usk, and the
rights to Cardiff, the largest town in the March, were withdrawn
from her joint lordship with Gilbert. The gesture was a victory
for the king in his struggle to rein in the traditional autonomy
of the Marcher lords. But for his daughter and son-in-law,
stripped of the lands where they had played king and queen, the
blow must have been exceptionally bitter.[5]

These moves emboldened the old enemies of Gilbert, and there
are signs he may have lost the will to keep fighting. In May, he
signed over the rights associated with several churches he held
in Glamorgan to his long-time adversary, the Bishop of Llandaff,
and he swapped some other churches in the March for ones in

Lincoln. At court in Westminster that August, a heavily pregnant Joanna was compelled by her victorious father to confirm Gilbert's charters. That summer must have been difficult for the countess – she had gained safety in England, but lost much of the autonomy to which she had grown accustomed. The words she spoke to her father on being forced to surrender parts of the estate that she had hoped to pass to her son are not recorded but, given her temperament, Joanna is unlikely to have held her tongue. She departed from court shortly after her interview, and probably headed for the Clare estate at Tewkesbury, to await the birth of her third daughter (whom she would name Elizabeth, for her youngest sister). Then, in October, the king relented and issued a charter restoring Glamorgan to the control of Gilbert and Joanna; in it, he made clear that he had not sought to deprive his daughter or grandson of their inheritance, but rather to demonstrate his ultimate authority over her husband, even in the lawless land of the March. The king's charter implied that Joanna played an active role in winning back her estate. But for Gilbert, it seems that the trauma of the rebellion and the confiscation of his lands had shattered his will.[6]

Despite the vast age difference between her and her husband, Joanna's decision to reside with Gilbert deep inside the March of Wales and in Ireland rather than in Clare, Suffolk, or their Gloucester estates, as well as her many pregnancies that occurred in quick succession, suggests a connection between the two beyond the legal one. It may be that her fiery and unflinching personality was well matched by the strident and bold earl. Certainly the choices she would make in the coming years suggest that she was anything but cowed by the confiscation and subsequent restoration of her estate by her father, or the ruinous effect that her father's actions had on her husband.

*

The king could not rest long after his subjugation of the Welsh rebels and his disobedient Marcher lord son-in-law. Just as Edward had been determined to demonstrate his authority throughout Wales and Scotland, the King of France was resolved to express his own control over the English-held province of Gascony. Tensions between the nations had been building throughout the early 1290s – there were regular violent skirmishes between English and Norman sailors, and in 1294 the French succeeded in tricking Edward into effectively surrendering Gascony and forfeiting his lordship. Though he was desperate to reclaim the province, the king had been preoccupied in Wales and was only able to send a small troop under inexperienced command, which gave the French king time to strengthen his position. By early 1296, France had forged an alliance of mutual protection with the ruling council of Scotland – the beginning of the so-called Auld Alliance – which fanned the flames between England and Scotland. Edward ordered his war-weary men north, and just after Easter they took Berwick-on-Tweed, sacking the Scottish border town and mercilessly slaughtering its inhabitants. The campaign was a rapid success: within five months, the castles at Dunbar, Roxburgh, Edinburgh, and Stirling had submitted to Edward, and the country was effectively conquered. He could now return to planning, none too soon, his campaign against the French in Gascony: the French had begun raiding English coastal towns – Winchelsea was attacked; at Dover, an elderly and infirm monk, left behind by his fleeing brothers, was killed when he refused to disclose where the church treasures were hidden – and the people were growing increasingly anxious. The intervening years, during which Edward had been prohibited from engaging with France directly, had also offered opportunities for the French king to win over the German and Low Country rulers with whom Edward had made pacts. By the time the

English were in a position to mount another continental campaign, Edward's northern alliances were breaking apart.

Late in 1296, Margaret and Eleanora – and the virtually indissoluble alliances they represented with the Duchy of Brabant and the County of Bar – were a lifeline to Edward, as he sought to retain control of his continental empire. Elizabeth's planned match with the heir to the County of Holland had been threatened in 1295 when the count, Floris V, frustrated by Edward's failure to back his own (weak) claim to the throne of Scotland and also by the closure of English wool ports in Holland that threatened the wealth of the province, abandoned the English alliance and instead sided with France. Despite this shift, Johan was not immediately returned from England, and when Floris was kidnapped and killed the following year by a group of nobles seeking to restore the wool trade, Edward capitalized on his guardianship of Johan to propel Holland back into the alliance, and plans for Elizabeth's marriage to him were pushed rapidly forward. While in Anglesey in the spring of 1295, Jan of Brabant had promised to bring two thousand knights to fight for his father-in-law in the war against France, opening up a northern front that would draw the French king's knights away from Gascony. Bolstered by this promise, Edward pledged Brabant forty thousand pounds to fund the effort. His son-in-law, the Count of Bar, also enlisted with great fervour, his personal ambitions being well aligned with those of England; Eleanora undoubtedly offered constant reminders to her husband of the vow he had made to fight with England.[7]

Following the tragic conclusion of their wedding festivities two years earlier, Eleanora and Henri had settled comfortably into their union. Aged twenty-five, Eleanora gave birth to a healthy son, and a daughter followed; both children were named in honour of Eleanora's family: the boy was Edward, the girl Joanna. The royal wardrobe books record frequent payments to messengers sent between Bar and England, suggesting that regular correspondence was maintained between the countess, her husband, and her father. Eleanora, the most political of King Edward's children, was well matched with a husband who enthusiastically embraced the opportunity to join the broad network of princes who were aligning against the expansionist ambitions of France (which now included Henri's own greatest rival, the Countess of Champagne, Queen Jeanne of France). The way that Henri seemingly modelled himself on his father-in-law suggests the influence of his wife, although she cannot have been without her own anxieties as the time for action approached. Unlike during Joanna's experience of rebellion, for Eleanora and her children there was no route for escape, nowhere to flee – Bar was landlocked and surrounded by powerful neighbouring lords, any of whom might seek to capitalize on the departure of the count and his family. While Henri gathered an army of a thousand mounted men, whose expenses were promised by England – ready to prove his worth and improve his position, like a hero from the romances that Eleanora had grown up reading – his wife prepared herself to undertake the management of Bar and the safeguarding of her household and her children, including her son Edward, who was still third-in-line to the throne of England.[8]

Writing a century later, the celebrated author Christine de Pisan commented that, since it is the responsibility of a nobleman to travel often, bearing arms at war:

> . . . his lady and companion stays behind, and she must take his place. Although there may be enough bailiffs, provosts, administrators and governors, there has to be someone in charge of them all, and therefore it is proper that she should take on this responsibility. She should conduct herself with such skill that she may be feared as well as loved.

This was the situation in which Eleanora found herself in the summer of 1297, when her husband went to war for her father. Daunting as it must have seemed, she would, at least, have been well-prepared for this eventuality: the scale of administration within her household was so great, and minor lords like Henri were away from home so frequently, that in practice their wives often shared the burden of management responsibilities. After four years in Bar, the twenty-nine-year-old countess had become knowledgeable about local law and customs, had learned which officials and servants were most capable and trustworthy, and understood the income and expenditure needed to maintain the security of her household. Eleanora, who long ago had practised to be a queen, now acted as chatelaine in her dower castle at the heart of her county, her young son and infant daughter close at hand. Though she was far from her family, she had her own abilities to guide her, along with those of Henri's councillors and his friends who were too old to join the fight.[9]

In May 1297, Henri and his men departed and headed west into Champagne. A French chronicle records that the Count of Bar commanded a 'great multitude of armed men' as they entered the countryside, attacking and burning villages as they travelled westwards. The news that initially filtered home to Eleanora must have been reassuring – the troops seemed to be progressing, unmolested by any large French forces. But suddenly, word arrived of villages within Bar itself being devastated: the Constable of France, avoiding Henri's army in open battle, had instead sent a contingent of men to invade the count's home territory, which was left unprotected while its knights were fighting in Champagne. 'By force and by fire [the French forces] devastated the land of the Count of Bar'. Eleanora knew what was expected of her in this situation – like all medieval noblewomen left in charge of an estate, she was responsible for overseeing its defence. Christine de Pisan wrote (in a phrase that poetically foreshadows Elizabeth I's famous speech on the eve of the Spanish Armada, three hundred years later) that in such circumstances a lady

> ought to have the heart of a man, that is, she ought to know how to use weapons and be familiar with everything that pertains to them, so that she may be ready to command her men if need arises. She should know how to launch an attack or to defend against one, if the situation calls for it.

In the summer of 1297, the situation in Bar called for Eleanora to rise to the defence of her county; for the sake of her husband, and to secure both her own dower estate and the inheritance of her heirs, she needed to protect Bar vigorously.[10]

She hastily dispatched messengers to recall Henri and his men, and sought the support of their allies, including her father. Close at hand, Henri's army turned and chased off the invaders, but the count was disheartened: his efforts in Champagne had achieved nothing more than the ruin of a handful of villages in both counties, and the loss of a number of lives. Though Eleanora had tried to enlist reinforcements, their allies could do little to help draw off the French forces: the Count of Flanders was locked in his own stand-off with the French at their southern border, and only a small English advance force, fighting far to the south-west, had reached the continent. Her father was still in England, making the final preparations for the launch of the fleet that would carry his main force. In response to entreaties from Bar, he wrote a letter on 4 June to the king of the Germans, begging him to come to the aid of Henri 'who has done more than our other allies in those parts . . . against our common enemy', but the German king was under intense pressure from the French-allied forces of the Duke of Austria and could not help.[11]

Throughout the summer, fighting across the border with France intensified; in the middle of June the French invaded Flanders with a large army, settling into a siege around the city of Lille and torching the countryside. When news of the siege reached Bar, Henri once again set out, travelling north to join his ally and fight the French. Back in Bar, once more the chatelaine, Eleanora learned that her husband had been captured in a skirmish with a French raiding party outside the village of Comines, near Lille on the river Lys. The king of England's 'dear son', who had had the temerity to invade the French queen's own province of Champagne, had been imprisoned by his greatest foe. When the messenger arrived in Bar with the news, Eleanora was unable to break down in fear or distress – she was now responsible for overseeing the estate, acting as an informal regent, and defending the province and her children to the best of her ability, with a diminished military force, but also for securing Henri's release. It was readily apparent to Eleanora that her husband's liberty, if he could be ransomed, would be dearly bought.[12]

X
Unconstrained

1295–6

BURY ST EDMUNDS

In the autumn of 1295, after their estates in Glamorgan had been returned to them, Gilbert and Joanna travelled back to Wales to pick up the pieces of their Welsh life. They had scarcely had time to settle into anything like a normal routine when, one month later, the earl was recalled to Westminster for a session of parliament. The Welsh rebellion had been expensive, and with Scotland on the cusp of war, the king needed approval for new taxes to refill the royal coffers. Gilbert travelled north-east out of Glamorgan, through his lordships of Newport, and Caerleon and Usk, and into Monmouthshire. He stayed overnight at Monmouth Castle, the newly refurbished and heavily fortified western residence of the king's brother, Edmund Crouchback and it was there, on 7 December, that he died suddenly of an unrecorded cause. His widow was twenty-three, mother to four small children, and now sole lord of one of the largest estates in the kingdom.[1]

The chronicles, which uniformly record his death, do not mention if Joanna was with her husband when he died, or if she had remained in Glamorgan when he was called to Westminster. Throughout their marriage, she normally travelled by his side, but it is possible that she had chosen that December to remain within their March estate, having had her fill of court and her family during the stressful summer of rebellion. After his death, she travelled to Monmouth to oversee the transfer of Gilbert's body to Tewkesbury, a distance of just over thirty miles. There, three days before Christmas, Joanna wrapped herself in a heavy cloak and made her way down the hill from the manor house south of the town towards the abbey church long patronized by Gilbert's ancestors. Inside the church, she heard Mass for the soul of her husband and watched as Gilbert's pall-draped coffin was lowered into the ground to the left of his father's and covered with heavy paving stones. No monument marks the site of his burial among the immense Romanesque piers that dominate Tewkesbury Abbey, but Gilbert was interred with his ancestors in the choir in front of the high altar – the most prestigious burial site within the church.[2]

After the funeral, Joanna spent a solemn Christmas at either Tewkesbury or another nearby Clare estate but, following the feast of Epiphany on 6 January, travelled to her father's court, which was then at Bury St Edmunds and heading slowly north to the Norfolk coast. News of Gilbert's death had reached court on 14 December, and the king had directed his men to take the Clare lands into their custody. This was common practice on the death of a lord who held lands directly from the king; the estate would be held and valued, and any outstanding royal debts would be taken, before it was released to the rightful heir following the performance of homage. Joanna's first priority after seeing her husband buried was to secure her estate so that it would provide her a suitable income, and to acquire the guardianship of her children, who were now legally orphaned. (Widowed mothers did not immediately gain control over their children because of concerns that the children's welfare might be endangered if she remarried, by a stepfather who wished his own children to inherit their mother's wealth.) By the terms that Gilbert had agreed at Amesbury in the weeks before his wedding to Joanna, all his lands were held jointly by her, which meant that, on his death, they all passed to her for the term of her life, before devolving to her heirs. Joanna's son and heir might have been embittered at being deprived of his entire inheritance until his mother's death, but on his father's death, little Gilbert was a decade and a half away from maturity. In the meantime, the young widow was assured of an economic power that few among even the greatest lords could boast.[3]

Like Eleanora, Joanna would have learned much about land management during the years of her marriage to Gilbert. As joint landholder she was legally required to agree significant actions such as buying, selling, and giving away properties and had even more reason and opportunity than her sister to understand how the immense and widely dispersed estates of the Clare family might be managed most profitably. However, as much as she had learned while her husband was alive, the prospect of being in sole command of such a vast landed interest after his death must have been daunting. Yet, whatever personal stress, anxiety, and grief may have accompanied Gilbert's passing, for a woman of Joanna's independent nature, the prospect of widowhood may have appealed. As a widow, the countess was freed from the control of her father or husband for the first time in her life – becoming a legally autonomous person and lord in her own right. While it was true that, in the heavily patriarchal society of medieval England, even widowed women were forbidden from holding royal office or sitting on the royal council, Joanna was now able to sue and to be sued, to conduct business in her own name with her tenants and peers, to pay her debts and claim those owed to her, and to appoint those servants she favoured to oversee the management of her properties. As a tenant-in-chief who held her land directly from the king, Joanna was also obliged to perform the customary feudal service, or military aid, when it was demanded; and though she would not personally be required to command men-at-arms in battle, she would need to gather and provision them, and to appoint a commander in her stead.

The enhanced legal status of widows like Joanna meant they were also able to exercise public authority in a more direct way than previously. The power wielded by as-yet unmarried or married women normally stemmed from their ability to influence a father or husband, but widows were free to act on their own decisions, and in their own names. Furthermore, aristocratic widows – particularly those who managed large landholdings, including heiresses and rare women like Joanna who had jointly held their husband's estates – were able to declare their interests publicly, without fear of the remonstrations they might have faced during their husbands' lives, that they were appropriating his rightful role as head of the household. Alongside these privileges, widowhood often brought considerable difficulties: for widows of the middle or lower classes, poverty was a significant concern; for those among the aristocracy, there were constant legal challenges to claiming dower, and anxiety and ill-feeling was not uncommon when a widow sued or was sued by her children or stepchildren. As a princess and joint landholder of

Gilbert's estates, and with an heir who was still only four years old, Joanna was fortunate to escape the most difficult and fraught aspects of widowhood. A long life was open to her in which she would no longer have to face the dangers of childbirth, and might enjoy influence at court, the respect that came from living chastely, and astonishing wealth. In Glamorgan, where she retained special privileges as a lord of the March of Wales, Joanna could live as a queen in her own right – the ultimate deci-sion-maker, a commanding patron, a woman unconstrained by the patriarchal system because she was above it.[4]

She could not, however, avoid the cultural impression strongly prevalent in medieval Europe that widows were emotionally unstable and incapable of managing a military force. The popular twelfth-century romance *Yvain, or the Knight with the Lion* featured a young widow who one moment was moaning, grieving, beating her breast, and threatening suicide over the death of her husband, and the next plotting to marry his murderer. Her counsellors' advice was unanimous: 'no woman wants to bear a shield and use a lance, so she would be much better for a marriage with some worthy lord, nor could there be a greater need. Advise her to be wed with speed . . .' Without husbands to sexually satisfy and control them, widows were also thought to be prone to lascivious behaviour that might scandalize their families. Even with full legal autonomy and economic independence, widows were subject to an underlying fear of unchecked female sexuality, as well as a persistent misogyny that questioned whether a woman really could fulfil the role normally occupied by a man. The young, beautiful, or those with vast resources of wealth that might tempt fortune hunters, were discouraged from following the path of pious celibacy, which was almost as highly prized as monastic virginity, since it carried the risk of encountering lechery, or even abduction and coerced marriage. Attempts had been made in the early history of Christianity to discourage priests from performing second marriages. But within feudal society, where power passed through generations of legitimate heirs, second marriages were often necessary to avoid the upheaval of failed dynastic lines. By the thirteenth century, women like Joanna – who was at least young and rich, though no record survives to attest to her beauty – were often positively encouraged to remarry, to avoid sin and provide a masculine protector. If her remarriage necessarily resulted in the dower estate falling back into male decision-making and control (which was assumed to be superior), this was thought to be no bad thing.[5]

Joanna would no doubt have known of, and possibly met, the formidable Marcher dowager and heiress Maud de Braose, whose Welsh tenants fought alongside Gilbert's men from Glamorgan during the king's Welsh wars. Maud was staunchly loyal to Edward, having herself devised the plan for his daring escape from enemy hands during the civil war of the 1260s, but her particular focus on supporting his efforts against the Welsh princes may have been influenced by her own father's execution on the orders of Llewelyn the Great. After the death of Maud's husband in 1282, she began to play a role remarkably similar to that of a male baron, with all the responsibilities that came with the position. Her men fought for the king, she fed his armies from her markets, she provided him with counsel and advisors, and she maintained his peace in her lands.[6]

In the early days of Joanna's widowhood, the model provided by Maud and other women like her – to hold her lands, perform the service that was due, conduct business, and maintain control of her own children – may have appealed to her. But if she hoped to succeed as Maud had, she would need to forge a place for herself in a social environment that restricted female autonomy;

success would not be easy. Joanna found court assembled at Bury St Edmunds around 18 January, and immediately sought an audience with her father. Her first piece of business was to negotiate the debts that Gilbert had owed to him; still outstanding were the ten thousand marks he had been fined for contempt in 1282, after he had ignored Edward's direct order to cease his private war with the Earl of Hereford over the March lands in and around the castle at Morlais. Whether out of filial concern and pity, or from practical reasoning that the sum, which amounted roughly to the total annual income of the Clare estate, was unlikely to be repaid, the executors of Gilbert's will were relieved of the fine 'at the instance of Joanna'. The earl's remaining debts amounted to roughly nine hundred pounds, and the executors were asked to secure these.[7]

Two days later at Bury St Edmunds, within the palatial precincts of the ancient abbey named for the martyred king of the East Angles, the countess knelt before her father. Placing her hands between his to show that she was subjecting herself to his protection, she spoke the words that bound her – as lord of the Clare estates – to her father. She would be his vassal, and he would become her feudal overlord: 'I do to you homage for the tenement that I hold of you, and faith to you will bear of earthly worship, and faith to you shall bear against all folk.' The pledge was very similar to that promised by a male vassal, with two exceptions. The first was that men began their vow with the words 'I become your man . . .' (the origin of the word homage was literally that the vassal became the 'homme', or 'man', of the lord), but it was considered inappropriate for a woman to give this pledge to any man other than her husband. Secondly, women paying homage were not obliged to bear faith 'of life and member', the words that implied an obligation to risk one's own life to the lord through military service. After she had spoken the pledge, Edward leaned forward and kissed his daughter, as he kissed all his tenants-in-chief who came to perform homage before receiving their lands. Joanna then stood and, placing her hand on a copy of the Gospels, said, 'Hear this my lord: I will bear faith to you of goods, chattels and earthly worship, so help me God and these holy Gospels of God'.[8]

The king and his daughter were accustomed to the solemn performance of public spectacle, and it seems likely that the ceremony was carried out with all the gravity that custom demanded. The strangeness of kneeling before her father and reciting a formal oath of allegiance must have underlined for Joanna the fact that her life would henceforth be different, given her sole command of her children and her vast estate. However, it was not particularly unusual for a women to be kneeling before the king. A century earlier, according to the great twelfth-century legal scholar Ranulf de Glanvill, women's inability to serve militarily precluded them from performing homage; his *Treatise on the Laws and Customs of the Kingdom of England*, written in the 1180s, stated that landholding women could *receive* the homage of men, but could not *perform* it. By the second half of the thirteenth century, practicality had overtaken the law and women – mostly, widows like Joanna – were performing homage fairly regularly, even for estates held in return for military service.[9]

The ceremony and negotiations relating to Gilbert's debts bound King Edward and his second-eldest daughter in a way that was unique within their family – the relationship between a feudal lord and his vassal was focused on the latter's loyalty and service, and Joanna, the king's least compliant daughter, was now doubly bound to honour the wishes of her father. But she was also now one of the pillars that supported his kingdom, given that she was among the largest landholders, and a Marcher lord. One of the first requirements her father made of her was that she promise not to remarry without his approval. This was, of course, a limitation on her freedom as a widow to do what she wanted, but more significantly, it was a way for the king to maintain control over which men gained access to the economic and military might that accompanied her estates. Male vassals were not required to make the same promise because their new wives posed little threat to the king, though they might prove a considerable nuisance to their husband's heirs if they lived too long. At a widow's remarriage, however, her husband would gain control of her lands, her money, and her fighting men. In the case of Joanna, now one of the foremost lords of his realm and a significant force within the March of Wales, the king naturally wanted a veto over which of his subjects or foreign peers might become so empowered.

With the ceremony and negotiations around Gilbert's debts complete, Edward issued declarations to his chief administrators to restore to 'Joanna, the king's daughter, late the wife of Gilbert de Clare, Earl of Gloucester and Hertford' all the lands she had held jointly with Gilbert from the king, 'as the king has taken her homage therefor'. A sense of the scale of Joanna's holdings in England can be gleaned from the fact that the order was sent to men governing estates in twenty-five counties – from Somerset in the south-west to York in the north-east, from Worcestershire in the western Midlands to Kent along the Channel coast. Other orders were sent to Ireland, and a week later Joanna appointed her own administrator to oversee her estates there. The census that recorded the full Clare domain at Gilbert's death provides further tantalizing details about Joanna's landholdings. The Amesbury agreement ensured that almost all of Gilbert's estate passed to Joanna intact, with the exception of

the dower lands like Thaxted in Essex, that had been assigned
to Gilbert's first wife, Alice de Lusignan, who was still alive. But
these were insignificant in comparison to the dozens of manors,
farms, meadows, rents, and tolls that came into Joanna's sole
lordship. She held towns such as Tewkesbury and Cardiff,
markets in Great Bardfield and Bletchingley, fairs in Sodbury
and Little Walsingham, and fisheries in the Severn, Medway,
and Wye rivers. She held a watermill near the confluence of
rivers at Yalding and a windmill at Hersham, a pottery at Hanley
and smithies at Rothwell, a warren near Gazeley, a dovecot at
Boverton, a ferry near Usk, and the toll paid by ships sailing
from Wells on the Norfolk coast. She held countless hunting
parks, chases, and woods, and the castles at Tonbridge, Clare,
Caerphilly, Neath, and Caerleon. In Little Haywode in Glamorgan,
she held a forest 'where there is a nest of sparrow-hawks', a
species of small hunting bird that was favoured by aristocratic
women. The estate Joanna now controlled was widespread and
extraordinarily diverse, and these lands, properties, and rights
were to yield her a formidable income. The *demesne*, or home
farm, that provided the foodstuffs and raw goods needed to cater
for her household was managed directly, but the bulk of the land
was let out for rents in cash and in kind. Some rents came in
the form of rare and imported commodities: from Camberwell
in Surrey, she was owed one pound of cumin at Christmas time,
from Crimplesham in Norfolk a pound of pepper and pair of
gloves, and from Mapledurham in Oxfordshire, a pair of gold
spurs. Other rents were provided in local produce: throughout
Essex, lands were held for payment in eggs and grain, capons,
lambs, and pigs. When its annual income was next accounted,
early in the fourteenth century, the estate was worth in excess
of six thousand pounds a year.[10]

After paying her homage, Joanna remained with her father

as he travelled north, stopping in the royal forest at Thetford to join a hunt. As she travelled with the court, spending time with her father, Joanna had plenty of time to work her usual persuasive magic, lobbying him for further financial indulgences. As was his way with his daughters, Edward softened easily, instructing his tax collectors in writing to delay taking up the new taxes due on the Clare estates until after Easter 'as the king wishes to show special favour . . . at the instance of his daughter Joanna.' A few days later, court arrived at Walsingham, home to a great shrine to the Virgin Mary, and among the most impor-tant holy sites in England, where the king could pray in humble preparation for the battles to come.[11]

In this village, mention of Joanna's children appears in the records for the first time since the death of her husband – they had by now been assigned to the guardianship of their mother. Though they were officially within her protection, however, the countess seems to have had concerns about her ability to guar-antee the children's safety within the lawless land of the March, and conveyed these thoughts to her father. Sensitive to his daughter's anxieties, and also perhaps hopeful that if young Gilbert grew up within an English court setting he might mature into a more compliant magnate than if his formative years were spent in the comparative wilds of Glamorgan, 'at the pleasure of the king and of her', he assigned his grandchildren a residence within England. Bristol seemed to offer the best choice – safely within the realm of England and subject to its laws and the king's influence, it was also immediately adjacent to Joanna's Gloucestershire and Welsh estates, thereby enabling visits to and from their mother. It was also home to one of the finest royal castles in the country, with plenty of room to house a noble nursery.[12]

Accordingly, the king wrote to his constable at Bristol Castle, issuing instructions to prepare for the arrival of the royal grand-children – Gilbert, Eleanor, Margaret, and Elizabeth – along with the guardians and attendants that would be chosen by their mother. The constable was to prepare the 'king's houses', free-standing structures within the inner courtyard that were enclosed by the castle's curtain wall and protected by a moat fed by the nearby Frome and Avon rivers, as well as a tall keep. Inside the keep itself was another royal grandchild, for whom the constable prepared a much less comfortable home: Owain ap Dafydd, the younger son of Dafydd ap Gruffydd, the last of the Welsh princely line, had been imprisoned by the English king at Bristol since his father's defeat a decade earlier, when he was only seven years old. He was around twenty when the young Clares came to live at Bristol Castle, but the Welsh prince would not have met his English counterparts. Owain lived closely guarded within the keep, and in years to come would have to suffer the indig-nity of sleeping in a cage to prevent his escape and a new uprising in Wales. If Joanna's young son ever learned of Bristol Castle's other royal inmate, he would have recognized in Owain's life enough parallels to make him nervous.[13]

After departing from Walsingham, the king and his men travelled on to the coast and boarded ships heading north for Newcastle, where Edward had summoned his earls, barons, and knights to gather, before marching on Scotland. His daughter, her first tasks as a widow concluded and needing to attend to her estate and assign guardians for her children in Bristol, headed to the south-west. Despite the fears that meant she did not want her children living in the chaotic and unpredictable land of the March, she herself returned to Glamorgan, moving between Caerphilly and the other castles in that region. Joanna's wilful personality may have relished the freedom of life as a rich widow in a land where her word was law. But the same wealth and power that promised independence made her an irresistible prize; her father might soon discover another ally in need of a wife, and with her vast estates to act as dowry, Joanna could be married off rapidly and cheaply. She would have to make the most of her independence while she had it.

XI

Acquiescence and Insubordination

1297

IPSWICH, GOODRICH CASTLE

Margaret, Elizabeth, and their companions had been sailing for days, when they exchanged their ship for a barge at Harwich, to transport them up the River Orwell. They were heading for Ipswich near the Suffolk coast; it was the end of December, when sitting still on the water for hours would have allowed the damp to seep through their fur mantles and the layers of silk and linen tunics that wrapped their bodies. But floating up the river was probably still more comfortable than bumping along the winter roads in wagons laden with furniture and trunks full of clothing, serving dishes, chapel fittings, and kitchen equipment. Despite the cold, the days ahead promised excitement, roaring fires, and glittering feasts.

First came the new year celebrations, with the traditional gift-giving. The royal children in attendance – Margaret, Elizabeth, and Edward – each received a jewelled brooch in the shape of an eagle from their father, a golden clasp to pin together their mantles against the East Anglian winter wind. In return, Margaret presented the king with knives carved from ivory and ebony, with silver handles. On 3 January, and again 6 January, there were further festivities, as two companions of the princesses were married in the priory church of Holy Trinity in Ipswich, with each bride receiving a silver cup as her gift from the king and his daughters. During these celebrations, fresh caravans of prelates and noblemen and -women arrived in the city for a further celebration. They came from religious houses (the Abbots of Colchester and Bury St Edmunds, the Bishops of Norwich and London), from castles and manors throughout England (the Earl and Countess of Norfolk and those of Oxford, the Earl of Hereford, and the Countess of Cornwall), and from across Holland in the Low Countries. They were all there to celebrate a royal wedding: the marriage between fourteen-year-old Elizabeth and the new twelve-year-old Count of Holland, Johan I.[1]

After Johan's father had been killed the summer before, Edward had invited a delegation of wealthy Dutch townsmen and nobles to Bury St Edmunds – easily accessible from ships docking on the east coast – to discuss trade and a renewal of the alliance between Holland and England. The priority of the Dutch embassy was to reclaim their new count from English custody, but Edward – anxious that Holland might once again fall under the sway of France – was reluctant to send Johan back before his marriage to Elizabeth could be solemnized. The wedding date was therefore brought forward, despite minor infelicities such as Elizabeth's dress being incomplete, as well as more significant challenges such as Johan being a full two years younger than the canonical age of fourteen at which males could marry. The royal coffers were much depleted from constant warfare; the Norwich monk Bartholomew Cotton records that the local populace was required to cover the cost of the event, which cannot have been popular. In return for their support, the common men and women of Ipswich and the surrounding villages may have been permitted to glimpse the bridal party or the king and his family, and they may at least have enjoyed the scores of entertainers who descended on the city – minstrels and fools, harpers and drummers, trumpeters and fiddlers – but they would not have had any opportunity to participate in the event they had financed. The friars of Ipswich did better out of the wedding – the king laid out a feast for them, at his expense, in return for their prayers for the newlyweds.[2]

Those inside the dimly lit Romanesque church would have seen the teenage bride in a silken robe festooned with silver and gold buttons (Elizabeth's twist on the silver-sequined buttons that her sister Eleanora had favoured); the dress must have been intricately embroidered, as its last-minute creation took thirty-five tailors four days and four nights to make, led by the princess's personal tailor Henry, who spent eight days in London overseeing its preparation. While undoubtedly sumptuous, the robe was incomplete: a *zone* of pearls intended to circle the bride's slim hips was not finished by the time a carriage drawn by five horses left London to swiftly carry the princess's jewels to Ipswich. Its loss evidently caused Elizabeth great displeasure, as her father gave her twelve marks to soothe her disappointment. On her head, the new Countess of Holland wore the most splendid of her bridal jewels, a gold coronet studded with pearls, large rubies, and emeralds. It was another crown to add to the collection she had inherited from her mother which, along with the golden cup she received as a wedding gift from Margaret, would have reminded her of home and her family in her new life as consort of one of the princes of Europe. Another gift was the exquisitely illustrated psalter commissioned more than a decade before by her mother for Alphonso, the elder brother Elizabeth could not have remembered: ornamented with the arms of England impaling those of Holland, the manuscript was a wedding gift to Elizabeth from her father, who had ordered that the part-finished book be finally completed, in his daughter's honour. An object of exquisite beauty, it is easy to imagine the young countess enthralled by the delicate marginal drawings of brightly feathered birds and elegant ladies hunting with hounds. Owning her own psalter would also offer Elizabeth regular opportunities for practising her reading skills, and it was therefore a gift of which her mother would have wholeheartedly approved.

Three days after the wedding, the young Count of Holland and his visiting noblemen, knights, and burgesses, requested the English king to arbitrate on their behalf in a disagreement with the Duke of Brabant, another of his sons-in-law. Edward was well-practised at arbitrating between European houses – he had spent much of the previous decade striving to build accord between France and Aragon, to enable Eleanora's marriage and the renewal of a united crusade – but the significance of his arbitration in this instance underlines the role played by Margaret and Elizabeth in international diplomacy. It was the two English sisters who provided a link between the opposing Brabaçon and Dutch camps, and it was the occasion of Elizabeth's marriage that offered the opportunity for reconciliation. Later the same day, the royal party left Ipswich, travelling back along the Orwell to Harwich, where a squadron of six oar-propelled galleys was docked, including the vessels of the visiting Dutch nobles and some of the grandest ships in the royal fleet. At the bustling port in Harwich, where wool from Joanna's Gloucestershire estates left England to be spun into cloth in her sisters' provinces of Brabant and Holland, the king not only oversaw the transfer of Elizabeth's trousseau aboard one of her new husband's ships, but also the magnificent trousseau of her sister Margaret. Aged twenty-one, the duchess had finally bowed to pressure from both the English and Brabaçon courts and, possibly in recognition of the much more active role her sister Eleanora was playing in supporting their father's war, was joining her husband in Brabant.[3]

The luxury of Margaret's trousseau was even more extravagant than those of her sisters, reflecting the importance of projecting England's wealth and sophistication at the ducal court, and perhaps also a sense of guilt on the part of her father, who was aware that he was forcing his child away, to her great unhappiness. The account of the king's goldsmith which lists the precious objects accompanying Margaret to her new home takes up a full folio page, in a minute and tightly packed script. Dozens of items of silver and silver-gilt are recorded among the inventory of her chamber and chapel goods: chalices, plates, and more than a hundred salt cellars; a censer for her chapel in the shape of a ship; alms dishes and candelabra; pitchers, cups, and large bowls for washing her hands and face. Her jewel caskets were full to bursting with more than three dozen gold clasps; ten rings; a golden *zone* and many made of silver; headdresses with interchangeable ornaments made of gold and pearls in the shapes of birds and the heraldic leopards of England; and a solid gold seal so the duchess could issue her own charters. More jewels had been made for Margaret and brought from London to Ipswich for her approval, but they were dismissed as insufficiently grand to please her and were returned unpurchased. She also took copper pans and cooking pots, and a new carriage, its interior trimmed in silken cushions, its chains and harness gilded. In total, the goods Margaret carried to her new life in Brabant cost thousands of pounds to procure. All this equipment, plus riding horses and transport carts, were packed aboard the *Swan of Yarmouth*, one of the king's largest galleys, and escorted across the sea by the Dutch royal ships in a fleet remembered as 'inestimably ornamented' in an early-fourteenth-century chronicle from Holland. The retinue chosen to sail with Margaret included the Earl of Hereford and Essex who had accompanied Eleanora to Bar, priests, and more than a dozen of the king's knights, clerks and commissioners, though only one of her men would be allowed to remain with the princess for any length of time. Margaret's lady Matilda de Statelyng and Isabella de Vescy, a close friend and lady of the princesses' late mother, are the only women recorded as travelling with the party.[4]

As the date for their departure approached, Elizabeth balked at the idea of leaving. She could easily have reasoned that Margaret had managed to stay in England for more than six years after her own marriage; she might have thrown back in her father's face the anxieties about young brides her mother and grandmother had expressed, when Eleanora's first marriage had been performed by proxy back in 1282. Her reason for refusing to travel to Holland is not recorded, but the reaction of her father is – already under intense pressure from his magnates about the never-ending wars, Edward was incandescent at the insubordination and wilful conduct of his youngest child, and what followed is the only known example of a violent flash of the monarch's temper towards one of his daughters. A note in the king's wardrobe book from the time records payment to Adam, the king's goldsmith 'for a great ruby and a great emerald bought to set into a certain coronet of the Countess of Holland, the king's daughter, in place of two stones which were lost when the king threw the coronet into the fire'. It seems that, in a fit of anger, the king tore Elizabeth's bridal coronet from her head and threw it into a fire so hot that, by the time he calmed down and retrieved the crown, two of its principal jewels had been lost. Regretting the violence of his action, he ordered the jewels to be replaced and guiltily, he also agreed that Elizabeth might remain a while longer in England and travel to Holland with his expeditionary force later that year. Elizabeth, therefore, had managed to buy herself some more time as an independent princess – she now had the freedom of being a married adult, but was still within the orbit of home. And so, rather than escorting his new wife to his dominions, Johan took with him only a small embassy assigned by her father, which was given the job of checking that the annual value of the dower lands assigned to the countess was as agreed.[5]

While Elizabeth had won a reprieve, her elder sister's independence in England was drawing rapidly to a close. Nearly seven years after she had married Jan, and almost two since he had returned to Brabant as duke without her, Margaret could no longer avoid her responsibility as a royal woman and consort of a foreign prince. She was to return to Harwich and the fleet, and depart eastwards across the sea with her new brother-in-law. Her father undoubtedly felt his child's reluctance, and in his parting gift to her of a gold ring set inside a golden *pyx*, or small jewel casket, it is tempting to perceive a touch of sorrow, as Margaret and Jan sailed away from the shores of England. With his daughter travelling across winter seas, the king took special precautions and placed extra crew on the *Swan of Yarmouth*: two pilots were aboard to steer the vessel, which was manned by more than fifty rowers, sailors, and deck-hands, and a lantern was hung by its prow at night to ensure none of the other ships in the small fleet crashed into her. In all, the crossing took three days and landed on the shore of the count's province of Zeeland. From there, the English party accompanying Margaret travelled on to Brussels, where they arrived in early February.[6]

Back in England, Elizabeth and Prince Edward headed southwards towards Windsor, while their father continued north, bound for Walsingham. He was at Castle Acre at the end of January when an almost unimaginable rumour reached his ears: that his second daughter Joanna, the Countess of Gloucester and Hertford, was romantically involved with a common man whom she planned to marry. Edward initially refused to believe that his daughter, wilful though she had always been, would dare to ignore the feudal vows she had pledged and remarry without his express consent. But he acted swiftly to safeguard his rights against this unexpected episode of filial intransigence, dispatching his men with orders to take all Joanna's properties and goods throughout England and Wales into the king's hands 'for certain reasons immediately on sight hereof'. A sense of Edward's fury can still be felt through the centuries in the clause in the letter that warned the royal messenger to carry out his lord's wishes 'as he loves himself and his things and wishes to escape the king's wrath.' Much was at stake – Joanna's estate was too large and gave its lord too much power for the countess to bestow the Earldom of Gloucester upon an unknown man, despite whatever ill-conceived notion of romance she may have entertained. In that moment, her father must have cursed the licentiousness and poor decision-making for which widows were popularly known. Despite his anger, however, Edward remained largely in the dark as to the truth behind the rumour, so sent his confessor to Glamorgan to seek out his daughter and discover her true intentions.[7]

However, the countess and her paramour – guiltier even than

her father might have guessed – had already fled her Welsh dominion, seeking a refuge and the advice of her friend, the recently widowed Countess of Pembroke. Joanna arrived at Goodrich Castle, just over the English border, in early February. Not yet realizing that her father had confiscated her whole estate, she nevertheless anticipated his fierce displeasure and summoned her children from Bristol. Meanwhile, Joanna's loyal constable at Tonbridge Castle in Kent refused to cede its command to the king's bailiffs, battling down the fortress in a defensive posture and sending Edward into ever greater fits of apoplexy. Lest Joanna's faithful servants at other sites follow his lead, the king ordered that all the lands and goods of the constable, and all the other defenders of Tonbridge Castle, be confiscated.[8]

The king's anger was no doubt exacerbated by the stress of planning for war; while he sought the truth about Joanna, he was also finalizing plans to travel to Flanders and attack the French from the north with his allies, while at the same time sending a separate force of English knights to take back Gascony in the south. Royal letters sent late that winter detailed these plans, as well as the king's efforts to cement his alliances around the marriages of his children: though Elizabeth remained in England, an English embassy travelled with Count Johan to examine the proposed dower estate and report back on its acceptability, and a potential union was proposed between Prince Edward of Caernarfon and one of the daughters of the Count of Flanders. Among the letters sent by the king in early 1297 was a warm response to a request from his cousin, Amadeus V, Count of Savoy, for Joanna's hand in marriage. The date that Amadeus first considered an approach is not mentioned, but the negotiations seem to have been exceedingly quick, with the king gladly assenting to the match, pleased with the solution to his predicament and hopeful that the count might open a further front on

France's south-eastern border with Savoy. Without having had a chance to consult his daughter, the king launched straight into his expectations regarding the lands and rents to be assigned to the countess as her dower, should she outlive Amadeus. This was by far the hastiest agreement of any relating to the many proposed betrothals of Edward's children, and because it concerned the remarriage of a widow – and one of the first lords of England – its rashness was, in fact, the least appropriate. Embroiled in wars all around him, with his barons on the brink of revolt at his ongoing demands for military service and new taxes, the king appeared to welcome a resolution to the problems posed by Joanna's action. And, as his plans progressed, news of them spread westwards to Goodrich, where Joanna soon realized that the time had come when she would need to confront her father before he went any further in arranging her marriage to Amadeus. For she knew what the king did not: she was already remarried.[9]

Among the squires in the retinue of the late Earl of Gloucester was a man in his mid-twenties named Ralph de Monthermer, whose origins and parentage are unknown. After Gilbert's death, he remained within the household of the countess, along with many of the earl's men. At some point during the year 1296, they fell in love. Ralph must have been driven nearly insane with desire for the great lady he served to even contemplate eloping with her and risking the wrath of the king. Though his adoration and longing for Joanna was undoubtedly affected and perhaps enhanced by her status, the risk that Ralph was putting himself in was too high to characterize him as a simple fortune hunter. Whether he seduced Joanna or she seduced him is not recorded, though it is difficult to imagine the boldness required for an unknown squire to seduce the daughter of his king. Ralph seems to have been a man of exceptional personal charisma and, according to a contemporary source, was 'elegantly formed'. Joanna must have been hopelessly enamoured with him to propose – as the almost infinitely more powerful partner, she must have been the one to do so – that the two marry in secret. Like the heroine Felice in *Guy of Warwick*, an almost exactly contemporary romance whose eponymous hero is the son of a steward but full of chivalric virtue, Joanna's pride would not countenance marrying a mere squire. According to the chronicler William Rishanger, Joanna arranged for Ralph to first be knighted (her request to her father explaining that Ralph had distinguished himself in her service); his new title better suited the romance narrative in which the pair seem to have cast themselves. The lovers were subsequently wed in secret sometime around January 1297, saying *per verba de praesenti*, or 'by words in the present tense', the vows that solemnized their union. No priests or witnesses were needed to legitimate a medieval marriage if both parties were unrelated and free from encumbrances. Declaring, 'I, Joanna, Countess of Gloucester and Hereford, daughter of the king, take you, Sir Ralph de Monthermer, as my husband', was all she needed to bind him, legally and indissolubly, to her.[10]

As simple as these words might have been to utter, Joanna's secret remarriage was a gesture of breathtaking bravado. She was risking everything she had; her actions contravened her vow to the king not to remarry without his consent, they disregarded whatever plans she must have expected her father would make for a second diplomatic marriage, and they threatened him with humiliation on an international stage – Edward would have to revoke his offer to Amadeus and admit he could not control his daughter. Unavoidably, Joanna knew she would eventually face the king's wrath, and yet she followed through, willing to endure the possibility that she would lose her estate. Her actions were possibly more calculated – by choosing a lower-born man she felt she could control she would avoid being subordinate to another noble husband; however, this would require forgiveness from her father, which she could not guarantee. She may, too, have been determined to avoid the fate that seemed to claim her sisters, one-by-one: exiled from England through royal duty, to live in the realm of a foreign husband, far from home and friends. If Joanna was determined to beat the system that had sent Eleanora and now Margaret away, and that would in time also push Elizabeth out of England, she would need to break the rules that conventionally governed remarriage.

Whatever her motive, Joanna knew that her actions, while bold, were not wholly without precedent, for she would have known well the story of her great-aunt, another English princess who had married a man of her choosing in secret. Eleanor, sister to Henry III, was married at a young age to an English nobleman, before being widowed in 1231 at the age of only sixteen. Soon after, the princess pledged before the Archbishop of Canterbury to remain piously celibate, wearing a ring similar to those worn by nuns as a token of her vow. However, at the age of twenty-two, she met the French-born Simon de Montfort, and, according to her brother the king, was willingly 'basely and clandestinely defiled' by him. Wanting to avoid scandal when he learned of their affair, Henry arranged for a secret wedding to be performed by his own chaplain at a small altar within his chamber. But the union was problematic from the start, with some objecting to a princess marrying a man so far beneath her rank, and others declaring it illegitimate, on account of Eleanor's vow of celibacy. Though her husband eventually acquired papal recognition for their marriage (by, it was rumoured, bribing the officials in Rome), it was easy for their enemies to portray the marriage as tainted, and Simon's subsequent leading role in the baronial uprising that nearly cost his brother-in-law, Henry III, his crown did little to improve popular perception of his secret marriage to an English princess.[11]

The story of Princess Eleanor and Simon de Montfort was therefore a cautionary tale for any noblewoman contemplating a covert second marriage to a man from a lower social background. At the time of Joanna's second wedding, however, more favourable examples could be found in popular romance stories, several of which detailed accounts of princesses falling in love with, and proposing marriage to, obscure knights and squires whose virtue shone through, despite their apparent low birth. In *King Horn*, Rimenhild, Princess of Westernesse, became wild in her desire for a mysterious young man, Horn, who had washed up on the shores of her father's kingdom. Rimenhild was desperate to marry him, but he refused until he had proven himself worthy by reclaiming his kingdom. In *Bevis of Hampton*, the Armenian princess Josian was so enamoured of an English teenager training to be a knight in her father's army, that she sought him out while he was naked in bed and there confessed her love; this time she was the one who had to undergo a transformation – to become a Christian – before Bevis would agree to marry her. In both romances, the lady ultimately succeeded in marrying her beloved who, after many trials, was both restored to his own rightful position and even elevated, through holding hers as well. These tales – of virtuous noblewomen marrying outside the normal social rules – are distinct from the more common recurring theme of adulterous noblewomen familiar from the Arthurian cycle or *Tristan and Isolde*, where the princesses Guinevere and Isolde are ultimately punished for indulging their love. Modern scholars are divided over whether romances such as *King Horn* and *Bevis of Hampton* were intended as pure fantasy and escapism for women inextricably trapped within loveless dynastic unions, or whether they could have provided models through which elite women might construct their own understandings of sexual behaviours. For a woman like Joanna with extraordinary wealth and the authority which came from her position as a widow, the prevalence of social narratives in which princesses openly declared their intention to marry a virtuous-but-unproven youth may have been enough to embolden her. Unlike Rimenhild and Josian, the real-world Joanna would never have been granted seven years to allow young Ralph to prove his worth, even if she had been willing to wait, and her father's swift offer of a union to Amadeus of Savoy certainly does not imply that Edward had the patience of the kingly fathers of fiction. And so, Joanna and her knight were married, swiftly and irrevocably.

At Goodrich Castle, unable to access the income from her estates, running out of money quickly, and only able to rely on her friends' support for so long, Joanna was in an increasingly precarious position. Around the time she learned her father was advancing plans to wed her to Amadeus of Savoy, she also faced a realization that must have added considerable pressure to the already anxious time: she had become pregnant with Ralph's child. This knowledge seems to have provoked an awareness that the time had come for full disclosure to her father; she sent her young children to their grandfather – a clear signal of submission – and travelled shortly after them to court. But if she thought her father would rapidly forgive her, she was wrong. Several chronicles record that when he learned Joanna had already married the obscure knight, the king was 'gravely offended' and reacted with 'excessive heated fury'. His anger is easily understood; Joanna had disregarded the king's authority as her feudal lord and as her father. She had broken the rules and now flaunted in his face her expanding belly.[12]

1. Modern view of a medieval princess, locked in her tower: the Lady of Shalott in an early twentieth-century painting by John William Waterhouse.

2. The gilded effigy of the princesses' mother, Eleanor of Castile, at Westminster Abbey.

3. Contemporary portrait of a king, possibly the only surviving image of the princesses' father, Edward I, at Westminster Abbey.

4. Royal ladies travelling in a coach, from the contemporary Luttrell Psalter.

5. Depiction of Caernarfon Castle, where Joanna celebrated her twelfth birthday with her mother and sisters, by J. M. W. Turner, *c.*1832.

6. Images of chivalric womanhood from the king's Painted Chamber at Westminster Palace: *Largesse* and *Debonereté*.

7. Holy women, saintly models: St Anne (with a young Virgin Mary), St Katherine, St Margaret, and St Barbara, from Elizabeth's Alphonso Psalter.

8. King Arthur and Queen Guinevere at court in Camelot, from a manuscript of *Lancelot du Lac* owned by Elizabeth's family.

9. Contemporary image of an ideal medieval noblewoman: Uta, Margravine of Meissen, at Naumburg Cathedral.

10. Exemplary scenes from the life of the Virgin Mary from the *Cantigas de Santa Maria*, written by Alfonso X, half-brother of Eleanor of Castile.

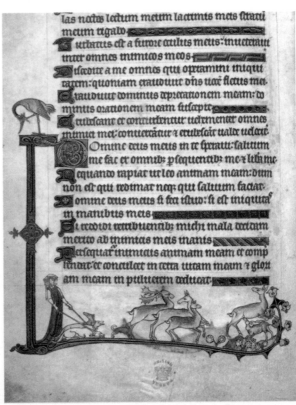

11. Lady hunting, Alphonso Psalter.

12. The reception and coronation of Queen Edith from Eleanor of Castile's copy of the *Life of Saint Edward the Confessor*.

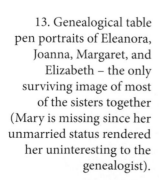

13. Genealogical table pen portraits of Eleanora, Joanna, Margaret, and Elizabeth – the only surviving image of most of the sisters together (Mary is missing since her unmarried status rendered her uninteresting to the genealogist).

14. Eleanor of Provence and Mary depicted as nuns, carved into the underside of Henry III's tomb at Westminster Abbey.

15. The great hall at Winchester Castle, site of the fabulous round table tournament in celebration of Joanna and Margaret's weddings, with Edward's Round Table now mounted on the wall.

16. View of later medieval London, with the Tower of London in the foreground and London Bridge and the City in the background, from a collection of poetry of Charles, Duke of Orléans.

17. Joanna's husband Gilbert de Clare depicted in glass alongside Clare ancestors and descendants at Tewkesbury Abbey, Gloucestershire.

18. Margaret and her ladies watching the festivities at her wedding from a scaffold, from the later *Brabantsche Yeesten*.

19. (*below left*) A *morse* (clasp for a mantle) showing the heraldry of Eleanor of Castile and Edward I, enamel on gilded copper with semi-precious stones, French.

20. (*below*) Engraving of the Eleanor Cross at Waltham, 1842.

21. Scene from a medieval birthing chamber, showing the mother attended by ladies and midwives with medicines, from John Lydgate's *Lives of Saints Edmund and Fremund*.

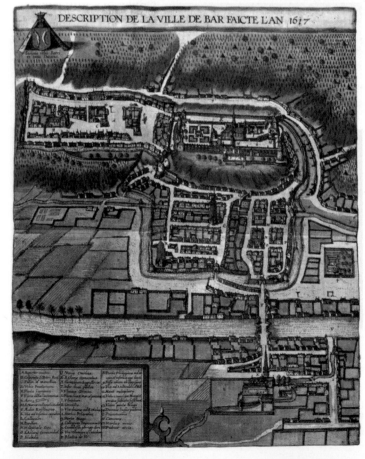

DESCRIPTION DE LA VILLE DE BAR FAICTE L'AN 1617

22. Map of Bar by Georg Braun, 1617, showing Eleanora's castle at the top.

23. Depiction of a knightly tournament from the chronicles of Jean Froissart.

24. Elizabeth as Countess of Holland. The illustrator mistakenly places her next to an earlier Count of Holland, William II, at his coronation in a later copy of the *Brabantsche Yeesten*.

25. *The Ridderzaal* (Knight's Hall), the great hall of the palace in The Hague, Elizabeth's principal residence in Holland, shown as it appeared in the seventeenth century.

26. Ivory mirror case showing lovers playing chess, Paris, *c.*1300.

27. Lady being attended in dressing by her maid, from the Luttrell Psalter.

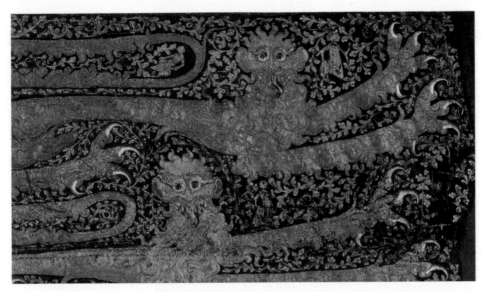

28. Contemporary horse-trapper embroidered with the royal arms of England, interwoven with images of noble ladies.

29. Crown of Blanche of Lancaster, the earliest surviving English royal crown, similar to those that would have been worn by the royal sisters. Gold, enamel, sapphires, rubies, emeralds, diamonds, and pearls, Paris, c.1370–80.

30. (*left*) The Bermondsey Mazer, depicting a lady placing a helmet on a kneeling knight, similar to dishes that would have been owned by the sisters. Silver, English, *c.*1335-45.

31. (*right*) Lady's seal, gold with jasper intaglio, showing fashionable noblewoman with inscription *CLAVSA. SECRETO TECO* ('I cover enclosed secrets'), English, fourteenth century.

32. View of the castle Margaret built at Tervuren, by Denijs van Alsloot, 1608.

33. Contemporary English depiction
of the funeral of a king.

34. Wedding of Edward II and Isabella of France at Boulogne,
from the later chronicle of Jean de Wavrin.

35. The Nine Worthy Women, female counterparts of the chivalric heroes the Nine Worthies, from Tommaso III di Saluzzo, *Le Chevalier Errant, c.*1404.

Orders were immediately dispatched for Ralph's arrest. He was taken – in a gesture that resounded with spite – to Bristol Castle, the usual nursery home of Joanna's Clare children, where he was held in the same prison that contained the caged Welsh prince Owain ap Dafydd. The king ordered his clerk to provide the pregnant countess with an allowance of 'reasonable maintenance' from the profits of her own lands, in order to support her and her children at court. This may resemble a nod towards reconciliation, but the king was still angry, and not above taking advantage of his daughter's insecure position to advance his long-term agenda to increase his control over the Welsh Marches. On the same day in May that he granted Joanna an income, he sent his own men, including Morgan ap Maredudd, who had rebelled so ferociously against Earl Gilbert, into her Welsh provinces to hear local grievances against the Marcher lords. In the middle of July, he instructed his men to seize all outstanding debts attached to the late Earl Gilbert from Joanna's estate since it remained in his possession; he was also still angry enough at his daughter to enrich his own men with the rents from her town of Cardiff and houses such as the castle at Neath. Court, meanwhile, whirled with gossip over the scandal, though Joanna's dual position as daughter of the king and the most powerful countess in the kingdom seems to have held the worst criticism in check. The king's adviser and friend, Anthony Bek, Bishop of Durham, reasoned with Edward that, since the marriage was legitimately made, it could not be undone, and advised the king to calm his wrath.[13]

Eventually, in late July, a visibly pregnant Joanna was ushered before her father at St Albans. She had come to present her case directly and, knowing her father intimately, she chose to frame her argument in a way designed to appeal to his conscious promotion of chivalry at his court. Extraordinarily, and uniquely in the history of the lives of Edward's daughters, the countess's own words on this occasion are recorded. They were noted and recalled by monks of the local abbey as words that paid vivid testimony to Joanna's character, and are recounted in a passage describing the spirit of King Edward and his family. Addressing her father before his court, in an effort to win not only her imprisoned husband's freedom but also to regain control of her estate and her independence, Joanna offered a powerful rationalization of her actions. 'It is not considered ignoble or disgraceful for a great and powerful earl to join himself in legal marriage with a poor and lesser woman,' she began. 'Therefore, in the same manner, it is not reprehensible or too difficult a thing for a countess to promote a gallant youth.'[14]

This was an extraordinary assertion because, despite the undeniable internal logic of her argument, it flew against contemporary opinion about the nature of marriage and social rank. An example of this may be found in the *De arte honeste amandi*, usually translated as *The Art of Courtly Love*, by the twelfth-century French thinker Andreas Capellanus, writing at the court of Marie de Champagne. In a section discussing courtly marriage, he wrote that the social status of an aristocratic woman changed on the occasion of her marriage, moving higher or lower to correspond with the social rank of her husband; in contrast, the social status of a man could never be socially elevated or demoted by marriage. In Capellanus' view, a man could confer aristocracy upon his wife, but a woman could not bestow nobility and promote her husband, however gallant he might be. Clearly, Joanna differed in her opinion, forged by a more direct reading of the contemporary romance narratives to which she was appealing. Hers was a rationale designed to appeal to a king who consciously promoted the chivalric sophistication of his court. This was Joanna's plan for breaking the rules and getting away with it, for marrying who she wanted, living where she wanted, and maintaining the wealth and power that provided her independence.[15]

Happily, her gamble worked; her words placated her father and, on 31 July, Edward restored Joanna's estate to her, withholding only the castle at Tonbridge (with its too-faithful constable), as a reminder to her that she held her lands at the pleasure of the king. Whatever warm feeling may have accompanied the resolution of the dispute between father and daughter, the business of war continued, and part of Joanna's settlement with the king was a promise to find one hundred men-at-arms, equipped with horses, to fight in his war with France. A curious stipulation appended to this agreement stated that Joanna would appoint a man other than Ralph, 'who will at present remain in England by license of the king', the captain of her forces; evidently Edward was sufficiently glad to be once more on good terms with his heavily pregnant daughter that he was willing to grant that she might enjoy some time with her new husband before he was sent off to war. Ralph must have been released from Bristol Castle around the same time his wife's lands were restored to her – as early as the morning of 2 August he was already with the king, Joanna, and her brother, at Anthony Bek's moated manor house near Eltham, south-east of London. Fittingly, it was there, in the great hall of the bishop who had advocated for acceptance of their marriage, that Joanna and her new husband knelt on the newly tiled floor and performed together the ceremony of homage for her lands – first to her father, the king, and then to her brother, Prince Edward.[16]

XII

Crisis

1297–9

GHENT, THE HAGUE

O n the same day that Joanna knelt before her father and
brother in another ceremony of feudal homage, the trousseau of her youngest sister Elizabeth was released from the
king's wardrobe, to be packed aboard a ship heading to Holland.
Among the countess's household items, jewellery, and robes was
the *zone* of pearls that had been unfinished at her wedding the
previous January, as well as a new purse with the arms of England
traced out in pearls, which matched an embroidered saddle that
the king had given Johan as a parting gift. The bridal goods
included the usual copious golden clasps and rings, silver-gilt
plates, and chalices, among them a silver cup with a cover that
had once belonged to the Archbishop of Canterbury, John
Peckham. Elizabeth had a new carriage and twenty-six horses
to stock her private stable; a large silver crucifix and service

books for her chapel (including the gloriously illustrated Alphonso Psalter); benches, candles, pitchers, and linens to furnish her table, and mixing bowls, cooking pots, knives, and mortars to equip her kitchen.[1]

For Elizabeth's sisters, 1297 was a year of crises – Joanna was estranged from her father, her husband was imprisoned, and her estates were confiscated; Eleanora was in command of the County of Bar, after her husband Henri had been captured by French forces near Lille, and in need of a vast ransom to set him free; Margaret was under acute pressure to produce an heir for her husband, while learning to navigate a foreign court. Their father's kingdom, meanwhile, teetered on the edge of civil war, as barons refused military summons and resentment grew at the king's incessant taxation to refill the coffers and pay off his allies. For the youngest princess, however, the months between her wedding in January and her departure for Holland in August were marked by an embrace of the freedom that remained to her. Wardrobe accounts from the year show Elizabeth travelling, often joining up with the itinerant courts of her father or her brother, or embarking on independent travel to various shrines and royal palaces throughout southern England, as well as numerous payments to minstrels hired to entertain her, and the purchase of adornments such as vibrantly coloured silken belts. In July, she and her brother visited their childhood home at Langley, where they were joined by Mary. During their time there, the siblings seem to have reminisced about their childhoods spent in the house their mother had built – itself the backdrop to many of their own earliest memories – because when Mary and Elizabeth arrived at Westminster together at the end of the month, they arranged for a Mass to be performed in their mother's memory. Alongside fond remembrances there would have been much conversation between the sisters about the future – Mary's extended visit was intended as a farewell to Elizabeth, who at fifteen was by far the youngest of Edward's daughters to venture into a new life abroad.[2]

Elizabeth arrived at the port of Winchelsea accompanied by her late mother's friend Isabella de Vescy – Mary's position may have afforded her extraordinary powers of movement, but even a princess could not stretch the rules to include voyages overseas, and Prince Edward, aged thirteen, was acting as official regent during his father's absence. Elizabeth would, at least, have his company. Any personal anxieties she may have felt at the point of leaving home may have been pushed to one side by the sight that greeted her, at least briefly: the fleet that had gathered for the king's continental campaign was among the largest of the age. Two hundred and seventy-three ships had been hired or commandeered from as far north as Newcastle-upon-Tyne and as far south as Portsmouth, with the bulk coming from the harbours of the Cinque Ports between Sandwich and Hastings, or along the east coast at Great Yarmouth, Harwich, and Ipswich. The *Swan*, which had conveyed Margaret to Brabant, was again among the fleet, joined now by galleys and barges, such as the *Godyere* and *La Blith*, as well as the *Nicholas* (for the patron saint of seamen) and the *Cog St Edward* (the king's own ship). As the countess's chests, packed to the brim with luxurious fabrics and delicate workmanship, were loaded aboard, workmen all around the port were building gangplanks, cargo boxes, and horse stalls, and stowing away immense quantities of food, weaponry, and carts.[3]

In stark contrast to the 'inestimably ornamented' fleet that had carried Margaret to her new home, Elizabeth's guard-of-honour was an army bound for war, consisting of nearly nine hundred knights and over eight thousand archers and foot soldiers from across England, Wales, and Scotland. Provisions to feed this enormous contingent as they crossed the sea and moved inland towards Flanders were collected from counties as far afield as Durham and Northumberland: 135 hogsheads, or tuns, of wheat flour; dozens of bushels of barley, oats, peas and beans; the carcasses of more than fifty cows, over three thousand hams, almost five thousand fish, thirteen hundred eels, 521 hogsheads of Rhenish wine and forty-one of ale, in addition to 21,300 bundles of hay to provide fodder for the thousand-odd assortment of warhorses, riders, and cart horses. Along with these provisions, the ships were loaded with thousands of arrows, hundreds of large iron crossbow bolts designed to topple stone walls, and nine *springalia* (or catapults), to defend and attack during a siege. Other heavy material included the vast sums of metal coinage with which King Edward had bought his northern allies – thirty-six barrels strengthened with extra nails to transport eighteen thousand pounds sterling to the Count of Flanders.

Elizabeth's ship put to sea at Winchelsea on 22 August, but ill omens plagued the fleet almost immediately. After drifting slowly up the Channel for six days, they stopped at the small harbour town of Hellevoetsluis, near the Hook of Holland and not far from Rotterdam. As the ships began docking, a disagreement arose between the seamen of Great Yarmouth and those of the Cinque Ports and, fuelled by a fierce and long-standing rivalry between them, burst into a frenzied riot. The harbour was rapidly engulfed in chaos, and thirty ships were lost to fire, before any enemy had even been engaged. Though the king was outraged, the ships carrying the royal party were unaffected by the pandemonium, and though Elizabeth may have felt anxious, it is unlikely that she was in real danger. After the rioters had been subdued and the cargo had been unloaded, the princess travelled south with her father, stopping first at the newly walled city of Aardenburg in the province of Zeeland to the south of

Holland. There, a messenger awaited with a gift from Margaret for her father: a fresh horse to welcome him to the continent. Elizabeth and Edward both paid their respects to the image of the Blessed Mary over the altar at the church in Aardenburg on 29 August, before travelling on to the banking port of Bruges. Among the principal cities of Flanders, it was a place of bustling markets and crammed canals – thanks to wool traders from Norfolk, Genoese merchants selling spices from the east, and ships from Bordeaux laden with barrels of claret, Bruges was fast becoming one of Europe's most prosperous cities. There they met the ally Edward had come to join, the aged Count of Flanders, whose daughter Philippa had been recently imprisoned in Paris by the French king, in order to prevent her marriage to Prince Edward. They learned from the count that the Flemish had been defeated at Furnes just two days before they had left England, and that Lille had surrendered five days later. With his army in tatters and his children in prison, the count could offer little assistance to the English. Instead, Edward's army moved on from Bruges; it was lucky they did, as within weeks, the citizens had handed the city to the French king.[4]

The English marched east, and seemed to find a more welcome reception at Ghent. There, on 19 September, in gratitude that their travels across the sea and through a foreign country at war had concluded safely, and perhaps wishing to listen to familiar sounds, Elizabeth sought out local friars and paid them to sing Masses for the soul of her mother. To protect themselves, their horses, and their provisions against French attack, her father's men set about building a *fosse*, or defensive ditch, around an undeveloped area of marshland to the south of the ancient abbey of St Peter, where the main forces were to be quartered as they awaited the arrival of their ally, the King of Germany. Elizabeth may have seen little of this building work, though as the weeks went by, she would have heard rumours that Edward's supposed allies were failing to challenge the French. She was lodged with her companion Isabella de Vescy and most of the king's immediate household, in a house inside the protection of the city's walls, which must have provided some reassurance of safety from hostile forces (her father sought to improve the comfort of their rooms, which were seemingly unrefined by royal standards, ordering a new chimney to be installed). It was here that Elizabeth learned the news sent from England that her sister Joanna had safely delivered a daughter, named Mary, for the only one of their sisters lacking a namesake among Joanna's children with her first husband, Gilbert. Despite all the ill-feeling about Joanna's secret remarriage earlier in the year, the child's birth was celebrated by her father and sister: the king sent word back to Prince Edward at Eltham to release ten does from the royal park at Raleigh, as a gift to Joanna.[5]

By early October, they were still waiting in Ghent, and it was increasingly clear that the King of Germany would not engage the French during that campaign season. The English army, despite the king's efforts, was simply insufficient on its own to hope for success against the French. Therefore, exactly one month after they had arrived in Ghent, Edward agreed a truce with France, and sent an embassy south to Tournai on the French border, to negotiate a peace treaty.

The king's continental campaign had been called off before it had really begun, but all those men, horses, and supplies could not be magically whisked back to England, and extricating his expeditionary force from Flanders took Edward some time. Elizabeth was once again offered a short respite, during which she might remain in the company of her father, before joining her new husband, Johan. As winter approached, the usual orders for apples, pears, and nuts to furnish the king and princess's table were supplemented by demands for richer and more exotic foodstuffs, including dates and pomegranates – suggesting the influence of Eleanor of Castile's Spanish palate long after her death.[6]

Amid the efforts to mitigate the wasted campaign, there were some glimmers of joy: Christmas would see a reunion between the king and three of his daughters, and would be the first time any of the family had seen Eleanora since she left England, three-and-a-half years earlier. The excitement built over several weeks, as a messenger arrived for the king with yet another horse, this time a gift from Eleanora. Though she was serving as informal regent of Bar while Henri languished in French captivity, she left the county in the hands of her husband's men and travelled more than 190 miles to Ghent, which would have taken her at least a week. If she brought the three-year-old Edward or the infant Joanna to meet their grandfather and aunts, their presence is not recorded; perhaps her grandmother's fears about the dangers of young children travelling in winter resonated with Eleanora, or perhaps it felt wise to ensure that Henri's heir remained safely ensconced within Bar while the count was still imprisoned. Arriving in Ghent, she made it her first business to plead with her father for a contribution towards Henri's ransom, to which the king – low on ready supplies of cash – offered the relatively modest sum of fifteen hundred pounds. As Christmas approached, Margaret and her husband Jan travelled from nearby Brussels to join her sisters and father in the city of wool weavers and waterways. Other nobles from the region also converged in Ghent for the holiday festivities, including Edward's ally the Count of Flanders and Marie of Brittany, the cousin of the English princesses and adolescent companion to Eleanora who had married the count of the small province of Saint-Pol near the border with Flanders. In the decades that followed the death of her mother – Edward's sister, Beatrice – Marie's family had developed closer ties with France than England; her presence at this family reunion illustrates how international politics could complicate personal and familial relationships. It also highlights how blood ties remained firm for many royal women and how they might maintain family ties, even in times of war. Marie's father and her husband had both fought for the French king, and one of her brothers-in-law was slowly dying from gruesome wounds he had received fighting against England's allies. And yet, despite the myriad reasons for *not* being there, Marie travelled to Ghent in late November to celebrate an extended Christmas holiday with her English relatives and their Flemish allies. She even brought gifts, presenting her uncle, King Edward, with a knife affixed with an enamelled silver handle and a crystal fork. Marie's visit is evidence of a strong attachment to her English cousins, and a tacit acknowledgement that her own allegiances might be distinct from those of her father and husband.[7]

For Eleanora, Margaret, and Elizabeth, Marie's arrival may have been a welcome reunion, but it was also a reminder that each of them might face similar estrangements between their marital and birth families, and offered a model for how a royal woman might navigate such a challenging situation. Conversations between the cousins must also have served to break down simplistic notions of 'ally' and 'enemy', countering a natural tendency to presume one's own side as innocent and the righteous victim of external aggressors. As Marie and her cousins reminisced and shared stories of their adult lives, they could hardly have spoken of husbands and children without also talking of the war. If Eleanora shared her fear and sorrow about Henri's imprisonment by the French king and the difficulties she faced acting as regent of Bar, Marie might have also spoken about the sadness and anxiety her sister was suffering as she watched her own husband slowly die from incurable wounds received at the hands of Edward's Flemish allies. Yet, through their continuing relationship with their cousin, Eleanora and her sisters had access to a form of embassy denied to men: the opportunity to hear about the horrific impact of war on the lives of individuals on the other side, first-hand and unfiltered.

On Christmas Day, the family and their allies watched as Edward knighted his son-in-law Jan of Brabant, and then joined in a feast that began the holiday celebrations. One week later, the family exchanged the gifts with which they traditionally welcomed the new year. Eleanora remained intent on gaining more support for Henri from her father, and sought to sweeten him with a gift of exceptional sophistication. In previous years, she had given him a simple gold ring, but as 1298 began, she presented him with a leather case containing a silver mirror, enamelled and gilded on the reverse, a comb (perhaps of ivory), and a silver bodkin to aid the king in drawing his laces.[8]

Eleanora and Elizabeth, along with Margaret and Jan, remained with the English party into the new year. The sisters clearly relished being together, and most likely took the opportunity to talk about the proposed marriage that would link their father with the youngest sister of the French king and end the war with France. Marguerite, the prospective bride was, at eighteen, the same age as their middle sister Mary. (They would probably have been less interested in two-year-old Isabella, whose betrothal to their brother Prince Edward was being discussed by the same ambassadors, though she would loom larger in later events.) But, alongside the renewal of their personal relationships with family, Eleanora and Margaret also aimed to capitalize on the chance for direct access to their father to practise the intercession that, as princesses of England, only they could do: before she left

Ghent, Margaret secured an official position as bailiff back in England for a courtier under her protection.[9]

Despite the ceremonial feasts and the exchange of gifts, records from their time in Ghent point to a court in disarray, and to the stresses created by the immense expense of Edward's never-ending wars. In January, the knights who dined in the king's hall became dissatisfied with the meagre provisions of food and, in protest, they sent their private servants into the city to buy bread, which they brought into the king's hall. For a monarch as intent as Edward on promotion of himself as a pattern of chivalry, the embarrassment of seeming unable to provide for his men provoked his 'manifest contempt'. Wealth was, after all, an important precursor to practising the virtue of *largesse*, and Edward had frequently expended vast sums to demonstrate the depths of his coffers. Now the same Low Country nobles who had been awed by the splendour of Margaret's wedding were witness to an English king who could scarcely feed his soldiers. The situation was made worse when the purveyor of the king's household, questioned about the lack of food, proclaimed publicly that he was unable to provide sufficient bread for the knights as there was not enough cash in the royal coffers to pay for it. At around the same time, a thief gained access to Eleanora's bedchamber and stole a silver-gilt cup belonging to the countess; her father insisted on replacing it, again embarrassed that his own reputation did not provide adequate protection for his daughter.[10]

Eleanora and Margaret eventually needed to return to their own dominions, and Elizabeth needed to travel north to begin her life in Holland. A Brabaçon chronicle records that Margaret received her father in Brussels later that winter, and she and Jan probably left Ghent at the start of February. The king was said to be delighted by Brabant's capital and gratified by the number of important lords who held land from his son-in-law. Elizabeth departed Ghent sometime before the middle of March, being escorted into Holland by a retinue of English noblemen who then returned, heading west across the sea with the king. It would be the last time one member of the family would see her relatives.[11]

The situation awaiting Elizabeth in Holland was nearly as precarious as that faced by Eleanora after Henri's capture. She was installed in the Binnenhof, the sprawling royal residence that Johan's father and grandfather had built in The Hague. Newly enlarged to replace a hunting lodge, the palace was Gothic in style, and was built around a magnificent timber-beamed great hall that rivalled the one at Westminster – the *Ridderzaal*, or Knight's Hall. A natural lake had been extended to form a moat surrounding the palace, and a growing town to the south served the court. Here, the fifteen-year-old English princess lived quietly while her young husband resided to the south in the trading centre of Dordrecht, near his watery province of Zeeland. Very little else is known of Elizabeth's life during her first year in Holland. She would have received letters from home and learned of her father's significant (yet frustratingly indecisive) victory over the Scottish rebel William Wallace at Falkirk in late July. She would have learned that her new brother-in-law Ralph had been called to Scotland to fight on behalf of his wife as Earl of Gloucester, but that the newlyweds had remained together long enough for Joanna to fall pregnant once again, and that she had delivered her fifth daughter, whom – having run out of sisters to honour – the countess named for herself. She would have heard that Mary had fallen seriously ill in 1298 and was moved from the priory at Amesbury to Ditton near Cambridge, where she recovered for several weeks. Elizabeth may also have learned that the nun – never one to eschew luxury on account of her vow of poverty – had run up such a large unpaid account to a goldsmith named Martin that he had been thrown into a debtors' prison for being unable to pay his own creditors, and that only the king's intervention in settling his daughter's account released him from jail. From Brussels, there was little in the way of good news. Margaret remained childless, even while her husband's mistress gallingly produced a healthy son, proving Jan's fertility.[12]

However, sometime near the end of Elizabeth's first year in Holland, some news arrived that devastated the countess. Her eldest sister Eleanora, ever loyal and dutiful to her family, had died of an unrecorded illness or injury in Bar on 29 August. All that is known about her death, other than the date (which was added into the calendar of her Alphonso Psalter, at Elizabeth's instruction) is that she probably did not die in childbirth, since her husband Henri was still stuck in prison in France at the time. The death of the twenty-nine-year-old countess was cursorily reported in only one minor contemporary chronicle, that of Hagnaby Abbey in Lincolnshire, which included in its account of the twenty-seventh year of Edward's reign the detail that 'this year died Eleanora daughter of King Edward, who had married the Count of Bar'. Given how richly detailed an account of the life and personality of England's eldest princess the wardrobe records and surviving charters have provided, the sparsity of information about her death feels both surprising and strangely painful. Had the wardrobe accounts of Bar survived, an illness might have been traced, through the purchase of medicinal herbs and resins or through the payment of physicians in attendance upon the countess, but these records have been lost, and no letters survive which passed the sad news back to England – though messengers must have been sent to Edward's court, as well as to Count Henri. The sudden gap in information about Eleanora's life is representative of the shift towards a reliance on chronicles as source material about the lives of medieval women. Many more chroniclers recorded Eleanora's marriage than either her birth or her death, and the same is also true of her sisters. The lack of detail pertaining to the princess's death is indicative of what little importance she was regarded as an *individual* by contemporary historians, who saw her predominately as a link between male-led dynasties. Yet, through the survival of the wardrobe rolls and other documents and material that illustrate her life, Eleanora's individuality is restored and the role she played in shaping her own life is recaptured.[13]

While Henri may have grieved the death of his wife, fearing the consequences of losing his connection to his powerful father-in-law, while he was still imprisoned he was powerless to mourn Eleanora in the manner appropriate for a member of the royal family. No memorial commemorating the English countess-regent remains in Bar; instead, her body seems to have been brought home by her father for burial among her own ancestors and siblings at Westminster. A seventeenth-century antiquarian survey of London and Westminster records a tomb in the chapter house of the abbey church that was dedicated to Eleanora, describing her as Countess of Bar and daughter of Edward the king. No further detail of the monument is given, but it is unlikely to have been as grand as those commissioned by the king to remember his wife and father. It may have been moved from elsewhere inside the church, but if it was intended to rest in the chapter house, the memorial may have been as simple as an inscription on a stone floor slab, perhaps surrounding a carved decorated cross. Eleanora's is the only royal tomb recorded as being in the chapter house; another nine graves in one of the side chapels located off the central pilgrimage circuit that included the shrine of Edward the Confessor and the monumental effigies to Henry III and Eleanor of Castile were recorded as belonging to royal children. One of these contained the remains of Katherine, the youngest child of Henry III and Eleanor of Provence, whose death at the age of three reputedly caused both her parents such acute grief that their health was considered endangered. Above Katherine's grave was an effigy sculpted out of solid silver, its extraordinary cost testimony to her parents' suffering. The other eight were probably Eleanora's sisters and brothers, born over more than two decades, who died in infancy or childhood in England: Katherine, Joanna, John, Henry, Alphonso, Berengaria, and a baby girl and boy whose lives were too short for any names to be recorded. This was the familial mausoleum to which Eleanora's body returned, at the behest of her father, who even though he sometimes forced his daughters abroad in life, gathered all his children together in death. Back in Bar, Eleanora's own small children Edward and Joanna were left practically orphaned in the care of Henri's councillors, who were still plotting for the return of their lord.[14]

The news of her eldest sister's death was a heavy blow to Elizabeth, and she would remember the anniversary of Eleanora's death for the rest of her life. But isolated, friendless, and far from home as she was, she was soon forced to contend with challenges closer to hand. Since his return to Holland shortly after their marriage, Johan had fallen under the influence of a courtier named Wolfert van Borselen, Lord of Veere, one of the southern islands of Zeeland. Edward had initially encouraged his impressionable son-in-law to look to Borselen for advice, and even helped retrieve the Dutch lord's sons from French imprisonment; he probably hoped Borselen would counter any French-leaning tendencies among the more established Dutch nobles. By 1299, however, Borselen's influence had grown to such an extent that he was effectively exercising command of

Holland through his control over the fifteen-year-old count, and – in a scenario that foreshadowed the troubles to come in England – the Dutch nobles rose in revolt. In August, Borselen fled Dordrecht into Zeeland, where his own power was greatest, taking Count Johan with him, either as a lover, a naive accomplice or a captive. The *Annals of Holland and Zeeland* record that, ensconced in her splendid palace at The Hague, Elizabeth received this news one morning, just after dawn.

She must have been genuinely terrified that Johan might come to share the fate of his father (who had been murdered at the hands of supposed friends) and also at her own exposure in the event, but as countess, she also had an important role to play in legitimizing the arrest of a nobleman who enjoyed the count's protection. As Johan's wife, she could make an emotional appeal that the people rise against Borselen out of loyalty *to* Johan, rather than as an act of treason *against* him. Her appeal could also mediate any negative feelings against the young count's judgment or anxieties about his sexuality, by painting him as an innocent who had been bewitched and stolen away from his loving wife by a cunning malefactor. As Johan's wife, she was therefore in a unique position to solve the problem of Borselen, restore Johan's authority and buttress her own position. In a set piece before her courtiers, Elizabeth wept bitter tears for the husband she had barely seen since being forced to move to his dominion two years earlier. She loudly bewailed the fate that seemed to await Johan, and accused Borselen of treacherously misleading the innocent count. A party of anti-Borselen nobles immediately gathered around the countess, who served as a natural focal point for those who proclaimed loyalty to Johan; they vowed – in the name of saving Holland – to hunt down the supposed abductor, free Johan, and restore him to his devoted countess. The abductor's own son-in-law – perhaps fearful that hatred of his father-in-law might negatively impact his own fortunes – offered himself in supplication to Elizabeth and convinced her to present herself in The Hague's market, only a few minutes' stroll from the Binnenhof. There, in front of a crowd, she repeated her performance; despairing over Johan's likely fate, the English princess 'made her grief and her fears pass into the souls of all the inhabitants'. Her performance had its intended effect: Borselen was captured and imprisoned, evidently without much protest from the count who had promoted him. Johan was returned to his wife at The Hague, while his abductor was taken to Delft, where, the countess's lamentations fresh in their minds, the local populace threatened to burn down the prison in which he was held, unless he was handed over. Unwilling to risk a riot, the jailors stripped Borselen of his armour and pushed him into the street, where he was immediately hacked to pieces by the frenzied mob.[15]

Though Borselen was gone, the Dutch nobles were not content to return the naive fifteen-year-old Johan to power, and his uncle, the Count of Hainault, was approached to act as regent. Elizabeth's role in Borselen's downfall seems to have won her a greater degree of influence than she had previously enjoyed: her own seal is affixed to the charter of 27 October 1299 alongside Johan's, in which the couple consented to the regency, and a codicil appended to the same document declared that Johan agreed to the arrangement, on the advice of his nobles *and his wife*. But, if Elizabeth had hoped for a quieter, more settled period after she and Johan attended the ceremony that officially confirmed Johan's uncle as regent in Dordrecht, she was tragically disappointed. Competing factions almost immediately formed around Johan and his regent uncle, and the latter decamped to the safety of his own dominion of Hainault. Johan fell suddenly ill with a fever soon afterwards; it rapidly turned to dysentery, and on

10 November he died, sparking centuries of speculation that he had been poisoned by the uncle who now became his heir. Whatever fears Elizabeth may have entertained when Johan absconded with Borselen had now been realized: she was now a childless widow at the court of a potentially murderous ruler. If Johan had been poisoned, she must have asked herself, would his killer hesitate to prescribe the same fate to a young widow whose dower would steal away immense portions of Dutch wealth? Elizabeth may have commented on a feeling of isolation or fear in letters to her father, for Edward sent two ladies to provide the countess with friendly companionship. Then, when early efforts to claim her dower were met with seemingly endless delays, he sent over his own men. In the letter accompanying their voyage in late March, her father instructed Elizabeth to follow closely the advice of his ambassadors and offered his 'treasured daughter' the 'blessings of a father'; the same day, he dispatched a series of further missives to Dutch nobles and whole communities in Holland, requesting their support for Elizabeth's cause. Still, no progress was forthcoming, and when more than half a year had elapsed after Johan's death and Elizabeth was evidently not carrying his heir, the widowed, seventeen-year-old countess, once again dependent upon her father for income, returned to England.[16]

XIII
Homecoming

1300–1
THE NORTH, WOODSTOCK

On her way back to England, Elizabeth stopped off in Brussels to bid farewell to Margaret who, after ten years of marriage and at the age of twenty-five, was finally pregnant, a cause of much rejoicing within Brabant. For Margaret, the pregnancy must have been an extraordinary relief – not only was she finally providing Brabant with a legitimate heir, but having a child of her own would go some way to make up for the loss of her sisters, whose proximity she had until recently enjoyed. If the death of her eldest sister Eleanora was surprising and saddening for the Duchess of Brabant, Elizabeth's departure for England left Margaret utterly isolated from her family. It was a loss the duchess seems to have felt keenly – references in the wardrobe records show that messengers were frequently dispatched to or from Brabant, carrying letters to her father and sisters.[1]

Elizabeth left Brussels in July, along with her travelling companions – the Dutch noblewoman Lady de Saux, and the two English ladies her father had sent over to comfort her after Johan's death, Alice de Breton and Joanna de Mereworth. The party travelled west through Brabant and Flanders, and across the sea, arriving in London in August. From there, they travelled two hundred miles north to Cawood in Yorkshire, where her father had established a northern court in a palace belonging to the Archbishop of York; this was to act as a base, while he attempted to draw the Scottish lords into battle and recreate the success he had found at Falkirk two years before.

Elizabeth had many weeks of travel with her ladies – long, boring days perched atop a palfrey or hidden within a richly ornamented carriage, with little to do but stare out at the countryside and gaze back at the awed faces of common labourers and pilgrims along the roads, her back perhaps straightening as she remembered the importance of projecting a regal image to her father's subjects. They stopped each evening to rest at different royal castles, monasteries, and at the manor homes of wealthy aristocrats who provided food and beds, before setting off again the next day. As they travelled north, Elizabeth had plenty of time in which to consider her future. Given the drama of Johan's death and the uncertainty which surrounded her dower from Holland, she might reasonably have anticipated to be granted a period at court before any remarriages were planned, although her father was undoubtedly mindful of the example set by Joanna's secret remarriage. The journey Elizabeth took led her past many sites familiar from her life before marriage, including Langley, her childhood home with its orchards and exotic pets, and the hunting lodge at Clipstone, where she had said goodbye to her mother a decade before.

Elizabeth was principally focused on reaching her father, and it is possible that her sister Joanna was also present in the north (along with their brother, Prince Edward, who was now sixteen): the Countess of Gloucester frequently accompanied her dearly won husband Ralph when he travelled to fight in her father's wars, and Ralph had certainly been present with the king in Scotland in July of that year, one of only three magnates who had come to serve the king's feudal summons in person rather than sending a member of their retinue to deputize. Ralph had returned earlier that summer from several months attending the Clare estates in Ireland, and he and his men made up a significant proportion of the roughly 850 knights and nine thousand men-at-arms who comprised Edward's campaigning army on the south-west coast of Scotland that year. In the list of noblemen appearing in the Anglo-Norman herald's roll, written the following year and detailing in heavily romanticized imagery the siege of Caerlaverock Castle, the following is the third entry:

> *He by whom [the king's men] were well supported,*
> *acquired, after great doubts and fears*
> *until it pleased God he should be delivered,*
> *the love of the Countess of Gloucester,*
> *for whom he a long time endured*
> *great sufferings. He had only a banner*
> *of fine gold with three red chevrons.*
> *He made no bad appearance*
> *when attired in his own arms,*
> *which were yellow with a green eagle.*
> *His name was Ralph de Monthermer.*

Joanna's husband was already making a name for himself as a worthy knight, but he remained of greatest interest to courtly society for his association with the king's daughter. When he fought, it was under the banner of her first husband; Joanna must have been proud to witness the 'gallant youth' she had promoted through marriage so splendidly arrayed and bolstered by the marker of nobility – the Clare banner – that his association with her had brought him. Seeing her sister, Elizabeth may have hoped to catch up on news of the niece who was named for her or Joanna's other children, and in return to share with her stories from Christmas in Ghent, the last time she had seen Eleanora before her death. The elder countess could have shared stories of the marvellous courtly feasts which her younger sister had missed while in Holland, including the fabulous event at the Tower of London in late 1299, at which the Countess of Gloucester had presided as the principal lady in the Great Chamber, refitted expressly for the occasion. Above all, Elizabeth may have hoped for her most fearless sister's frank perspective on Marguerite, the French princess whom the year before had become their father's second wife, and whom Joanna had met in March.[2]

Marguerite was the younger half-sister of the French king who had invaded Gascony, precipitating a war with Edward and imprisoning Henri of Bar. As was common in the entwined royal families of the day, she was a cousin of her new husband: the granddaughter of Edward's aunt, Margaret (wife of the French king St Louis and eldest sister of Eleanor of Provence). Marguerite was born the same year as Mary of Woodstock, making her about twenty in September 1299 when she travelled to Canterbury, to marry the sixty-year-old widower king in the shadow of the great shrine to St Thomas Becket. Edward's living children at that time ranged in age from twenty-seven (Joanna) to fifteen (Prince Edward). The marriage between the aged king and the youthful princess was a key part of the treaty that brought peace between France and England, and its agreement allowed Edward and his expeditionary force to depart Flanders, after months of expensive inaction. A young bride also offered Edward the possibility of further sons to secure the future of his throne, which, in the event of Prince Edward's childless death, would pass by default to Eleanora's son Edward, the future Count of Bar. The English king had been very close to his first wife, and few could have expected the strong emotional attachment he would form to Marguerite, or the great affection that would grow between the new queen and her stepchildren.

As Elizabeth and her companions rode into the walled precinct of the archbishop's castellated house at Cawood, nestled between his hunting forest and an important ferry point on the great northern River Ouse, she might have been anxious to meet the woman – barely her senior – who stood in her mother's place. It is possible that Elizabeth had already had been reassured in a letter from her sister Mary, who had gladly accepted her father's invitation to spend some time at court soon after Marguerite's arrival in England. Any reluctance to love her mother's replacement may have melted away when Elizabeth was presented with her two-month-old baby brother, Thomas of Brotherton, to whom Marguerite had given birth early and in apparently dramatic circumstances – Langtoft's chronicle records that the king flew to his wife 'like a falcon before the wind' on hearing news of the premature arrival. The little prince was sickly from birth, though he was said by the chronicler Rishanger to thrive once the French wet nurse appointed by his mother was replaced by an Englishwoman. The baby was certainly doted upon: elaborate cradles were curtained in scarlet and deep blue using huge amounts of the finest English cloth, topped with fur covers and bed sheets of linen imported from Rheims, and surrounded by hangings embroidered with heraldry that marked out Thomas as a prince of England. Marguerite's personality may also have won her easy friends: she was remembered as 'good without lack' by an English chronicle of the early fourteenth century. Either way, both at Cawood and as they travelled north together towards Carlisle to rendezvous with the king, Elizabeth and her new stepmother found in each other an important friend. In the years that followed, the women were only rarely apart from one another, and they are often seen in the records playing the part of twin intercessors with the king.[3]

The pair departed on 9 September and arrived in the north eight days later. They settled into the Bishop of Carlisle's house at Rose Castle, nestled among gently undulating hills to the south of the city. For Elizabeth, the reunion with her family had been a long time coming – nearly a year had elapsed since Johan's death had thrown her future into disarray, and although she was far from Langley and the other houses of her childhood, once she was at court with her father and brother, she was essentially home. For Edward, the arrival of his youngest daughter would have proved a welcome distraction from what had been a dispiriting season of campaigning, with little in the way of successful military action; beyond the capture of Caerlaverock Castle (described somewhat disdainfully by the chronicler Peter Langtoft as a *'chastelet'*), there had been little meaningful progress against the Scots, and his army was fading rapidly, as thousands of men-at-arms deserted. That autumn, while residing at Rose Castle and the nearby Cistercian abbey of Holme Cultram, Edward and Elizabeth rediscovered a companionship that they would regularly seek in years to come. Her brother came and went from the main court, his growing independence expressing itself in short visits to other parts of the region, in the way that the royal children had always done. While staying with his father's household, the prince is likely to have met a youth who had recently arrived from Gascony and joined the king's men in July that year; he was a young man whose charm the prince would ultimately find irresistible. His name was Piers Gaveston.[4]

Early in November as court prepared to return south, joyful news arrived from Brussels: Margaret had safely delivered a healthy baby boy, an heir for Brabant. The future duke was named Jan for his father, seemingly at the latter's request. (Margaret's husband was so fond of bestowing his own name on his progeny that there are records of at least six Jans among his many illegitimate children.) The whole family's pleasure at the safe and successful birth of little Jan is evident in the extravagant rewards they bestowed on the Dutch messenger who brought news of baby Jan's birth: Edward gave him one hundred marks, Marguerite offered fifty, and Prince Edward a further forty. Elizabeth seems not to have been with her family when the message arrived from Brabant on 8 November – her own gift to the messenger of thirteen-and-a-half pounds is post-dated. Along with the good wishes of her family, a sensitive diplomatic message was sent back to Brussels, conveyed by word-of-mouth to a clerk who was instructed to discuss the matter with both the Duke of Brabant and with Margaret, 'the king's daughter'. Within weeks of giving birth, Margaret – her influence as consort perhaps at its peak, now that an heir had been born – was required as a friendly voice for England in Brabant. Her support would be needed again in the next year when an emissary would come bearing gifts for the princess and her baby, as well as a message 'concerning the king's arduous affairs' that was intended for the ears of the duke and duchess only.[5]

Two days after learning that her sister had safely given birth, Elizabeth entered the city of Carlisle. She was heading for the Dominican priory near the bottom end of the city market, away from the bustle and the crude exchanges of commerce and flesh that occupied the top of the marketplace. There she paid the

friars to sing Masses in commemoration of the first anniversary
of Johan of Holland's death – special prayers meant to speed his
soul on its journey through purgatory and towards heaven – and
afterwards, she provided a feast for all Dominican friars within
the city. Her new friend Marguerite stood by her side as the
young countess marked one year as a widow, hundreds of miles
away from Holland. For this ceremony, Elizabeth most likely
wore the new blue robe embroidered with gold thread that her
tailor, Peter of Guildford, had made for the feast of All Saints
nine days earlier; it was the first new gown made for her
since her arrival back in England. That she chose to hear Mass
in the Dominican friary rather than the nearby house of the
Franciscans suggests the enduring influence of her mother on
Elizabeth's life. In the days following, Elizabeth and her small
household – now headed by a clerk named Stephen de Brewode
– left Carlisle and headed south. They stopped briefly at a
decaying wooden motte-and-bailey castle in Kirkby Fleetham in
Yorkshire, near a convergence of medieval roads. The party
arrived at Ripon at the end of the month, where Elizabeth, her
brother, their father, and stepmother observed the tenth anniversary of her mother's death, with Masses sung before the high
altar of Ripon Minster (the church would have to wait many
centuries before it obtained cathedral status). The eastern end
of the minster had collapsed two decades before – the result of
building the immense Gothic structure atop an uneven,
seventh-century crypt – and work constructing the gloriously
delicate east window that survives today continued well into the
fourteenth century. But Edward and his family were long-
accustomed to carrying out the solemn ceremonies that
punctuated their lives in the middle of building sites. From the
surviving Alphonso Psalter, which includes the anniversary dates
of the deaths of her mother, grandmother, and those sisters who

predeceased her, we know that Elizabeth was a keen observer of remembrance ceremonies, but her dedication to the memory of her mother was particularly fierce: more than a decade after the queen's death, Elizabeth was still making the case to her father that Eleanor's former servants should be granted special privileges for the devotion they showed her.[6]

From Ripon, the royal party continued their southern trajectory. By 11 December they had arrived at Leicester, and Elizabeth felt sufficiently secure in her position within her father's household to order an expensive new fur cape, lined with vair and embellished with gold thread and forty-four silver buttons. Peter the tailor was dispatched to acquire the silks he would need for making the countess a new wardrobe as well as to buy candles to enable him and the furrier to finish the cape in time for Christmas by working into the night. She also dispatched a page back to London to collect her jewels – including the magnificent crowns she had taken to Holland after her marriage. Over Christmas, Elizabeth, her brother, father, and stepmother were splendidly entertained at Northampton by minstrels including two German 'giants' employed by the king, whose repertoire may have included feats of strength as well as song. Prince Edward's pleasure at being reconnected with his childhood companion is recorded – he made sure to include her among his new year's gifts, giving her a smooth-riding, slim-backed palfrey on 8 January 1301, but he departed from the group shortly afterwards, heading for Langley to represent the royal family at the funeral of an important magnate.[7]

Throughout the winter and spring, seemingly unhurried at deciding on the path her life would take next, Elizabeth travelled regularly around the centre of England, stopping at Towcester, venturing north to Lincoln, and west as far as Winchcombe in Gloucestershire, where she visited Hailes Abbey with its famous phial of Holy Blood, the rare and immensely valued relic of Christ's physical presence on earth that had comforted Joanna in the delivery of her first child. Winchcombe was also near Tewkesbury, one of Joanna's principal residences, and Elizabeth's visit there may have included a meeting with her oldest living sister. She often returned to the company of her father and stepmother, and was with them in Worcester in April, interceding with the king on behalf of a retainer granted lands 'by reason of his services to Elizabeth, Countess of Holland, the king's daughter', and at Kempsey in May, when she requested a posting at Wallingford Castle for another servant in her patronage. Her Dutch companion, Lady de Saux, left the countess's household during this time, returning to Holland with a gift of silver plate for her service. Lady de Saux may have travelled home in the company of Sir Gerald de Freney, whom Edward posted to Holland, in a continuing effort to make progress in obtaining Elizabeth's dower estate, 'as the affairs of the countess in those parts progress badly nowadays owing to the hindrances of certain men'. Another English embassy that spring had achieved, with the intervention of Marguerite, one of Edward's long-held ambitions: the freedom of Henri of Bar, husband of the late Princess Eleanora. After four years imprisoned in France, the count was released in early June, under a treaty that required him not only to pay a hefty ransom but to relinquish significant portions of his province and to place the entirety of it under French feudal overlordship. He returned to Bar and to his children Edward and Joanna, but the remonstrations of his nobles, incensed at the terms he had agreed, rang in his ears loudly enough to drive Henri swiftly away again on Crusade.[8]

Back in England, Marguerite, whose influence with her brother in France had helped to win Henri his freedom, was pregnant again. Anxious not to be caught unprepared, as she had been with the birth of her first child at Brotherton the year before, she decided early in her pregnancy to stay in the large castellated manor at Woodstock, just north of Oxford; early in June, when her husband's attentions again turned north to Scotland, Marguerite retired to the rambling palace on a hill overlooking a large royal park, which would be demolished during the building of Blenheim Palace in the early eighteenth century. By 1301, the lions and leopards with which Henry I had stocked the space almost two centuries earlier, were already long gone. But the intricate pleasure gardens that may originally have been planted for Henry II's favourite mistress, 'Fair Rosamund' Clifford, remained, surrounding a secluded Gothic chamber remembered in her honour as 'Rosamund's Bower'. To this luxurious compound, Henry III had added multiple chapels, a wine cellar and larder, stables and a gatehouse. The house had been comfortable enough to tempt Eleanor of Castile to give birth to Mary there late in the winter of 1279, and its extensive gardens would have made it even more attractive for a summer sojourn when the flowers would have been in full bloom.

Elizabeth, by now among the new queen's most intimate friends, accompanied her stepmother to Woodstock, but she was not the only one of Edward's children whose company was requested. Edward wrote from Berwick, where he was poised to move up the east coast of Scotland, to Mary at Amesbury to pass on his wife's request that she also travel to Woodstock to attend the new queen, a journey which would require her to withstand three days of bumpy riding over the North Wessex Downs. Throughout the late spring and summer and into autumn, the three royal women – more like sisters than mother and daughters – stayed together at Woodstock. Like most elite women in medieval Europe, Elizabeth and Marguerite spent most of their lives ensconced within heavily male-dominated house-holds and had fewer opportunities to build and sustain close friendships with other women than their male counterparts, who might remain in attendance on a lord together, or travel on campaign for years in each other's company. Women also had fewer ceremonial options for marking the importance of a particular bond (unlike men, who might, for example, be knighted together or form a team at a tournament), but chief among those open to them was witnessing a birth. Among royal women, the practice of waiting for a baby to arrive with a close friend or relative was well-established by the early fourteenth century: a generation before, King Edward's sister, Margaret, had travelled back to England from her home in Scotland to give birth to a Scottish heir at Windsor in the presence of her mother, Eleanor of Provence. Mary would serve again as companion for her niece (one of Joanna's daughters) when she gave birth a decade later, and one of Elizabeth's deliveries would also be attended by her sister-in-law, the future Queen Isabella of France.

For Elizabeth, the summer of 1301 at Woodstock was the most settled period of her life since her return to England following Johan's death. The long summer days awaiting the onset of labour provided opportunity to deepen her relationship with Marguerite, and a chance to reconnect with her closest sister, Mary, whom she had not seen since their time at Langley just after her wedding, four years earlier. Elizabeth had faced extraor-dinary pressures and potentially grave danger abroad since saying goodbye to Mary, and stories of her experiences in Holland during the intervening years must have featured in her conver-sations with her sister. For Mary, insulated as she was from the experiences of marriage and life as a consort at a foreign court, Elizabeth's tales of intrigue and conspiracy and Marguerite's ever-growing belly would have served as reminders of how different her own life was from most royal women. Eleanora, Margaret, Elizabeth, and Marguerite – even Joanna, who had in essence been a bride in a foreign province when she first accompanied Gilbert de Clare to the wild lands of Glamorgan – all shared many essential experiences. The constant itinerancy, the travel across seas and into unfamiliar landscapes where the natives spoke incomprehensible tongues, the unrelenting pressure to produce heirs for expectant husbands, the fears associated with pregnancy and delivery, and the difficulty in settling into life in a different culture; all these things drew those women together and their shared familiarity of uncommon experiences made them natural allies and confidants, and easy friends to turn to in times of trial. However, the same ties that bound most royal women together, also set them apart from Mary. The disparity cannot have escaped the regular acknowledgement of the nun, for whom daily life centred around one constant home, whose life could never include children or husbands, and whose travel was necessarily limited. If the gulf between their experiences occasionally made Mary feel isolated from her sisters and other relatives, the feeling was never so great that the nun refused an invitation to join court and renew her association as an intimate member of the royal family. Perhaps she felt her position, free as it was from the usual expectations on royal women, was the more desirable one – certainly she never sought out opportunities, which would have been open to her, to embrace the challenge of life in a foreign land and transfer to Fontevrault, as her grandmother had intended.

On 5 August, a second prince, yet another spare for the king's seventeen-year-old heir Prince Edward of Caernarfon, was born to Queen Marguerite. The delivery this time seems to have been less dramatic than Thomas's. The name chosen for the baby boy,

Edmund (for the martyred boy-king of the East Angles), completed the triumvirate of favourite saints of the English royal line – alongside his surviving brothers Edward (for the great pre-Norman Conquest Confessor king) and Thomas (Becket, the canonized archbishop murdered by knights loyal to Henry II). As his mother recuperated in the company of his much older sisters, the baby's father, the king, was marching north to Glasgow.

Joanna spent the summer between her various estates in the western counties of England, but she did not travel to Woodstock to join her sisters and the new queen. Her adored husband Ralph was in Scotland once again, struggling to make decisive headway against the Scottish forces as one of the half-dozen earls who led the army in that year's campaign, nominally under the command of Prince Edward. Joanna had remained in England rather than accompanying him because she was preparing, aged twenty-nine, for the delivery of her seventh child. Her older Clare daughters – Eleanor (nine), Margaret (eight), and Elizabeth (six) – were most likely by this time already at Amesbury Priory, where they were being educated under the guidance of their aunt Mary, when she was in residence. Joanna's younger Monthermer daughters – Mary (four) and Joanna (two) – probably remained with their mother, though they would in due course follow their sisters to Amesbury, with young Joanna Monthermer ultimately joining the priory as a vowed nun (as would one of Margaret de Clare's daughters). Joanna's only son and heir, ten-year-old Gilbert, had effectively been head of his own itinerant household for several years, but he seems to have been residing with or near his mother in the autumn of 1301, as it was to her that King Edward wrote at the end of September, with a mandate that Joanna relinquish custody of the boy.

The letter, with its stiff formal instruction that the countess should 'deliver to Marguerite, queen consort, on her demand, Gilbert, son and heir of Gilbert de Clare . . . as it is the king's will that he shall stay in the queen consort's custody until further order', feels to the modern reader cruel in its separation of a mother from her child. There is even a hint in the letter that Joanna's father expected that his feisty daughter might resist the order: its final words, 'for this [order] the present letter shall be her warrant', underlined the non-negotiable nature of his instruction. And yet, prior to this, the king's daughter had been allowed an unusually long period of time as the foremost influence on her son: most noble children like Gilbert would have entered the service of a lord or relative soon after their seventh birthday, becoming a page before acting as squire to a knight. It was through service within another household that boys like Gilbert learned the arts of the nobility, of war and administration, of chivalry and diplomacy. This tradition also forged powerful bonds within and between families that often continued throughout their lives. For young Gilbert, the king's eldest grandson and a future leading magnate of England, there could be no better training ground than the royal household, where he would grow up at the centre of power in England, developing intimate knowledge of its machinations as well as its most powerful personalities; Joanna could not have failed to acknowledge this truth.[9]

The king's messenger, dispatched from Edward's camp near Falkirk on 27 September, may not yet have reached Joanna when, on 4 October, she gave birth to a baby boy, an heir at last for Ralph. Again, there are hints in the baby's name – he was christened Thomas, rather than after his father or kingly grandfather, as might be expected – that the countess had reason to appeal to a saintly intercessor during the birth. Nevertheless, Thomas was healthy enough not to be considered in grave danger – his baptism was delayed until December, by which time the baby had travelled with his mother into her dominion of Glamorgan, and he was baptized there by the Bishop of Llandaff. If Joanna remained aggrieved by her father's demand that she send Gilbert to serve her new stepmother, she had also received the much more welcome news that Ralph's service in Scotland had won back her castle of Tonbridge in Kent, the last remaining portion of Gilbert de Clare's estate that her father had continued to withhold, in punishment for her secret marriage almost five years earlier.[10]

Mary and Elizabeth remained with Marguerite and baby Edmund at Woodstock until October, when the queen was considered strong enough to recommence the endless journeying across the country that characterized the lives of the English royal family at that time. The three women and their sizable households must have presented an astonishing sight as they paraded slowly on their prized palfreys and in their painted carriages, their furniture and goods following behind in a dozen or more carts, north from Woodstock and then west, heading for Hereford. Their pilgrimage was intended as one of thanksgiving for the safe delivery and health of the child – the party stopped in each of the principal shrines along the road, making offerings to affirm in public their pious gratitude. But the occasion also afforded an opportunity for the queen and princesses to present an image of regal grandeur and *largesse* in all the villages they passed, as well as proof of the continued virility of the king who, despite his sixty-two years, was still producing healthy heirs for England. After hearing Mass and making offerings at Hereford Cathedral, the party separated. The baby safely born and the pilgrimage complete, it was time for Mary to return to her cloister at Amesbury and resume her role overseeing the education of her

Clare nieces. She was escorted south in the protection of one of her father's clerks while, in the second half of November, Marguerite turned north, bound on a long journey to Linlithgow in Scotland, where she would be reunited with her husband as he settled in for a cold winter in which scores of horses would die from lack of fodder and the king's army would once again face desertion because of a lack of money to pay their wages. As she set off on the long journey, she was accompanied by young Gilbert de Clare, as well as his aunt, the countess Elizabeth.

XIV
Companionship

1302–4
TYNEMOUTH, DUNFERMLINE, KNARESBOROUGH

Elizabeth had probably met Humphrey de Bohun – the Earl of Hereford and Essex and Constable of England – when he visited Langley while she was living there in the late 1280s, but the young widow became reacquainted with him while staying with her father and stepmother at Carlisle and Linlithgow. Humphrey had succeeded his father (the earl with whom Gilbert de Clare had maintained a long-running and mutual animosity) only a few years earlier, and by the time Elizabeth met him again he was among the first lords of England and the March. By the spring of 1302, plans were being put in place for Humphrey and Elizabeth to marry. The papal dispensation required for the union was approved on 4 August 1302; it noted that King Edward particularly hoped the match would promote peace and reconciliation after the 'great dissention' between the king and Humphrey's father.[1]

It is not hard to see what the twenty-year-old Elizabeth might have liked about Humphrey. The herald of the *Siege of Caerlaverock* described him in 1300 as 'a rich and elegant young man', noting that his age at that date was not older than twenty-five. He was, therefore, young and courtly, but his Englishness would also have appealed to the princess, who had been made wary by her previous experiences in the uncertain world beyond her father's realm. Unless and until Elizabeth's dower income was secured, allowing her to enjoy the independence that she had experienced during her brief widowhood, she and her household were also a large drain on her father's resources. Short of declaring a wish to join Mary in holy orders at Amesbury, the countess would need to remarry, and soon. She did not have the freedom Joanna had enjoyed to marry a penniless young gallant; furthermore, a match with a young lord, whose wealth would provide for her in suitable style, while also allowing her to remain close to friends and family, was surely preferable to a match with an aged ruler of a foreign land. She would have appealed to Humphrey, too; Elizabeth was not only young but also potentially extremely wealthy (if her dower in Holland, which was still proving irretrievable, despite the continuing efforts of Gerald de Freney, was ever successfully claimed), and she embodied a powerful connection to the king.

Accordingly, the pair were married at Westminster Abbey as soon as Humphrey had signed over his whole estate to the king and been re-granted it on roughly the same terms that Gilbert de Clare had agreed a dozen years earlier (in which all the de Bohun estates were jointly held by Humphrey and Elizabeth). The ceremony took place on 14 November 1302, the bride attended by her close friend and stepmother Marguerite. The bridal coronet was solid gold, studded with rubies and emeralds and surmounted by a circlet that provided a second tier of gemstones: eighty-two pearls and a dozen large rubies and emeralds, as well as twenty-four small plaques depicting animal and human figures moulded in gold. A surviving wardrobe entry suggests that the crown had formerly belonged to Blanche, Duchess of Austria and sister to Marguerite – if so, it was almost certainly given to Elizabeth as a personal gift from the queen, who filled the mother-of-the-bride role with panache but also bestowed special favour on her closest friend. After the wedding, Elizabeth remained at court with her new husband, as he joined in the preparations for the renewed large-scale assault against Scotland being planned for the following summer.[2]

The Maid of Norway, who died on the way to marry Prince Edward in 1290, had been the granddaughter and last living heir of Alexander III, King of Scotland and brother-in-law to Edward I of England. Without a direct heir, the kingdom suffered instability in the aftermath of the Maid's death, as competing claimants emerged to compete for the crown. Edward supported the installation of John Balliol as king, but also sought to exploit the insecurity of Balliol's position to undermine Scottish autonomy, aiming to turn Scotland into a vassal fiefdom of England. When the Scots retaliated, forming an aggressive alliance with the French in 1295, Edward invaded, beginning a cycle of wars of conquest and independence that would last for five decades. Beginning in 1296, the English had spent four campaigning seasons north of the border, culminating in a truce in 1301. But, by the summer of 1302 this had expired, and rumours were circulating of a planned Scottish invasion of England.

After decades of fighting, Edward needed to arm another force, and this time his daughters helped him to pay for it: Magna

Carta allowed the King of England the right to levy a tax on the marriage of his first daughter. Twelve years earlier, on the eve of Joanna's marriage to Gilbert, Edward had been granted the right to raise a tax to support her dowry, but this had never been fulfilled. Now, lacking ready funds, the king appealed, and on 7 November 1302 his men were authorized to collect the taxes owed. If fully realized, the king expected 10,465 pounds, but although only 6,832 pounds was collected, the funds helped him mount a fresh force before heading north for Scotland once more. Humphrey set out to meet the king's muster at Roxburgh, just to the north of the border, late the following spring, and Elizabeth went with him, most likely in the company of Joanna, who accompanied Ralph, as well as Marguerite, who followed in the wake of the king with her young sons, Thomas (aged two) and Edmund (one).[3]

Whether the women peeled off before arriving at Roxburgh or remained with the main body of the eight-thousand-strong army until it struck out into the as-yet-unconquered territories north of the 'Scottish Sea' (as Edward termed the Firth of Forth), is not clear. What is readily apparent is that, when the English forces moved into unfamiliar terrain where there was an increased threat of ambush, safeguarding royal women and babies would be an encumbrance. In any case, Elizabeth was by this time heavily pregnant and could not risk childbirth so far into hostile territory, especially with the Scottish rebel leader William Wallace still at large and sporadically mounting attacks; she required a secure residence for her confinement and subsequent recovery. While their husbands, brother, and Joanna's eldest son, Gilbert – now ensconced with a tutor within the household of his uncle Prince Edward and training to be a knight (for which his grandfather had bought him a small suit of armour) – continued north, the women turned back to England.[4]

By 6 June, Elizabeth, Joanna, and Marguerite arrived at Tynemouth Castle, a highly developed defensive site on the east coast, near Newcastle. Tynemouth was far away from any fighting and well-positioned to receive food, wine, and salt from merchant ships – an acute challenge for the cash-strapped English captains, as they struggled to feed their men on the march north. The castle's direct access to the sea also provided a means of escape in the unlikely event that it was besieged. Though lacking the manicured gardens and idyllic parkland of Woodstock where they had awaited Prince Edmund's birth the year before, Tynemouth was a practical and secure choice for Elizabeth's confinement while the armies of England pushed north towards Aberdeen.[5]

A surviving letter from the king's camp at Aberdeen late that August, casts light both on the constant flow of letters to and from Tynemouth, as well as the active intercessory role that Elizabeth played, even during her pregnancy. Since the formation of the alliance with France that was part of Edward's marriage to Marguerite, he had sought to support his new brother-in-law and ally, the King of France. Among Edward's actions had been to direct the seizure of goods held by all Flemish merchants in London after Flanders had rebelled against the French, in the summer of 1302. When the cloth merchant, Walter de Bruges, was arrested, he appealed – not directly to the king but to his daughter, Elizabeth, for whom he may have procured items she had developed a taste for while living in the Low Countries. Identifying himself as 'clerk and merchant of Elizabeth', Walter got word of his arrest to the countess. From Tynemouth, she wrote directly to her father, explaining that Walter, 'although born in Flanders, did not adhere to the Flemish enemies and rebels of the King of France'. Walter had good reason to feel grateful to his patron: on the word of his daughter, Edward directed a renewed investigation and eventually released Walter's stock, which amounted to over two hundred pounds' worth of cloth and other items.[6]

At Tynemouth, Elizabeth gave birth to her first child, a baby girl she named Margaret, almost certainly in honour of her stepmother and friend Marguerite, though the name of course also recalled her sister in Brabant. We are able to surmise from the recorded gift-giving that followed Margaret's birth that the delivery had proceeded smoothly: a buoyant Elizabeth purchased and distributed a number of silver cups (ubiquitous as gifts in this era) to her companions, including Joanna de Mereworth, who had continued in the countess's service ever since King Edward had sent her to collect Elizabeth from Holland in 1300. With autumn closing in and the king and his men intending to stay in Scotland, Elizabeth, Marguerite, and Joanna – who was pregnant once again – planned to return north. Each woman seemed to want to be with her husband, and it is difficult to avoid the conclusion that something we would recognize today as romantic love linked the princesses with their husbands: Joanna's passion for Ralph had clearly been demonstrated by the trials she endured to marry him; Marguerite would, on Edward's death, remain a widow, proclaiming that 'when Edward died, all men died' for her; Elizabeth and Humphrey would go on to produce nine further children during the next twelve years of their marriage, suggesting at the very least a persistent intimacy. But although love may have drawn the young countesses and queen back towards the theatre of war, they recognized that Scotland in the winter among an army struggling with food supplies was not an ideal environment for small children, and Elizabeth's baby Margaret was sent to the royal nursery at Windsor with her uncles, the toddler princes, Thomas and Edmund. Back in the security of the castle, Margaret's needs were catered to by a dedicated wet nurse, as well as teams of maids and cradle-rockers who managed the nursery, under the guidance of a royal administrator, who oversaw the broader requirements of the household. The king's minstrel Martinet was assigned to entertain the children, one of whom got hold of his *tabor*, a small snare drum often played in accompaniment with a pipe, and managed to break it. The minstrel's wages were supplemented for the repair of his instrument.[7]

By November, the queen and her two stepdaughters had rejoined the king's court. Edward had chosen to spend the winter at the abbey and royal palace at Dunfermline, the ancient capital of Scotland and by tradition the burial site for the country's kings – as at Aberconwy in Wales, Edward knew his occupation of this sacred royal ground would symbolically reinforce the completeness of his conquest of Scotland. The site will also have appealed for more practical reasons: the chronicler Matthew Paris described the thirteenth-century compound as large enough to house the retinues of three kings at once without them inconveniencing one another. All the available chambers and horse stalls would have been occupied by the assembled retinues of the king (with his nearly five hundred knights and dozens of personal servants), as well as Marguerite, Joanna, and Elizabeth. Prince Edward had departed for Perth with his own household late in November, hinting perhaps at early signs of estrangement with his father that would burst forth in the years to come. But the king's two sons-in-law, Humphrey and Ralph (who by this point, was so well-beloved by his father-in-law, that he had been granted the extraordinary privilege of a licence to hunt and carry away game as he pleased from any royal forest) remained at Dunfermline to welcome their wives north.[8]

On their arrival, Elizabeth and Joanna were greeted with the happy news that a rupture that had threatened the friendly relationship between England and their sister Margaret's Duchy of Brabant had finally been resolved. English merchants all along the east coast had been protesting that they were unable to recover debts owed them by Duke Jan, and after many months of complaints Edward was forced to allow them to confiscate the goods of local Brabaçon merchants in turn as compensation. In June, Margaret wrote a letter replete with expressions of filial love and obligation to 'her very dear and well-beloved lord and father', deploying sentiment in the service of international diplomacy. Margaret, 'his humble daughter, gives all the affection and reverence that she can send him, with a daughter's love', in informing the king in the Anglo-Norman they spoke to each other that:

> in no place have [Edward's English] merchants been arrested or detained . . . even when the merchants of our lands have been detained and arrested: so, I pray you, dearest sire, that, for reason and right, and also for the love of me, you will command that their goods be restored and delivered to them.

When Margaret's pleas were not sufficient to stop the king's actions against the merchants of Brabant, Jan seized the goods of an English merchant, before rapidly thinking better of it. By November, yielding to the entreaties of counsellors that included his wife, Jan wrote to his father-in-law, promising that he would honour any debts owed, thereby de-escalating the diplomatic situation. Although Margaret's name is not mentioned in the final charter, her influence was very important in negotiating a peaceful outcome.[9]

The presence of Elizabeth and Joanna, so deep into hostile territory during the darkest months of the year, demonstrated once again the impact of their mother's influence on these adult women: just as Eleanor of Castile had accompanied her husband to war in the Holy Land and into Wales (perhaps inspired by her own mother's journeys in Spain), her daughters Joanna and Elizabeth did not shy away from travelling into the warring territories of Scotland with their own husbands. From their base in Dunfermline, the princesses – ever accustomed to itinerant journeying – took several extended journeys throughout the southern region of Scotland and down the east coast of England. For Christmas that year, Elizabeth travelled south to Hovingham at the bottom of the North York Moors with her father and stepmother, and after the holiday they continued as far as Frodingham in Lincolnshire, before turning north. Nearly two hundred horses were required to transport all the furnishings and personal items that they took with them, encircling the royal family in a sea of courtiers and servants. Elizabeth's household alone required provision for thirty horses: seven for her carriage, seven more to pull the carts that held her personal suite of furniture and goods, three for the countess to ride, and a further fifteen to transport her ladies and chief attendants. Labourers idling along the roads in the winter months who hoped to glimpse their monarch would have needed to strain their eyes as the entourage passed to pick out the king and queen amid the sizable retinue, but their impression of royal power would have been reinforced.[10]

As spring arrived and the king's army left Dunfermline, having turned the palace and all its monastic buildings apart from the magnificent abbey church itself to rubble, Joanna safely delivered her eighth child, a baby boy she named Edward, in honour of her father. Elizabeth and Marguerite, meanwhile, remained with the army. Behind an oriel window constructed for the purpose of providing them with a view safe from projectiles and shrapnel, the royal ladies watched as Edward's men lay siege to Stirling

Castle. From their protected vantage point, they would have heard the king declaring a lengthy oration of the legal rationale for his overlordship of Scotland, and seen the deployment of battering rams and giant siege engines, which hurled huge stones and 'Greek fire' (so-called because it sought to replicate an incendiary weapon used by the Byzantines – an explosive mix of sulphur and saltpetre) over the walls. Elizabeth's husband Humphrey, leading a contingent of knights on horseback, managed to fight off a Scottish force aiming to break the siege, while her father paraded boldly along the castle walls to demonstrate his bravery and boost the morale of his men – at one point narrowly escaping a cross-bow bolt shot from inside the castle that dramatically pierced the saddle of his horse. The appearance of the royal ladies within the besieging camp attests to the confidence of the English forces in their control of the area outside the castle, but also offers vivid evidence of the interest of these women in the business of war, even if only as spectators.

Late in July, Stirling Castle fell, effectively concluding Edward's conquest of Scotland. Joanna remained at court, which was still only as far south as Jedburgh in the border region, where she interceded with the king for mercy on behalf of an Englishman charged with murder. Her twenty-two-year-old sister Elizabeth, pregnant for the second time, meanwhile departed for the safety of England. She left on 21 July, heading for the royal castle in picturesque Knaresborough near Harrogate in Yorkshire, where she would remain for her second confinement. That fortress's defences had been strengthened under King John a century before; a broad moat to enhance its security had been installed, and its chambers had been updated to house the king and his retinue while they hunted in nearby Knaresborough Forest. But the standards of comfort expected of nobles by the early fourteenth century had increased considerably, and the castle seems to have been found wanting. In 1307 King Edward would set about reconstructing it, adding a modern keep with vaulted cellars and three upper storeys housing a great hall and a chamber with large Gothic windows. Three years before those works began, however, his daughter travelled south in a carriage refitted for the journey with feather cushions to soften the constant jolts caused by the bumpy roads. Following her were carts with trunks filled with household goods to enhance the comforts of Knaresborough: seven tapestries to cover the dusty walls, woven with the arms of England and Hereford, on a background of deep green; two new benches for her chamber and three to furnish her hall; six large, canopied beds for the countess and the five lady companions who accompanied her. Her kitchen was provisioned by the royal storehouses that dotted the north of England and the captured stores of Scotland: bread came from Stirling, Edinburgh and Berwick-on-Tweed; fish was sent from Newcastle; wine from York, with the sheriff of that county also asked to procure salt.[11]

Despite frequent visits by her husband, Elizabeth began to feel a creeping anxiety about her impending labour as autumn set in. Her concern was not without precedent – Marguerite's first delivery, and one of Joanna's more recent experiences, had led both mothers to appeal during labour to one of the royal family's favourite saints, Thomas Becket, and to feel sufficient gratitude after their safe deliveries that they named their healthy sons after the martyr. Statistics on maternal mortality in the pre-modern era are notoriously difficult to gauge, but studies that use both archaeological and textual sources and span the medieval centuries demonstrate a consistently high rate of death for women in labour – a fact made all the more harrowing when considering the number of children born to women like Eleanor of Castile and Joanna. Even when the babies had not lived, Elizabeth's mother and all her sisters had survived by that date a total of twenty-six deliveries, though other women close to the royal family had succumbed during or shortly after childbirth: Aveline de Forz, the heiress who had married Elizabeth's uncle Edmund, the Earl of Lancaster in 1273, had died giving birth to twins who were either stillborn or died very soon after their birth. Tellingly, the sole historical record of Aveline's death is in the chronicle written by Nicholas Trivet, commissioned by Mary in the decades to come, which suggests that the death was remembered as significant within the family. In September 1304 Elizabeth's anxiety eventually became so great that she sought divine protection beyond simple prayers to St Thomas – a messenger was sent to Westminster Abbey, requesting that one of the kingdom's most prized relics be sent north to Knaresborough to comfort her.[12]

The Girdle of the Virgin at Westminster is a mostly forgotten cousin to the relic still venerated at Prato, just outside Florence, but like that knotted cord – supposedly woven by the Virgin's own hands and seen encircling her waist in surviving works by Raphael and Titian – its veneration rose sharply in the thirteenth century with the increased popularity of the cult of the Virgin Mary. The most well-known version of the girdle story came from *The Golden Legend*, a compendium of Latin tales about the lives of important saints that was compiled in Italy during the late thirteenth century by a Dominican monk-turned-archbishop, Jacobus de Voragine. The story follows the episode in which St Thomas the Apostle missed the appearance of Jesus to his fellow disciples after his resurrection and 'doubted' the veracity of his friends' words. Despite his doubts, the saint nevertheless travelled to India to preach the Christian gospel, but in doing so missed the death and bodily Assumption of the

Virgin Mary to Heaven. The Virgin, recognizing Thomas's scepticism, appeared to him in the sky as he travelled back to Judea from India and dropped down to him the cord that served as her belt, offering physical proof of his vision. How this ancient object had survived the centuries intact or made its way to Europe was less important to the medieval mind than its direct, physical link to the pre-eminent saint of the Christian Church (although the detailed provenance story that became attached to the Prato Girdle perhaps lent greater weight to its authenticity than the Westminster Girdle, which was reputed to have come miraculously into the possession of Edward the Confessor and was given by him to the abbey). Relics – whether parts of the bodies of saints, or 'contact relics' like the girdle that acquired holiness through its association with the Virgin's body – functioned as physical proofs of the stories within *The Golden Legend*, linking medieval Europe directly to the ancient Near East of Jesus's time. Many who, like Thomas, doubted the historic truths of Bible tales, were convinced by the remarkably well-preserved phials of holy blood, breast milk, tears, and the thousand-year-old bodies encased in glass coffins that displayed early martyrs to crowds of pilgrims, as well as the girdles and veils that had touched Jesus or Mary at critical moments on their way to heaven.[13]

From early in its veneration, the Girdle of the Virgin was particularly associated with pregnant women, unsurprising given the primacy of motherhood in the life of the Virgin Mary. If she was 'immaculate' from birth (preserved from the taint of original sin), it was in the act of giving birth to Jesus that she helped save humanity; her position as Queen of Heaven derives exclusively from her relation to Christ. It is apparent that the veneration of Mary, widespread across Europe at the start of the fourteenth century, suggested to medieval women that they too might enjoy enhanced authority once they became mothers. First, however, the women had to survive childbirth; it was to help with this that two monks from Westminster travelled north with the holy Girdle to the Countess Elizabeth in Knaresborough. They remained there until 15 September, when she gave them forty shillings to cover the expenses related to their travel.[14]

Elizabeth gave birth on or before 10 September. Like all medieval noblewomen, she would have been tended by an experienced midwife and her ladies, who would have drawn the curtains and burned herbs to create a soothing, dark environment. Prayers would have been chanted to request the saints' aid for a safe delivery, but medieval medicine could offer little in the way of solutions to major obstetric dangers, or pain management. When the time for delivery came, Elizabeth would have sat upright on a birthing chair rather than lying in the large bed she had brought from Scotland, though she would have moved to the bed to rest afterwards while the baby was bathed and swaddled, and – in the case of noble children – given to a wet nurse to suckle.

Elizabeth remained at Knaresborough until 11 October, when she had recovered sufficiently to be entertained by the king's minstrel Robert and fifteen of his fellow musicians, following her purification mass, a ceremonial re-entry to society after childbirth, in which thanks were given for her survival. Her father sent her six bream from the King's Pool in York to aid the celebration. But all had not gone well, as the muted response of the king to the messenger who brought him the news offers sad testimony. Elizabeth gave birth to a boy, christened Humphrey, after his father and the three earlier generations of Earls of Hereford who preceded him. The family name, however, could not protect Humphrey, who died soon after birth. On 15 October, four grooms collected the body of the infant, and started a slow journey south to Fulham, where on the thirtieth a lead worker was commissioned to cast a tiny coffin. He was buried at Westminster Abbey on 8 November, in the chapel of St John the Baptist and only a few feet from the ambulatory passage which took pilgrims past the shrine of Edward the Confessor and the delicate effigy commemorating the child's great-grand-father, Henry III. One hundred and twenty candles (made of 524 pounds of wax) surrounded the funeral bier, while Masses were said for the infant's soul by the canons at Westminster and the Dominican friars of London, and the bell-ringer William and his companions rang the bells.[15]

Late that autumn or early in the next year, another tragedy struck: one-year-old Margaret, Elizabeth's first-born child, died at Windsor. The little girl's death itself is unrecorded in surviving sources – an indication of the harrowing frequency of infant mortality; instead, Margaret's name merely ceases to appear in the household accounts of the royal nursery at Windsor, only entering the historical record again attached to the tomb she shared at Westminster with her brother Humphrey. From the records, it was as though the baby simply disappeared. Given the period's astonishingly high mortality rates for infants and young children, modern commentators have often portrayed the death of children like Humphrey and Margaret as less traumatic for medieval parents than we might expect. Certainly, noble and royal children frequently lived separately from their parents, nurtured by wet nurses so their mothers might rapidly become pregnant again, and Margaret was no different. Living at Windsor with her royal uncles while her parents were in Scotland and Knaresborough, she may not have known her parents. Yet first-hand accounts of grieving mothers and fathers depict the enormously damaging emotional toll of losing a child, even in royal households. The chronicler Matthew Paris recorded that, after the death of three-year-old Princess Katherine in May 1257, her mother, Eleanor of Provence, 'was so overcome with grief that it brought on a disease, which was thought to be incurable, as she could obtain no relief either from medical skill or human consolation.' By the end of the month, the little girl's father, Henry III, was suffering badly from tertian fever, brought on 'by the accumulation of sorrows.' There is no reason to believe that Elizabeth and Humphrey did not suffer similarly with the deaths of their children.[16]

Though the youngest of Eleanor of Castile's many daughters, Elizabeth was the first to experience the pain of losing a child, an agony which her mother had known well. The Castilian queen had given birth to at least fifteen children over a period of twenty-five years or more, but nine of them died during her life – despite the advantages she enjoyed of a superior diet, access to physicians, and a relatively clean living environment. Though shocking to the modern reader, Eleanor of Castile's familiarity with infant mortality reflected the prevalence of death among young children in families of all social classes across Europe. Her experience, bleak as it seems to us, was not rare, even among royal women: Queen Marguerite's only sister gave birth to two children who died early before succumbing at a young age herself, possibly through complications surrounding a failed third pregnancy. In contrast, what was unusual – remarkable, even – was the accomplishment of the English princesses in providing such a large group of grandchildren for Eleanor of Castile. All eight of Joanna's children, from the baby Edward to Gilbert, who was aged twelve in the spring of 1304, flourished in health – and extraordinarily, they would all live into adulthood. Eleanora's son and daughter, both safely out of the most dangerous years of early childhood, remained in good health in Bar even after the death of their father Henri, while on Crusade in 1302, placed them in the guardianship of a council of elders and, ultimately, their grandfather, the English king. Both would live into middle age, and beyond. Margaret's sole offspring, three-year-old Jan, and the handful of illegitimate half-siblings who shared his name, all prospered in youth and into adulthood, despite the odds being stacked against any babies born before the advent of modern medicine.[17]

A small, grey marble tomb set into a recess in the north wall of the chapel was identified by the antiquary William Camden in 1600 as belonging to Elizabeth's young children. The chest and delicately carved, trefoil canopy which surmounts it were exceedingly expensive to make, outstripping in their cost the funerary monuments of all but the richest lords at the beginning of the fourteenth century. This was a grave memorial designed to guarantee that the children would not be forgotten, its grandeur and expense offering vivid testimony, if it were needed, to the suffering of Elizabeth and Humphrey after the deaths of their young children.[18]

XV
Opulence

1305
LUDGERSHALL, WESTMINSTER

Late in the summer of 1305, the king's youngest children, Thomas and Edmund, escaped the heat of their nursery quarters at Windsor for the cool shade of the parklands of Ludgershall Castle, near Andover in Wiltshire. The fortified manor house was an ideal summer retreat, compact and yet recently modernized, and equipped with separate chambers for the king, queen, and royal children, each with fireplaces and privy chambers catering to the comfort of their occupants. Visible from the windows of the royal apartments was an enclosed park to the north, too small to house deer but probably used for rabbit hunting and the staging of lesser tournaments. Ludgershall may also have been selected for its close proximity to the usual home of their sister Mary, who was the young princes' guardian during their summer sojourn. Fourteen years after her grandmother's death, the king's fourth daughter was still described as a 'nun of Fontevrault, dwelling at Amesbury', hinting that the decades-old plan that she would eventually join her cousin Eleanor of Brittany at the mother church of their religious order had not yet been forgotten. Mary's reason for remaining at Amesbury, fifteen years after her cousin had first travelled to Fontevrault, is not known, but as late as 1305, her father's grants included the explicit prerequisite that she continue to reside within his realm – she seemingly did not wish to lose the privileges she enjoyed living within her father's kingdom.[1]

Foremost among the exceptional freedoms granted to Mary as a nun, was the ability to visit her family. In the years since Edmund's birth, Mary had remained close to Marguerite, and she increasingly took on the role of educating the young members of her extended family – Joanna's many daughters, by both Gilbert and Ralph, spent significant amounts of time at Amesbury under the tutelage of their aunt. Aged twenty-six, Mary could have been forgiven for preferring to spend her time among the excitement of court rather than deep in the countryside, charged with the care of two little boys, aged five and four. But, having never learned to live within her income, she was not in a position to resist a request made by her father or stepmother – four months earlier she had been saved once again by a loan from her father in order to pay off extremely heavy debts. A letter survives in which Edward ordered his men to pay Mary the sum of two hundred pounds, 'as speedily as possible, as she is indebted to diverse men' – this was an immense loan, which the king can have had little faith he would see repaid. He also forgave his daughter rents she owed to him in May of that year, knowing they could not be paid.[2]

This was not the first time that Mary's debts had spiralled so wildly out of control (including the time her father had to pay off the goldsmith of London who had been thrown into debtors' prison). What is clear though, is that her constant debts were not due to any meagreness in her income. From her first entrance into the priory, when she was assigned a generous annual income of one hundred pounds, her allowance had risen twice: it doubled on the death of her grandmother in 1291, to ensure she might maintain her comfort without recourse to the dowager queen's income; and was enlarged again in 1302, when that allowance was replaced with a portfolio of estates spread across Wiltshire, Dorset, Somerset, and the Isle of Wight worth more than 266 pounds each year. By 1305, in addition to the funds received from her manors, she was given sixty oaks each year from her father's forests, which were transported to Amesbury for the hearth in her chamber. She was also a recipient of royal wardships, taking in the income from estates held by major landowners who had died while their heirs were still children. The following year, the king granted her more lands to supplement her daily needs, and when a competing claim to the lands emerged, he made up the difference from the royal coffers, 'as the king wills that his daughter shall not be prejudiced in any way.'[3]

As a nun, the requirements on Mary's income should have been limited, since her vow of poverty was intended to prevent copious expenditure. While her sisters favoured sumptuous gold-embroidered silk gowns, embellished with silver buttons, and headdresses festooned with large pearls, sapphires, rubies, and emeralds, Mary – like all nuns in the Benedictine order – was meant to wear the plain black robe that marked her out as a religious woman. Frequent exhortations by bishops throughout the later medieval period (often blaming the independent incomes that increasingly accompanied noble nuns like Mary into their convents) suggest, however, that nuns regularly eschewed the simplicity of their prescribed dress, instead wearing gowns crafted of the same fine silks that clothed their secular sisters. The bishops also lamented the propensity of nuns to wear jewels that were deemed inappropriate to their status. As well as the sapphire ring presented to Mary by her father when she took her vows, she is known to have worn golden clasps, and her indebtedness to goldsmiths indicates the purchase of additional jewels for her use. Nor was personal adornment the only inappropriate expense for which the bishops blamed aristocratic nuns; they were also chastised for keeping pampered lapdogs, which seem to have been often brought into chapel, where they interrupted services, and even hunting hounds. Mary was therefore well positioned, should she desire, to participate in many of the noble activities that entertained her sisters. Whether or not she pursued the hunt with vigour, she was certainly a patron of travelling minstrels, who sang songs of romance and epic heroism far removed from the devotional chanting that marked the hours at Amesbury. Churchmen's chastisements against the conduct of aristocratic nuns also included complaints about the frequent appearance of these musicians, their concern not only exercised by the impropriety of popular song but also by the way their music encouraged the nuns to dance, a physical expression that was felt to be dangerously close to sin. Mary also spent money on literature, commissioning a chronicle of her father's reign from the Dominican friar Nicholas Trivet, whom she may have first met through contacts associated with her mother.[4]

Mary may, therefore, have run up considerable – and to the modern reader, unexpected – expenses on clothes and jewellery, as well as on the patronage of musicians and writers. The bulk of her remaining income was concentrated on supplying her chamber with the richest foods, wines, furnishings, and entertainment available, and in travelling in a style to rival the king.

Her bed – almost always the most costly and intricate item of furniture within a medieval chamber – was purchased at the king's expense in 1305. It was hung with heavy woven tapestries and covered in fine linen sheets topped with heavy velvets, which – together with the constant glow of fire from her hearth – would have kept her warm in the cold of winter on the Salisbury Plain. This opulent bed, and the green benches cushioned with down feathers that lined three walls within her chamber, set Mary's rooms apart from the simpler dwellings of the other Amesbury nuns, and provided a luxuriously comfortable alternative meeting place to the prioress's chamber or chapter house. In Mary's chamber, visiting magnates and bishops could be entertained, and senior nuns – themselves mostly from aristocratic families and likely accustomed to modern comforts – could gather to make decisions on behalf of the priory. It was with a deep appreciation of the princess's potential for influencing the outside world that her cousin, Eleanor of Brittany, now Abbess of Fontevrault, declared Mary her deputy in inspecting the other houses of the order within England – at Nuneaton in Warwickshire, and the small priory at Westwood in Worcestershire – and bestowed upon her the power to discipline and correct any behaviours that were deemed unsuitable.[5]

By all accounts, Mary's quarters at Amesbury were impressive, and she evidently considered entertaining a serious means of building and maintaining her influence, providing a forum where petitioners could appeal to the princess for her intercession. The private dining table within her chamber at the priory required more than one hundred *ells* – or 125 yards – of linens to make napkins and tablecloths for dozens of guests, and she had her own pond stocked with two thousand fish for making pies, soups, and sauces which were prepared away from the priory's main kitchens. Guests at her table also sampled more exotic delicacies, such as the sixteen giant Atlantic wolffish (capable of growing over four feet long and each weighing thirty pounds or more) which were sent as a gift to Mary from the king. When she travelled on pilgrimage or to visit her family, her expenses normally fell to her father, and her profligacy can be glimpsed in the surviving royal wardrobe entries. Over one twenty-nine-day period during a pilgrimage to the great shrines at Bury St Edmunds and Walsingham, her household expenditure – on beer and wine, fish (clearly a favourite food) and venison, oats and hay for her large stable of horses, and on paying the wages of the many ladies, clerks, and messengers in her regular employment – totalled almost forty-nine pounds, more than the annual income required by a knight. Nor was even this amount sufficient: no fewer than three times during the pilgrimage, Mary sent her men to the king to borrow twenty additional pounds. This level of expenditure is scarcely believable for the household of a single woman, and especially one who was pledged to poverty.[6]

Even when visiting court – which, by 1305, normally accounted for at least one extended period each year, during which she renewed her acquaintance with her siblings and stepmother – Mary was not content to promote the virtues of asceticism and poverty that were usually associated with the monastic vocation. While the household of her sister Elizabeth, one of the foremost ladies of England in her capacity as Countess of Hereford, used up to thirty horses when it travelled to Scotland and back, Mary's required no fewer than twenty-four (for riding by the nun and her entourage, and to pull carts carrying baggage), merely to travel between Amesbury and Westminster, each animal being attended by its own groom, whose wages would be supplied by the king. And it was almost certainly during one of her extended stays at court that Mary developed one of her most expensive habits of all.

The vice of gambling, which was most commonly undertaken with dice but also with chess, was fairly conventional among the noble class – Mary's brother, Prince Edward, lost about thirty-two pounds in 1302 while betting against other young noblemen, and was not considered to have a gambling problem. Her parents had favoured chess, a game very commonly played in Eleanor's childhood home of Castile. Mary's mother evidently retained a strong affection for the game into adulthood: she is known to have borrowed a treatise on tactics so that it could be copied by her scribes, and she received an exceptionally fine set of pieces carved from jasper and rock crystal as a gift from her husband. At least during the early years of his reign, Edward also gambled at chess, losing small sums before either improving his game or learning to play only for the pride of winning. Mary preferred to gamble with dice, playing a variety of popular games from the simple raffle, in which players took turns rolling three dice, with the highest matching pair or sets of three winning, to the more complicated hazard, which has evolved, in a simplified form, as craps, still played today. When it came to gambling, the difference between Mary and her parents or brother, apart from the incompatibility of betting with her religious vocation, was that her income was comparatively limited. Her predilection for dice games nevertheless remained strong throughout her life. On one occasion while travelling (her expenses therefore recorded within the king's wardrobe accounts), she lost all the cash she had playing dice, but – in a gesture familiar to many who have gambled – she was so determined to make back her loss, she borrowed from her companions, money which was inevitably also lost.[7]

Her penchant for gambling and her unrepentant taste for luxury marked Mary out even among the other mostly aristocratic nuns with whom she lived, yet her position as daughter of the king preserved her not only from penury in times of debt but also from censure. Moreover, while Mary, as a nun, may have seemed too fond of luxury, she was firmly within the prescribed behaviours for female members of the royal family, who were positively encouraged to model conspicuous consumption. In addition to the intricately embroidered gowns speckled with silver buttons, and the heavily jewelled headdresses and girdles that added lustre and further embellishment to their dress, the royal sisters were taught to furnish their lives in a manner that advertised the wealth, prestige, and sophistication of their dynasty.

Their parents had not held back. Eleanor of Castile had possessed exceptionally cosmopolitan tastes, that were variously drawn from the courts of Castile where she grew up and Ponthieu in northern France, the home of her mother, but she also understood the expectation that her surroundings should reflect her own status as queen. Thus, she imported silks from Tripoli and Damascus, furs and feathers from France, glass vessels from the workshops of Venice, and caskets from Limoges. Her mirrors were backed with silver, her combs were carved from ivory. Her chambers featured glazed windows and were invariably painted in rich colours, often in a deep green, and cushioned with pillows, linens, velvet covers, and 'pictured cloths', figural tapestries bought from Cologne. The chronicler Matthew Paris described the queen's use of fabric coverings for walls and floor as displaying 'excessive pride', reporting that her rooms were 'hung with palls of silk and tapestry, like a temple'. Their father, who reportedly eschewed elaborate dress in favour of simple tunics, nevertheless spent lavishly on the tournaments, feasts, and weddings that were designed to promote his *largesse* and the perception of his wealth. He patronized many sweeping architectural and decorative programmes, including the extraordinarily detailed cycle of narrative paintings at Westminster

Palace, which depicted stories of heroic warriors and kings of the Old Testament, that were completed under his instruction late in the thirteenth century. At court, table settings gleamed over fine linens, with plates, chalices, and pitchers made of gold and silver and etched with the intertwined heraldic arms of Castile and England, and knives and forks with handles vibrantly coloured in delicate enamelwork. Just as rich as the vessels in which they were served were the foods themselves: there were casks of olive oil, lemons, and oranges imported from Spain; wheels of delicate cheese received as special gifts from relatives in Brie; dates and pomegranates, figs and raisins, and cherries, apples, and pears from across England and Europe. Eleanor of Castile had equally high tastes in other consumables, including books – her own scriptorium turned out treatises on religion and war, while the queen purchased more refined illuminated works from specialist artisans.[8]

Mary, like her mother and grandmother (whose own substantial collection of manuscripts, including those focusing on stories from Arthur's court at Camelot, may have been passed to Mary after her death), demonstrated a decidedly secular interest in books. Her own commission, a chronicle of her father's reign by the Dominican friar Nicholas Trivet, shows that she possessed a significant interest in the world of politics and war. Family histories formed an important part of literature in the chivalric age – their stories linked real knights and kings directly to the fabled heroes whose songs were sung by the travelling minstrels. In commissioning this chronicle, Mary was promoting the prestige of her father's lineage, and by extension, her own.[9]

As a nun, Mary would never enjoy the status that provided her countess and duchess sisters with opportunities for influence, but she could nevertheless project her royal connections through the luxurious appointment of her rooms, which she filled with costly imported goods and foods, specially commissioned literary works, music and games. What may appear as unbecoming flamboyance in a religious woman can therefore rather be understood as the princess-nun deploying her income to reaffirm her position and affiliation as a member of the royal family. Her ostentatious travelling entourage, over-stuffed interiors, mirthmaking, and extraordinary consumption of fuel and food in her chamber – so utterly ill-seeming in a religious woman – forcefully demonstrated her economic power and connection. Mary needed those around her to remember she was a princess, perhaps even more than her sisters did – she, after all, was without a wealthy husband to provide a secondary opportunity for accessing power and influence. Hers came only through her connection to court and her birth family, and she understood that her role required her to be surrounded by the trappings of worldly honour.

As Mary's sisters became increasingly established within their own households, they each demonstrated the same understanding of the way that conspicuous luxury reflected positively on their status as leading noblewomen. Early in the fourteenth century, Clare Castle in Suffolk, one of Joanna's principal residences in England, boasted fabulous luxuries, including a swannery, an embroidery studio, and a goldsmith's workshop, as well as an aviary and a lion house where exotic beasts were kept – recalling the camel that lived at Langley during Joanna's adolescence. The castle itself was surrounded by fountained gardens criss-crossed with flint paths, a nod to her mother's passion for the gardens of her Castilian youth. Joanna was also a patron of building works at Clare Priory, a house of Augustinian friars to the immediate south-west, across the River Stour from the castle. The priory had been established in the middle of the thirteenth century by the father of her first husband, and by 1305 Joanna seems to have determined that it would be her final resting place. Indeed, it may have been to secure burial rights within that church that Joanna made her benefaction to the friars, as she does not otherwise appear to have been concerned with religious patronage, and nor does anything about her personality suggest that she was more than conventionally pious. In supporting Clare Priory and opting to be buried there, Joanna chose to forever associate her memory with the Clare family, whose vast estates granted her the independence she cherished; it is, moreover, clear from her rejection of a burial alongside Gilbert at the Clare mausoleum at Tewkesbury that it was her independence, rather than any lingering emotional connection to her first husband, that was foremost in her mind.[10]

Across the sea in Brabant, Margaret – who was often distanced from her husband at court, as he indulged in very public love affairs – began crafting her own memorial. Her ambitions could not be contained within a church: instead, harking back to her father's works in Wales, she built a castle on a magnificent scale. The castle at Tervuren replaced an earlier royal hunting lodge on a site traditionally associated with St Hubert, patron saint of hunters, deep in the Sonian Forest, east of Brussels. It was demolished in the eighteenth century, but an early-seventeenth-century landscape painting that may be considered a portrait of the castle (albeit set in an idealized landscape) after a later renovation survives. Looking beyond the steep gables and many-windowed façades that were added in the seventeenth century, Margaret's castle – with its many turrets and large great hall – can be glimpsed rising out of the surrounding mere, with a view of the nearby ducal church of St John the Evangelist (retaining the Romanesque tower it has since lost) in the background. The painting also contains a view of the wide, flat path which Margaret directed should encircle the castle and lake, and which quickly became a favourite place for Jan to stroll with his counsellors and hunting companions. Though surrounded by water, the low walls at Tervuren indicate that the castle was never intended for defensive purposes; rather its aim seems to have been to please Duke Jan, and Margaret may have hoped it might lure him away from his mistresses. In building on such a scale, Margaret also knew she was demonstrating her ducal family's wealth and sophistication to the courtiers and ambassadors who visited.[11]

Back in England, Elizabeth also promoted cultural refinement. Like her mother and the elegant lady who appears painted in the lower margins of the Alphonso Psalter, she hunted with dogs, including a white greyhound that was of such beauty that her brother, Prince Edward, wrote to his 'beautiful sister' in 1304 to ask if he could borrow the dog to mate it with a grey bitch in his kennel. She presumably accommodated his request, since she was herself so frequently the recipient of gifts from her brother; nor was she shy about asking him for favours in return. Prince Edward was a consummate lover of music, to the extent that he once sent a musician in his household to Shrewsbury Abbey near the Welsh border, armed with a letter of introduction and the instruction to remain there until he had learned to play the *crwth*, a stringed, partly bowed instrument resembling a primitive hybrid of guitar and violin. Elizabeth wrote to the prince, asking him to send his choirmaster to her at Pleshey Castle for a time, so that he might teach the children of her chapel to sing in polyphony, or multiple parts. The request sounds simple enough, but Elizabeth's desire to import fashionable new music into her own home was itself a gesture at demonstrating her connection to court. Polyphonic singing, with its blended harmonies, opportunities for showing off virtuosic voices, and even occasional dissonance, was utterly distinct from the traditional religious chanting that still dominated church services throughout England in the early fourteenth century. Many prelates considered the application of multiple parts to sacred songs inappropriately frivolous and likely to distract from the meaning of the words; within twenty years, the Pope had forbidden polyphonic music during liturgical services. Elizabeth's efforts to introduce polyphony into her own chapel shows that she had retained a genuine interest in music from the minstrels who had entertained the children at Langley. But in bringing the latest musical trends to rural Essex – especially when imported through the person of the prince's own choirmaster – she was also demonstrating the metropolitan refinement of the Bohun family, as well as reinforcing local recognition of her own royalty. It was a connection that would have been further emphasized by the fur-lined mantles and the hoods emblazoned with the royal arms that her father purchased several times each year for his daughter and her chief personal attendants, turning Elizabeth's household into an extended royal household. Like all Edward's daughters, Elizabeth never forgot the lesson she had learned from her parents – that displays of luxury could serve to enhance a reputation and maintain the influence that came with it.[12]

For Mary, it is clear that, despite the luxurious chamber and heaving table she cultivated at Amesbury, her most prized indulgence was the freedom of movement afforded to her as daughter of the king. It is even possible that her liberty to move freely may have enabled Mary to indulge in the most forbidden activity of all for a nun: an illicit love affair. In May 1305, Mary's niece, Joanna of Bar (Eleanora's daughter), became betrothed to John de Warenne, heir to the great Earldom of Surrey, and when they married the following year in a lavish ceremony, the bridegroom was aged twenty-one and his wife was only ten or eleven. Many years later, John de Warenne claimed his marriage to Joanna of Bar was invalid because he had conducted an affair with her aunt, Mary, prior to the wedding – carnal relations with such a close relative would place John and Joanna's union firmly within the prohibited degree of consanguinity, and could only have been resolved with an explicit dispensation from the Pope.[13]

The acute sexual frustration experienced by nuns was a theme commonly explored in a popular genre known as the *chansons des nonnes*, or nuns' songs, one example of which included the lamentation:

> I should be learning about love and turning my mind to its delightful ways; but I have been put in prison . . . In the convent I live in great misery – God! – for I am too young. I feel the sweet pangs beneath my little belt: may God curse the one who made me a nun!

Other literary nuns, like the nun Dame Peronelle in William Langland's *Piers Plowman*, who could not serve as prioress because she once 'had a child in cherry time', succumbed to such temptation. Nor were these examples wholly based on fantasy. The bishops' registers – which contain the court cases of nuns whose sins were exposed – abound with stories of nuns who gave in to the lure of local priests and confessors, or who eloped to live with secular men, in flagrant violation of their vows. Whole convents might even be closed down following widespread scandal; the priest John Bale, for example, called St Radegund's Priory in Cambridge 'a community of spiritual harlots' following its dissolution in the fifteenth century. Amesbury itself had also suffered from scandal: its dissolution in the twelfth century (before its royal refoundation by Henry II) was caused, at least in part, by rumours that its abbess had given birth to three children and that its nuns were notorious fornicators. In Mary's day there were no such accusations levelled at her priory, and any liaison with John de Warenne would have been much more likely to occur during her frequent and lengthy periods of residence at court, when there would have been more opportunity for the courtly youth and the older princess-nun to fall into sin. Mary's reckless extravagance and blatant disregard for her vow of poverty may well have been matched by a willingness to ignore her vow of chastity, and it is easy to imagine that a princess so frequently at court might have wished, like the nun in the *chanson*, to experience – if only fleetingly – love's 'delightful ways', and to indulge its 'sweet pangs'. Yet John de Warenne sought through several arguments (this claim being just one example) to win a divorce from his unhappy wife. The couple were estranged within only a few short years after their marriage and, given her young age, well before they might have lived as husband and wife in the full sense. To make such a bold claim about a bride of Christ and the daughter of a king – especially if it was untrue – might have been dangerous for the earl, but since John's divorce from Joanna of Bar was never granted, it seems that little credence was given to his assertion of an affair with Mary.[14]

As the autumn of 1305 approached, Mary and the two little princes left their summer lodgings at Ludgershall and travelled to Reading Abbey, where they made offerings before its relics that included the hand of St James the Greater (one of Jesus's twelve Apostles, and therefore a hand that had literally touched Christ), and at nearby Caversham they visited the holy well of St Anne, the waters of which were thought to possess sacred healing properties. By the time they turned back towards Westminster in November, they had been travelling together for more than two months, and the travel-weary nun could have been forgiven for longing for the peace of her chamber at Amesbury, with its blazing hearth, sumptuous furnishings, and small library, with only liturgical songs or occasional appearances by her Clare nieces to disturb her. But Mary's travels were far from complete. At Westminster, she was reunited with Marguerite. The women would spend the next several months perambulating together throughout southern and middle England, from their principal abode at Winchester Castle – comfortably refurbished following a fire in 1302 that nearly claimed the lives of Marguerite and Edward – to the lodge at Clipstone and as far north as Doncaster in Yorkshire.

Early the following year they were joined by Mary's youngest sister, who had given birth to another boy the previous autumn. While her family was growing again, some of the old challenges remained. After many years of trying, Elizabeth still had not succeeded in claiming the large dower she was due as widow of the Count of Holland. Every spring, faithfully, Gerald de Freney returned to Holland to argue before administrators of the Count of Hainaut (who held Holland after the death of Elizabeth's first husband). His efforts were often supplemented with separate embassies made by various clerks and yeomen from the countess's household, which at times also included visits to nearby provinces, including Brabant.[15]

Despite these appeals, the eight thousand *livres Tournois* (roughly two thousand pounds) which had been promised to her as annual income was not released, and Elizabeth could rely only on the Bohun estate she held jointly with Humphrey. Helpfully, her father agreed to forgive a large debt of four thousand pounds that had been owing following the death of Humphrey's father. In 1306, he further enhanced his daughter's income by granting the couple the province of Annandale, on the southern Scottish coast near Carlisle, which was considered forfeited through the rebellion of its Scottish lord. In the same year, Edward also enriched Joanna by granting Ralph the Earldom of Atholl, in the Scottish Highlands, which had been taken into Edward's control after the capture and execution of its lord, who joined the 1306 rebellion. Despite the wealth of Joanna's Clare estates, her expenditure was such that the additional income from this land would have been very welcome – only the year before, her father had helped to ease her situation by forgiving 340 pounds' worth of loans he had advanced her.[16]

Near the end of Edward's reign, the king's daughters began personally to profit from their father's war in Scotland. As members of the royal family and noblewomen accustomed to the norms of feudal society, they are unlikely to have questioned the morality of their own income being supplemented by the estates of those conquered by their father.

XVI
The Storm Approaches

1305–6
WINDSOR, WESTMINSTER

The year of 1305 was Edward's thirty-third on the English throne, and though he was sixty-six, the king remained strong in body and will – indeed, his determination to impose his rule over Britain would soon be shown to be as fierce as ever. Even so, his four daughters could not have failed by this time to have begun planning for life after his reign. Principally, this meant looking to secure good relationships with their brother, who at twenty-one had recently been granted large estates to manage, with the assistance of dozens of knights and clerks on the ground in each locality. Edward of Caernarfon was now Prince of Wales, Earl of Chester, and Count of Ponthieu, his mother's province – these extensive lands provided him with a suitable income and also the opportunity to practise governing before the whole of England fell under his command. His role was to keep an eye on income and expenditure, and to use his authority to inspire loyalty and to keep unruly or troublesome lords in check – essential skills for a successful king. Around him, even in peacetime, was a household of two hundred courtiers and servants, including by this time a circle of close friends – many of them former royal wards and other childhood acquaintances – to whom the prince had a strong attachment that was already proving worrisome to some. According to the chronicler Ranulf Higden, Prince Edward preferred the rough labours of the countryside – digging ditches and thatching – and the company of sailors and craftsmen, to the genteel pursuits of the hunt and the tournament. He was uncontrolled in his speech and his behaviour, speaking crudely, lashing out, and prone to overly lavish expenditure. Worst of all for a future king, he failed to exercise his own judgment, instead being easily controlled by the most charismatic of his friends.[1]

In the middle of June that year, the Prince had an altercation with Walter Langton, Bishop of Coventry and Lichfield, the king's Treasurer, and one of his most senior advisors. Langton had been a loyal servant to the Crown for more than a decade and served as Keeper of the Wardrobe throughout the early 1290s; he would have known the prince since boyhood, and it was perhaps this familiarity that he felt gave him licence to reprimand Prince Edward for his behaviour and his company. The prince responded with caustic fury; his precise words are unrecorded, but his father's reaction is well attested; the king, livid at his son's disrespect, was determined to teach him a lesson. He banished the prince from his presence, disbanded the detested gang of courtiers, and cut Edward off financially. A few weeks later, the prince was sent to Windsor Castle and ordered to remain there, with only two servants chosen for his company and the most meagre of allowances to enable him to eat. King

Edward was aiming to chasten his heir, to shape his behaviour while he could, and to remove him from the negative influence of his friends, including the Gascon courtier Piers Gaveston, who the year before had been enriched with the guardianship of a royal ward at the behest of the prince. For young Edward, stripped of his household, his substantial income, and his close companions, it must have been a bitter blow, but he was powerless to change the situation as long as his father remained angry and alive – for surely none would dare to defy the king.

Almost no one did, but early in July a messenger arrived at court with a letter bemoaning the king's harsh treatment of his son and containing the seal of a great lord whose whole estate and purse had been placed at the hands of Prince Edward to procure whatever he needed. The act unambiguously sought to remedy the prince's position, in direct confrontation with the king's wishes. This bold gesture of open defiance could only have come from one of his subjects: his daughter, Joanna. Ever-ready to stand firm and without fear against her father, Joanna's audacity in sending her seal to her brother shocked even the prince. He replied by letter to Ralph, offering assurance that his situation was not as dire as rumour suggested, and explaining that he did not suffer from any want. This, however, was not sufficient to distance himself from Joanna's act of defiance, and the prince was careful to ensure he did not incur any additional wrath from their father. To that end, he gathered a group of knights in the private chamber of the Archbishop of Canterbury at Lambeth Palace, to witness him dictate a formal deed in Latin, returning the seal to his sister, citing it as unnecessary, since their father provided for his sustenance. Joanna was not cowed, sending her own messenger back to tell Edward he should come and stay with her; he did not possess her unique readiness boldly to disobey their father's orders, and politely declined.[2]

Mary and Elizabeth also rose to their brother's defence, as did their stepmother, though in less dramatic ways than Joanna. Mary first gained the permission of her father, before writing to suggest that her brother spend time at her comfortable apartments in Amesbury. As one of the king's principal motives was to separate his son from the influence and company of his male favourites, an interlude within the walls of a nunnery would prove effective. Elizabeth, residing often at court with the king and queen, also wrote to her brother. She may have been involved with the queen's request late in July that Edward lift the harshest aspects of his son's punishment, including a ban the king placed on lenders in London from providing money to the prince. Writing from Windsor in early August, Prince Edward replied to his sister that he was well, but would be better if their father allowed Piers Gaveston and another close friend to join him at Windsor – and asked their stepmother Marguerite to pass the request to the king. The form of this letter provides a clear indication of the deep and apparent intimacy that had formed between Elizabeth and Marguerite, and also demonstrates Prince Edward's understanding of the role that female intercession might play, even within families. While he did not dare ask his father to reinstate his favourites directly, he felt able both to appeal to his stepmother (which he did, directly, two days later in another letter), and to ask for the help of his sister, the queen's companion and confidante. With the help of his sister and stepmother, by autumn the prince was forgiven and returned to court. Gaveston, however, remained out of favour for several months longer.[3]

Undoubtedly the months before he returned to the king's graces were uncomfortable for Prince Edward, who had learned he must bide his time as long as the old king lived. As for his sisters, the situation was far from straightforward – aiding their brother in his time of need might strengthen a bond with him as the future king, but alienating their father would be unwise. Mary was, of course, utterly reliant on her father's generosity to maintain her lifestyle, and Elizabeth's proximity to the king and queen may have checked any impulses she felt to defend her brother directly, so each focused their efforts on conventional intercession and made any offers to help only after checking with their father first. Only Joanna's actions fell outside the boundaries of sanctioned behaviour – the gift of her seal presented an alternative financial dependency to her brother that threatened to undermine the lesson the king sought to teach him. She was able to make her bold offer not only because she remained throughout life unawed by her father's position, but also because she had the independent means and lifestyle to withstand a degree of royal anger. Her father had seemingly learned to tolerate his daughter's independent frame of mind – there is no evidence of friction between the king and the countess, who joined court for Christmas that year and received a golden clasp studded with emeralds from him as a new year's gift.[4]

Early in 1306, while the family were gathered at court, news arrived that rebellion had broken out again in Scotland, and the king once more rallied his son and his men for war in the north. In March, a Scottish nobleman who had previously pledged his allegiance to Edward dared to allow himself to be crowned king of an independent Scotland at Scone. His name was Robert Bruce – the Earl of Carrick in the ancient kingdom of Galloway and Lord of Annandale near the border with north-west England. For King Edward's daughters and their stepmother, this fresh outbreak of war meant their husbands left for the north once again – that summer the king's armies, captained by Humphrey de Bohun and Ralph de Monthermer, met the enemy with a vengeance. The conventions of gentlemanly warfare – by which local populations might be mercilessly slaughtered, but captured nobles were allowed to purchase their freedom through ransom payments – were swept aside, in a manner suggesting that the English noblemen had tired of incessant war and were determined to crush the rebellion once and for all. King Robert's own brother, Neil, and other Scottish nobles were executed without the traditional recourse of ransom, such as that which had ultimately freed Henri of Bar after his captivity in France. Nor were the usual modes of intercession given credence: when Queen Marguerite and others pleaded with Edward to spare John de Strathbogie, the Earl of Atholl, on account of his status, the king reportedly replied he should merely be hanged higher than the others.[5]

Far to the south, Elizabeth and Joanna knew about Scotland from their previous journeys there, and about the nature of war from their experiences during rebellions in Holland and Glamorgan, as well as from witnessing the siege at Stirling Castle. As they awaited messengers from the north, news also arrived from Brabant, where tensions had been simmering for years between the weavers, whose skilled labour was enriching the Low Countries, and the patrician merchant class who were enriched by it. That spring, the weavers of Brussels rose in revolt, ransacking the townhouses of the duchy's most prosperous merchants, and threatening the great ducal palace that was perched at the top of Coudenberg, the hill overlooking the city, and where Margaret was in residence. According to a Brabaçon annalist, rather than flee the rampaging crowds, the duchess appeared before the weavers, urging them to disband and return to their homes and workshops. It is not known exactly what she said, but her words and the sturdy walls of the fortress were enough to keep the mob at bay, and when Jan returned from a hunting expedition at Tervuren, he and his men chased the rebels from the city and reconfirmed the privileges of the patrician merchant class.[6]

Given the real dangers that Joanna, Elizabeth, and Margaret had been exposed to on account of their position as noble ladies, it is impossible not to wonder what these princesses made of their father's treatment of Robert Bruce's wife, daughter, and sister – their counterparts in Scotland – who were caught up in the hostilities of 1306. They had taken refuge at Kildrummy Castle, one of the great strongholds of Scotland, which was wrapped within a tall curtain wall and set against a deep ravine. The ladies were under the protection of King Robert's brother, Neil, when the fortress was besieged by Prince Edward's army, under the command of Humphrey de Bohun. The ladies escaped (with the unfortunate Earl of Atholl, hanged 'higher than the rest', as their escort) before the siege broke, and fled north to Tain in the Highlands, where by local tradition they claimed sanctuary in the chapel of St Duthac. However, any notion of sanctuary was ignored, and they were soon handed over to the English. Robert's queen, Elizabeth de Burgh, was the daughter of one of Edward's staunchest Irish allies and had close links to the English court, which may have ameliorated her treatment. She, her young stepdaughter, and one of her sisters-in-law, would spend the next eight years imprisoned, albeit in relative comfort, at various castles and convents in England, until they were released in 1314 as part of a prisoner exchange of English lords taken captive at the Battle of Bannockburn. The imprisonment of the Scottish royal ladies cannot but have served once again to remind Joanna, Mary, and Elizabeth of the danger they would face as representatives of the English royal family, should their own father or brother be overthrown. Special horror awaited Robert's youngest sister Mary, at twenty-one an exact contemporary of Elizabeth, who was taken to Roxburgh Castle near the border with England, and kept inside a cage that was probably outdoors or exposed to the elements, where her punishment could be observed by passing Scots and serve as a reminder of the power of the English king.[7]

One other Scottish noblewoman shared Mary Bruce's fate: Isabella MacDuff, the daughter of the Earl of Fife and one of Earl Gilbert's two disinherited daughters with Alice Lusignan. Isabella had boldly claimed, on behalf of her brother (a minor residing at Edward's court in England), the Earl of Fife's traditional ceremonial privilege of crowning the new King of Scotland. When she learned of the plan to crown Robert, she travelled to Scone, but arrived the day after the ceremony, which had therefore to be repeated. Her husband, one of King Robert's greatest foes among the Scottish nobility and a supporter of the English king, reputedly wished his wife dead on learning that she had personally placed the crown on the head of his enemy. As the only member of the MacDuff family who was able to exercise their historic right, Isabella faced a dilemma – and she sided ultimately with preserving the privileges of the earls of Fife, to great personal cost. For her temerity, Edward ordered that she waste away, in a cage in the shape of a crown, placed outside the border town of Berwick-upon-Tweed; there she languished, for all to see, through four cold Scottish winters, before being transferred to more humane conditions. Her disappearance from the records soon after her transfer suggests she likely died from the effects of her long-term torture. Even while she was his prisoner-on-display, the English king arranged a marriage between Isabella's brother and his granddaughter, Mary de Monthermer. How galling it must have been for Isabella that the woman responsible for her mother's disinheritance – Joanna of Acre – would also claim for her progeny the proud Earldom of Fife, Scotland's most prestigious noble lineage.

During the eight years that the Scottish women languished in various prisons – convents, castles, and cages – there is no record that Edward's wife or any of his daughters sought to intercede or plead for clemency on their behalf, despite their regular efforts to secure pardons for those implicated in serious crimes, including murder. Perhaps the parallels between them and their Scottish counterparts were too upsetting for the princesses of England to contemplate, or perhaps they did attempt to argue with their father and were rebuffed. A further possibility, however, was that none of the English royal ladies desired or tried to intercede on behalf of their Scottish counterparts because they felt little solidarity with them, despite the obvious parallels in their lives. For royal women in the age of chivalry, identity was ultimately wrapped up in family rather than gender, and if they felt little sympathy with Isabella MacDuff and Mary Bruce, it was because those women were the enemies of their father, of their family, and of England. Perhaps they felt the Scottish women deserved what they got.

At Winchester in the spring of 1306, Elizabeth, Mary, and Marguerite were joined by two young relatives, each of whom was on the cusp of marriage: Joanna of Bar and Eleanor de Clare. Joanna was the only daughter of the late Princess Eleanora and Count Henri of Bar. She had arrived in her mother's homeland for the first time in the autumn of 1305, aged about ten – considerably younger than any of her aunts when they had travelled abroad – in preparation for her marriage to a young English nobleman. Her grandmother, Eleanor of Castile, would have been horrified at the prospect of such a young child marrying but, as an orphan, Joanna of Bar had few advocates to argue on her behalf, and none who could outrank her grandfather and guardian, the King of England. For his part, Edward undoubtedly intended to do his best by his granddaughter in bringing her to live with his wife and securing her marriage into one of the English nobility's foremost families. Weeks before her wedding, the king also sought to secure the future of her brother, finalizing a prestigious marriage and helping him recover his patrimony from the French king; clearly the future of his grandchildren weighed heavily on Edward's mind.[8]

The second niece was Eleanor de Clare, the eldest daughter of Joanna of Acre by her first husband, Gilbert. Eleanor was thirteen in 1306 and knew her aunt Mary well, having spent at least part of her childhood under her tutelage at Amesbury. Edward doted on his granddaughter, buying her a robe of costly deep-green silk, imported from Tripoli in Lebanon, and providing her with a dowry of two thousand pounds. Her bridegroom was to be Hugh le Despenser (remembered as 'the Younger'), the son of the Earl of Winchester. Hugh was aged about twenty and was a close friend of Prince Edward – he would soon be knighted alongside the prince. Hugh's connections meant it was an excellent match. As plans for the two weddings progressed, none could have foreseen the unhappiness that awaited Joanna in her marriage to John de Warenne, nor how Eleanor's husband would tear apart her family and play a leading role in the tragic downfall of her uncle's reign.[9]

The women were at Winchester on 6 May, when Marguerite gave birth to a baby girl. The new princess was given the name Eleanor – a perhaps surprising gesture in honour of the king's first wife, as well as his mother and eldest daughter. Within three weeks after the child's birth, and after far fewer than the forty days traditionally granted new mothers to recover before travelling, Marguerite and her friends were required back at court in Westminster. There they were met by Joanna, who had travelled to court to see her daughter get married to Hugh le Despenser. Her fifteen-year-old son Gilbert most likely accompanied her, interrupting his intensive military training, as well as her other daughters, Margaret and Elizabeth. On arrival in Westminster, the royal family found that court was filled with carpenters and food deliveries, as the final preparations were being made for the knighting of Prince Edward. The prince had turned twenty-two in late April, and in celebration of this birthday his knighting ceremony was to be held on 22 May – Whitsuntide, or the great Christian feast of Pentecost. It was not only his age that meant it was time to knight the prince but, for the king, the ceremony also brought the opportunity to levy another tax – guaranteed by Magna Carta – needed to support the renewed war in Scotland. By the end of the following year, 26,500 pounds had been raised in support of the prince's knighting ceremony. Counting on some of these funds, and keen to gather a body of warriors who would be loyal to his son, the king proclaimed that all young men of sufficient age wishing to obtain a knighthood, and possessing sufficient income to fund the expensive enterprise, were to travel to Westminster to be knighted at royal expense, alongside their future king. Nearly three hundred young men answered the summons, so many that overflow housing had to be provided at the compound of the Knights Templar, on the River Thames between Westminster and London. Fruit trees and courtyard walls were pulled down at the Temple to accommodate a field of colourful tents, where the young nobility of England slept and ate in the days leading up to the feast. There, and back at the royal Palace of Westminster where the royal women were staying, enormous quantities of meats and bread were delivered, and pavilions and scaffolding were erected to stage the celebrations.[10]

In the midst of these preparations – with the carpenters' hammering outside only dulled by the great thickness of the abbey walls – Joanna of Bar married John de Warenne before an altar spread with glittering cloths-of-gold. Minstrels hired by the king entertained the bridal party, which included the bride's aunts and cousins, as well as the king and queen. For Joanna of Acre, the ceremony must have sparked memories of her own wedding to Gilbert de Clare in the same place sixteen years earlier. But, while the countess had been eighteen on her first marriage, her niece was only ten or eleven – so far beneath the age of canonical consent that consummation may not have taken place immediately after the wedding. Certainly, on the second night of her married life, the bride slept back in the royal household, with her aunts and her cousins. In the years ahead, as she negotiated a difficult marriage, Joanna of Bar would spend much of her time living primarily with her mother's sisters – most particularly with her aunt Elizabeth – and it seems that this initial period together was one of intense bonding between the women.

On the night of 21 May, the eve of Pentecost, Joanna of Bar's new husband was among the companions of her uncle Prince Edward as the mass ceremony of knighthood – so heavily ritualized as to be almost a sacrament – began. According to an early-fourteenth-century description of the ceremony, presumptive knights-to-be ritually bathed in rose water on the eve of their knighthood, the bath symbolizing a new baptism and the rose water serving as a link to the purity of the Virgin Mary. They dressed simply and spent the night in silent, prayerful vigil in church, hearing Mass the following morning. In late

May 1306, a large contingent of the hundreds of young squires would have knelt huddled under the circular dome of Temple Church, visions of crusading glory doubtless filling their heads, but Prince Edward and his closest friends remained at Westminster Abbey. He stayed close to the spot where his father had been crowned, near the shrine of their great forebear and namesake, Edward the Confessor, and among the gilded effigies of his mother and kingly grandfather. Also surrounding him were the memorials to the siblings he had never known – all those princes who would have had his place in the line of kings if only they had lived – and to his sister Eleanora, who must have seemed almost like a mother to him during their years together at Langley in the 1280s. The prince's brothers-in-law, Ralph de Monthermer and Humphrey de Bohun, were most likely present for at least part of the vigil, and Humphrey's attention could hardly have failed to be drawn towards the grave of his own son and eldest daughter, so recently interred in the chapel of St Thomas just to the north of the high altar. Yet the evening was not all solemn contemplation: according to one chronicle, the monks struggled to sing the overnight offices, unable to hear each other's chants over the noisy chatter of the prince and his company.[11]

The following morning, the prince walked across the broad court that separated the abbey from the royal palace. Inside the palace chapel – overlooked by brilliantly colourful murals showing scenes from the Old Testament, and knights and kings kneeling before the Madonna and Child – he heard Mass. By tradition, he would have been given the *collée*, a light ritual blow, taken vows of fidelity to his lord and father, and promised to protect the weak and faithful, praying that God might bless his knighthood. As Prince Edward stood, his father, the king, girded him with the sword belt that represented his new status.

Humphrey de Bohun, the husband of his closest sister, was chosen to stand beside the prince as a sponsor and fasten one of the new knight's golden spurs. After his formal vesting, Sir Edward – now armed with his sword and wearing spurs of gold – walked with his companions back across the court to the abbey and there he stood in the place of the king, personally girding with the belt of knighthood all the young noblemen who had come to share his day, although his closest friend Piers Gaveston was denied the honour of participating (and was instead knighted a few days later). Inside the great church, the clamour of trumpets and the excitement of the crowd were so great that enormous warhorses, the great beasts used for battle, were required to clear a path for Prince Edward to make his way to the high altar.

Joanna, Elizabeth, Mary, and Marguerite were most likely not present at the knighting ceremony itself. Even in romance stories, the ceremony that created a knight was an exclusively male ritual: though the princess Rimenhild, the heroine of *King Horn*, arranges for her lover to receive a knighthood, she is forbidden from witnessing the ceremony itself. Women were, however, participants at the feasts which followed knighthood ceremonies, and the queen, her stepdaughters and step-granddaughters were all present for the celebration that followed. After many hours of watching swords girded and spurs affixed, and of listening to triumphal fanfares, the guests made their way into the great hall while eighty minstrels entered to serenade the company. The climax of the feast was a display so theatrical it seems lifted from fiction: before the assembled guests, two live swans were presented to the king, who stood and vowed solemnly to bring down Robert Bruce and after that only to draw a sword on Crusade. After these words, the prince and then all the new knights stood and each vowed to the majestic white birds that they would bring Scotland to heel. The pledging of oaths at a feast is a frequent scene in the stories of the Round Table at Camelot. The swans – after which the event is remembered as the Feast of the Swans – gestured toward another popular romance that interwove aristocratic lineage and the glory of the Crusades: *The Swan Knight,* whose eponymous and courtly hero was purportedly an ancestor of the first Christian King of Jerusalem. As ever, King Edward was a master at deploying chivalric cultural themes to draw parallels between his court and romanticized visions of history. With his son's knighting feast, he also sought to pass his own ambition for a renewed Crusade down to the next generation of noble warriors. Contemporary chroniclers were quick to draw parallels between the Feast of the Swans and the court of Britain's most perfect Christian king, Arthur: the chronicler Peter Langtoft asserted that nothing so splendid had been seen in Britain since Arthur's own coronation at Caerleon. For Edward's daughters, who had grown up participating in their father's chivalric showpieces and often showed themselves adept at deploying theatricality for their own ends, this was nothing new. As royal women, they likely sat centrally within the Hall, and they may even have participated in the performance.[12]

In the days that followed, additional noble weddings took place at Westminster, including that of Joanna's thirteen-year-old daughter, Eleanor de Clare, and more knights were girded by the prince. But war in Scotland still beckoned, and by the end of May the king and his men had were heading north once again. As his armies travelled under the nominal command of his son, the king's progress was slowed to a frustrating pace by illness – his decline was increasingly apparent, and unavoidable. The need for his daughters and wife to plan for a future without him was growing by the day. By August, the queen's position was secured: at the end of that month, with his progress towards

Carlisle grinding to a halt at the northern tip of the Pennines, Edward granted Margaret's young sons lands and rents worth ten thousand marks each year and her infant daughter, Eleanor, a dowry of ten thousand marks with a further five thousand set aside to build a trousseau worthy of an English princess.[13]

As the summer progressed, the three princesses left court: Joanna returned to her estates, while Mary headed north-east. She travelled in a litter and was accompanied by a train of minstrels to provide her entertainment as she embarked on a lengthy pilgrimage of thanksgiving to Bury St Edmunds and Walsingham, where she offered alms and prayers of thanks on behalf of her stepmother for the safe delivery of baby Eleanor. Elizabeth travelled north to Scotland, to Lochmaben Castle in Annandale, formally granted to her and Humphrey in April that year, but only captured by her husband from forces still loyal to Robert Bruce on 11 July. She arrived at the castle, which was perched on top of a motte, on a promontory that jutted beautifully out into a serene, arrow-shaped lake renowned for its fisheries, at its most glorious season. It was a time of calm for Elizabeth, but the clouds were gathering on the horizon.[14]

XVII
Death Returns

1307

CLARE, NORTHAMPTON

The old king never made it to Scotland for the summer campaign in 1306. And despite some successes, in the absence of the king, the army nominally commanded by Prince Edward failed to draw out and defeat Robert Bruce. By October, Edward had made it as far as Lanercost Priory in Cumbria, but he languished there all through the winter and into the following year, restrained by aching legs and a bad neck, suffering from dysentery, and unable to travel even the short distance to Carlisle, where Parliament had been summoned for January. His doctors sought cures and emoluments – potion-like cordials, and sugared lozenges made of gemstones and other rare and expensive ingredients that had been ground to powder, including amber, pearls, musk, jacinth, coral, gold and silver, rose water imported from Damascus, and pomegranate wine – but Edward was not fit enough to travel until 4 March 1307. In the intervening time his men realized that the king's days were numbered, and his command began to waver: in October, his son-in-law Humphrey de Bohun departed Scotland, without authorized leave, in the company of several young members of Prince Edward's household, including Piers Gaveston. To add insult to injury, the knights were reported to be intent on displaying their martial skills in a tournament, despite the king's prohibition on their participation in such activities during wartime, when he most required his men to be fit and healthy. Edward was furious at this act of desertion and immediately ordered the men to be arrested and all their lands, goods, and chattels confiscated by the Crown. This act not only cast Elizabeth's husband as an outlaw, but also stripped her of the estate she held jointly with him. Late in 1306, therefore, Elizabeth experienced the acute anxiety familiar to her sister Joanna when their father had seized her estates after her secret marriage to Ralph Monthermer. Luckily for Elizabeth, Marguerite was soon able to convince her husband to forgive the men and restore their estates. Within three weeks of this reprieve, Humphrey was once again proving his loyalty in the field, this time around Ayr on the west coast, leading a contingent of men against Scottish forces loyal to Robert Bruce. In this campaign, Humphrey was joined by Joanna's husband Ralph, recently elevated to the Earldom of Atholl. The effort to rout and defeat the Scots did not seem to be going well, since on 11 February the king wrote, clearly frustrated, to chide his sons-in-law for their failure to report progress.[1]

Nor did King Edward's mood improve once he had arrived at Carlisle. Late in February at Lanercost, in a scene recorded by the chronicler Walter of Guisborough, Prince Edward, newly enriched through possession of the great Duchy of Aquitaine, approached his father, desiring to grant the County of Ponthieu (which he had inherited from his mother on her death in 1290) to Piers Gaveston. The king's rage was enough to overcome his lingering weakness: he lunged at his son, ripping out handfuls of his hair, and shouting,

> You base-born whoreson, do you want to give away lands now, you who never gained any? As the Lord lives, if it were not for fear of breaking up the kingdom, you should never enjoy your inheritance.

As he contemplated his own end, King Edward could not have made his feelings clearer about the son whom custom dictated would succeed him. With the damning words ringing in his ears, the prince was chased from his father's presence, and Gaveston was banished to Gascony, paid off with an annuity of one hundred marks from the Crown – a paltry sum compared to the county his friend had wished to bestow on him.[2]

Far to the south of the battlefields around Ayr and secluded from the drama enveloping the king's son, spring arrived at the gardens of Clare Castle. With her eldest daughter now married, Joanna seems to have turned her mind to securing matches for her heir Gilbert and his two Clare sisters, who remained unmarried. A double wedding was planned for the following year between Joanna's children and the son and daughter of the Earl of Ulster in Ireland, siblings to Robert Bruce's imprisoned wife, Elizabeth. The eldest Monthermer daughter, Mary, was also married during that year to Duncan, the young Earl of Fife, whose elder sister still languished in the cage outside Berwick for having crowned King Robert. Her sister Joanna de Monthermer likely resided at Amesbury by this date, where she would eventually become a nun. Ralph's boys, Thomas and Edward, were aged five and two, and still young enough to remain within their mother's household. Whether or not the young children were with her in April 1307 is unrecorded, when, without warning or expectation, Joanna died suddenly on the twenty-third of the month. The cause of her death is unknown; she was only thirty-five, no indications of long-term illness are apparent from family letters or charters, and nor were medicines purchased on her behalf during her stay at court during the previous summer. In January of that year, she had sent a minstrel in her employment to Wetheral Priory in Cumbria, to entertain her brother's household during the long wait for their father's health to improve sufficiently for Parliament to commence. Near the end of March, she and Ralph were engaged in the business of searching through their estate records and finding where ancient rights might allow them to leverage more money. Then, suddenly, she was dead. She possibly succumbed to a rapid fever or fell from a horse, but her easy fertility coupled with the regularity of her many pregnancies (with a new child arriving every two or three years) suggests rather that Joanna might have been carrying her ninth child and had died from complications following a premature labour or miscarriage.[3]

The death of the king's most obstinate and audacious daughter was shocking. Her father, far to the north at Carlisle, learned of it only nine days later, on 1 May. The king, forced to face his own impending mortality, was clearly shaken by the loss of his eldest living child, who had seemed in her prime. That day, he wrote to the Chancellor, Bishop of London Ralph Baldock, to demand that 'as Joanna, our dear daughter . . . was commanded to go to God,' Bishop Ralph should require all priests within the realm, including archbishops and bishops, abbots and priors, as well as those at cathedral chapters, colleges, universities, and Dominican and Franciscan friaries to perform funeral rites and solemn Masses, and offer private prayers for Joanna's soul. On the next day, and the two that followed, he travelled into Carlisle and listened as the friars of the Franciscan house sang Masses for her soul. Unappeased, and perhaps especially anxious, given how Joanna's strident independence of thought was misaligned with conventional female virtues, on the sixth he wrote to all bishops, as well as the Archbishop of Canterbury and the abbots of Westminster, Waltham, St Albans, St Augustine's Canterbury, and Evesham, requesting further prayers:

> Since it is considered a pious and worthwhile task to pray for the dead, that they may be freed more easily from sin, and God has called Joanna our dearest daughter to himself from this life, which news I deliver with a bitter heart; we pray that you will encourage all priests and religious persons and subjects within your cities and dioceses to commend her soul to God through the chanting of masses and other pious works.

Frustratingly for a man of action, issuing demands that priests pray for the soul of his child was all the king could do.[4]

In his infirmity, despite his evident grief, Edward could not travel south to Clare to lead the funerary rites for his child. Nor was her husband, Ralph – the man for whose love Joanna had risked everything – able to attend his wife's funeral. He may not even have learned of her death until later that month since, soon after the news arrived in the north, Ralph's army was defeated by Robert Bruce, and he and his companions were forced to retreat to Ayr Castle, where they were besieged, until the king's forces arrived to chase off the Scots. Instead of her father or her beloved husband, therefore, Joanna's brother Prince Edward was chosen to represent the family at her funeral. Given her staunch defence of her youngest sibling during his quarrels with their father, she would likely have approved the choice, but the prince's participation was mostly a practical decision. He was already far to the south on 5 May, escorting Gaveston to his ship at Dover, lavishing him to the end with expensive presents such as silk tunics and tapestries, when he would have learned of his sister's death and his expected role in her burial. In the days after bidding farewell to his friend, the prince oversaw the transfer of his sister's body from her castle, across the River Stour and to the Chapel of St Vincent in the nearby priory of Clare, which she had established. According to a chronicle written at Little Dunmow Priory, only twenty miles south of Clare, Prince Edward was attended at Joanna's funeral by 'all the magnates of England', but this must surely be an exaggeration, since most of the kingdom's great men were at that time attending the king at Carlisle or engaged in battle even further north. Elizabeth's castle at Pleshey was only twenty-six miles away from Clare, but though she felt Joanna's death keenly enough to commit the anniversary to her calendar, she was at Lochmaben in Scotland, and heavily pregnant. Her brother therefore travelled alone after the funeral to his favourite home at Langley, which he had first shared with his sisters; he spent several days there, no doubt full of emotion after the loss of his friend to exile and his sibling and strident defender to death.[5]

Other than committing her body to burial at Clare Priory, nothing is known of Joanna's wishes in death; no will has survived to record which of her dresses or jewels she might have bequeathed to sisters or daughters, or which special friends were picked out to receive furnishings or books. No letter remains to attest how her sisters reacted on hearing the news, although Mary soon afterward left Amesbury once again, seeking the company of her stepmother at Northampton. Because she was a great lord, however, the business of dividing Joanna's estate is attested in the historical record in documents, and these demonstrate a clear distinction between the grief her father experienced at his child's death and the reality of managing the transfer of a large estate. Nowhere is this distinction more apparent than in the king's first action after Joanna's lands had been taken into the Crown's possession. After more than a decade of constant warfare, Edward struggled to keep his armies replenished with fresh recruits, and the vacancy of the Earldom of Gloucester – unfilled after Joanna's death because of the minority of her son Gilbert – presented an opportunity not to be dismissed. The king directed his sheriffs to select five hundred men from her Glamorgan estates and to send them to Carlisle 'ready to set forth against the Scots, the king being in want of men to pursue Robert Bruce and his accomplices'. Without emotion, he resupplied his army by forcibly drafting the most able-bodied labourers from his daughter's Marcher dominion, at a time when none could stop him.[6]

After the men were called up, the estates were resettled in a manner that displays a mix of emotional and practical response. Since Joanna's eldest child and heir, Gilbert, was only sixteen at the time of his mother's death, he was unable to perform the homage required to possess the great Clare estates. The Clare lands therefore required a custodian. The king granted Joanna's ever-impoverished sister, Mary, possession of two manors from the estate for the duration of her nephew's minority, an influx of cash over five years that was clearly intended to help the nun pay off her spiralling debts and learn to live within more constrained means. Edward may also have hoped the transfer would encourage Mary to often remember her sister in prayer; as a virgin dedicated to Christ, Mary's prayers would have been seen to have special value in speeding her sister's soul to heaven. Ralph, Joanna's widower – by this time freed from the siege at Ayr Castle – was entrusted with many of the remaining lands, including all those in Glamorgan, whose men he had captained at Carlisle. Ralph was probably chosen as a trustworthy guardian of his stepson's estate: since his own children would not inherit the Clare estate unless all of Gilbert's children were dead, and as he had been stepfather to young Gilbert from the age of five, he was perhaps more likely than other noblemen to guard the estate without seeking to exploit its long-term potential for short-term gain. But his continued possession of parts of the country's largest estate served another purpose for King Edward: Ralph, who had no significant patrimony of his own, needed money to buy a new estate, or else the king's own grandchildren (Joanna's Monthermer children) would be cast into obscurity. Though Ralph had been granted the Earldom of Atholl the year before, King Edward now sought to restore that title and associated lands to the son of the previous earl, who swore fealty in Scotland to the English Crown. A deal was struck in which Ralph surrendered his Scottish earldom for five thousand pounds cash, paid by its new holder, plus an estimated additional five thousand from the Clare estate during Gilbert's minority. The king directed the custodians of the castles at Cardiff, Caerphilly, Newport and Caerleon, Usk, Neath, Llantrissant, and Kenfig to release them to Ralph's men, and forgave his son-in-law any outstanding debts owed by Joanna or Gilbert. Together, these sums were intended to provide Ralph with enough money to purchase a new estate that would produce an income of one thousand marks, or about six hundred and seventy pounds, which he could pass to his and Joanna's children. These negotiations were among the last that King Edward led.[7]

Late in June, while her father enriched her pockets with her late sister's manors, Mary was staying at Northampton Castle with Marguerite and her children. The castle was a favourite of the queen, well-defended with its curtain walls and forbidding keep, and nestled along a meandering river in a landscape that hid little from view. The fortress had also been enhanced by Edward's parents with a comfortable queen's suite that included lower and upper chambers and a private chapel, and therefore amply accommodated Marguerite as well as the royal nursery. Mary's visit was probably timed to coincide with that of her brother Prince Edward, who arrived around 16 June as he lingered in the south after Joanna's funeral, seemingly dreading his return northwards to Carlisle and the disappointed father whose banishment of Gaveston remained bitter to the prince. Mary's appearance at Northampton offered her brother opportunities for reassurance as well as a chance to discuss the loss of their sister. Her death was not to be the last grief they shared that summer.

The prince could not delay rejoining his father forever, despite his good excuse of spending time with his stepmother and siblings but, after her brother's departure, Mary remained with Marguerite and her young children. The queen's eldest son, Thomas, had just celebrated his seventh birthday and was soon to move into a new phase of his education, taught by noblemen and male scholars focused on forging a future lord steeped in the culture of chivalry, with military training paramount, rather than the women in his family who had provided his earliest lessons in reading and arithmetic. His brother, Edmund, not yet six, would soon follow, while their baby sister, Eleanor, who had only just turned one, was probably expected to remain within the royal nursery for several more years, before gradually joining court, as her elder half-sisters had done. But the lives of the youngest royal children were about to be upended: in the first days of July, a messenger arrived from the north, with the news (already several days old) that the king's acute illness had returned and that his men feared his end was near. On learning this news, Mary, Marguerite, and the two young princes set out from Northampton on the fifth, on a pilgrimage to Canterbury and Dover. The party progressed at a pace that must have challenged the children, bumping along inside a carriage or riding pillion with their nurses over long days in which they covered over forty miles. They stopped first before the great shrine of St Thomas Becket at Canterbury, especially revered by the royal family, in part out of lingering guilt at the role their forefather Henry II had played in the archbishop's murder. They then moved on to Dover Priory and the shrine of Thomas Hale, the elderly monk killed by French sailors during a brief invasion in 1295. After making offerings and desperate, pleading prayers, the royal women turned back. It was only on the return journey that another messenger finally caught up with them. Their prayers had been too late: King Edward was dead, having expired on the seventh, as his daughter and wife sped south. Fiercely determined to the last, he had died at Burgh by Sands, a few miles north-west of Carlisle, during one last attempt to reach Scotland, in a futile effort to quash rumours that he was already dead.[8]

The king's household and his treasury kept his death secret until Prince Edward had arrived in Carlisle to receive the homage of the realm's principal magnates on 18 July – and Mary only learned the news so soon after the event because she was with her stepmother when the messenger sent to inform the queen arrived. Marguerite was distraught, and most likely exhausted from their now-futile pilgrimage. Unable to continue riding at the gruelling pace they had maintained for more than a week, she ordered that her sons should quickly return to Northampton Castle – she may have felt anxious about their safety following their father's death. The queen continued to travel more slowly in the same direction, but her stepdaughter Mary turned instead south-west, making her own way back to Amesbury, where she arrived as late as 25 July.

No record survives of the reactions of the king's other daughters, Elizabeth and Margaret, to the news of their father's death, which likely only reached them in late July. The emotional blow would have been greatest for Elizabeth, who had spent most time as an adult in the company of her father and his second wife. After her return from Holland in 1300, Elizabeth seems to have considered court her primary home, even after her marriage to Humphrey de Bohun: the only lengthy periods in which she lived apart from her father were the months of confinement around the birth of her or Marguerite's children, and the few campaigns in Scotland that the women did not accompany. The death of her father would have truly devastated Elizabeth, but for Margaret, the more affecting loss had occurred many years earlier, when she stood with the king at Ipswich before her departure to Brabant and he gifted her a gold ring for remembrance. Though she had visited the English court at Ghent during the failed campaign in 1297 and continued to trade messages with her family back in England, Margaret had not been present with her other siblings to plan and worry during their father's decline. She had not come to love the stepmother who shared her name, or the young siblings whose future seemed suddenly in jeopardy. She had not witnessed the great feasts, or the fights between their father and the brother whom she last saw when he was aged twelve, had not sheltered through cold winters with the English armies in Scotland when horses died for lack of fodder, or shared the fear with her sisters as their husbands rode into battle under the banner of their own dynasty. By 1307 Margaret had long been on the periphery of her family's emotional existence, isolated considerably more than she could have anticipated after Eleanora's early death and Elizabeth's departure from Holland.

What she nevertheless shared with her surviving sisters on the death of their father, was the threat of diminished status.

Each woman had enjoyed special privileges well into adulthood that derived from her filial bond – as 'daughters of the king', Elizabeth, Mary, and Margaret had received exceptional loans and grants of lands, titles, and wardships from a father willing to prioritize the comfort of his children. Under their brother, despite the clear efforts his sisters made to cultivate strong relationships with him, these advantages could not be guaranteed, especially as Prince Edward had already, in seeking to enrich his favourite friends, demonstrated a clear disregard for his family. While their father lived, each woman could rely on gaining an audience with the king and on interceding successfully on behalf of friends, abbesses, and merchants of Holland or Brabant, or rewarding faithful servants by requesting grants of royal office. This special access made the king's daughters even more influential than they would have been by right of their noble husbands' statuses – and for Mary, it was the sole guarantor of her exceptional freedoms. Another important element of Mary and Elizabeth's influence with the king was the friendship they formed with Queen Marguerite, who appears often in charters and letters joining in the requests for clemency or for advancement made by her stepdaughters. The court of Prince Edward included no analogous female presence, and although the prince was betrothed to marry Marguerite's young niece, Isabella of France, she was only twelve and unlikely any time soon to supplant in her husband's affections the young gallants whose opinions shaped his judgments. And history did not favour lasting influence for the sisters of English kings: their father's own sisters had died shortly after his succession to the throne, and while King Edward initially remained close to the brothers-in-law, nieces, and nephews left by his two sisters, the Scottish branch died out and the relationship with his sister's family in Brittany soured during the war with France in the 1290s.

As his daughters were coming to terms with their father's death and the impact it would have on their lives, his body made its way slowly south. From mid-August until late October, the king's body rested inside Waltham Abbey in Essex, almost overlooked by the serene gaze of a statue at the crossroads depicting his first wife, whose own remains had stopped there overnight seventeen years before. On 27 October, before his widow and six of his surviving children – including Mary and Elizabeth – King Edward was interred in a tomb next to his father near the centre of Westminster Abbey, after a funeral ceremony led by his old friend Anthony Bek, Bishop of Durham. For Elizabeth, the ceremony would have conjured memories of her mother's funeral, and her eyes probably flicked more than once to the golden queen who lay atop the tall chest opposite her father's grave. But this funeral also held an important distinction from that of their mother; with Edward's burial, they mourned not only the loss of their father, but of the central figure around which their lives had revolved.

None of the children who saw the king to his grave had been alive when their father was crowned in the same space thirty-five years earlier, but each had lived their entire life surrounded by the aura of Edward's kingship. To his contemporaries – subjects, magnates, and family members – the dead king was close to an ideal ruler, a man whose mastery of chivalric virtues might be compared with that of King Arthur – courageous and strong, loyal to his followers, and faithful to the Church. He had cultivated this image throughout his reign, performing the role of a king as he understood it from the many examples provided to him by romance and epic poetry, by saints' lives and the Old Testament, and constructing at every opportunity tangible parallels with an ancient, united Britain, from the reburial of Arthur and the construction of Caernarfon Castle, to the Round Table at Winchester and the vows proclaimed at his Feast of the Swans. His daughters, having grown up inhabiting roles within this performance – at which their mother, Eleanor of Castile, had also particularly excelled – had long been adept at performing the part of 'daughters of the King of England', presiding in splendid gowns and jewels at major spectacles, piously offering prayers and votives at important shrines, frequently by their father's side. Their public identity – and very likely their self-concept – was constantly being forged and reinforced as children of the monarch, through their participation in the rituals of kingship. After King Edward's funeral, they would need to learn to play new parts.

XVIII
Another Coronation

1308

BOULOGNE, WESTMINSTER

Near the middle of January 1308, Margaret, Duchess of Brabant left Brussels with a large retinue, bound for the ancient port city of Boulogne-sur-Mer on the French coast. With her was Jan, her husband of seventeen years, and likely also her seven-year-old son, the future duke. On their arrival in Boulogne, Margaret and Jan were installed in a house within the city walls, while the bulk of her household joined the growing crowds in the brilliantly coloured tented encampment that was fast springing up outside the city. Despite her age of thirty-three and the many years she had spent living among European courtiers, the duchess can hardly have failed to feel a growing sense of excitement when, on 23 January, news arrived that the English king had at last landed at nearby Wissant and would be in Boulogne the following day. For the first time in eight years,

Margaret was to see a member of her own family – her brother, Edward. If she was disappointed that her surviving sisters, Mary and Elizabeth, had not joined the English delegation accompanying their brother to be married, she at least had the promise of seeing them at Edward's coronation at Westminster the following month. After more than a decade abroad, Margaret was finally going home – but first, Boulogne and the royal wedding. In the eleven years since she had departed England for Brabant, the twelve-year-old little brother she remembered had become a man, who was now to be king. He had travelled to be married to a French princess, further strengthening the always-uneasy peace that had existed between England and France since their father married Marguerite in 1299 – a peace that Margaret must especially have prized, located as Brabant was, so close to French territory and influence.

Crossing the English Channel in the dead of winter made for an unpredictable journey, and Edward of Caernarfon, the not-yet-anointed King of England, was late to arrive for his wedding to the twelve-year-old Princess Isabella. He sailed from Dover on the twenty-second after a week awaiting the right winds. The company of lords that travelled with him included his brother-in-law, Humphrey de Bohun, and his niece's husband, John de Warenne. They had been among the first to be shocked when the new king had unexpectedly and controversially delivered the regency of England to Piers Gaveston in his absence. Among Edward's first acts after his father's death had been to recall Piers from exile and to elevate him to the prestigious Earldom of Cornwall, a noble title normally held by a junior member of the royal family. The earldom had been intended by his father to pass to one of Marguerite's sons, the new king's young half-brothers, and the dowager queen was mortified to find her son's estate so carelessly given away. Compounding this insensitivity, within one week of his father's funeral, Edward further secured his favourite's position by bringing Piers within the royal family itself, by arranging for him to marry the fourteen-year-old, recently orphaned Margaret de Clare (Joanna's second-eldest daughter) at Berkhamsted Castle in Hertfordshire, which was also gifted to the groom. By giving away his niece, despite the plans her mother had already made for her marriage to the heir of Ulster (her younger sister, Elizabeth, was substituted in that match), Edward ensured that Piers' heirs would have royal blood – a notion that scandalized the nobility and would have horrified his father.[1]

Elizabeth attended the wedding at Berkhamsted, where she took the opportunity to appeal to her brother for his help in her continuing battle to access her promised dower from the County of Holland. Many of her nieces and nephews accompanied their aunt to Margaret and Piers' wedding, and they were likely also present at the tournament that followed it at Wallingford, staged by Edward to celebrate his friend's ennoblement and entry into the heart of the royal family; Piers led a band of mostly obscure young knights to victory over the more established earls including Humphrey de Bohun, further fuelling their dislike of him. If, however, late in 1307, Elizabeth had concerns about linking her young niece Margaret's fate to that of Piers Gaveston, neither she nor her husband appear to have voiced them. That autumn, Edward was confident enough in the unquestioning loyalty of his 'dearest sisters' Elizabeth and Mary to reconfirm their right to own all the lands they had held during their father's life, and Humphrey was among the new king's closest circle of advisors.[2]

When Edward and his entourage arrived at Boulogne, they settled into lodgings near Notre Dame, the enormous church that for centuries dominated the city. Named for a miraculous statue of the Virgin Mary that had purportedly been discovered floating mysteriously offshore on an unmanned boat in the seventh century, the medieval church would be pulled down after the French Revolution and reconstructed as a neoclassical basilica. All that survives from the medieval period is an unusually long Romanesque crypt with stout pillars holding up a low ceiling shaped by round archways, but above this heavy underground space had been a delicate Gothic nave and choir with soaring stained-glass windows that cast bright, jewel-coloured light onto those within. On 25 January, that light would have reflected off dozens of gem-encrusted crowns and golden headdresses, as a magnificent assemblage of royalty and nobles from across Europe gathered in their embroidered silks and sumptuous velvet cloaks to witness the union between the royal families of England and France. Aside from the groom, the company included four additional kings: Philippe le Bel, the bride's father and King of France; her eldest brother Louis, already King of Navarre through his deceased mother; Charles II of Sicily, a cousin of both bride and groom; and Albert von Habsburg, King of the Romans and brother of the ill-fated Prince Hartman, to whom Joanna had been betrothed in childhood. There were also three queens (including Marguerite, the groom's stepmother, who was also aunt to the bride), and scores of dukes and duchesses such as Jan and Margaret, counts and countesses from France and Germany, English earls, and assorted political allies and distant cousins drawn from noble families across the continent.

For eight days following the ceremony, guests were entertained at lavish feasts put on by the French and English kings, and opulent gifts were exchanged. During these days and the period of travelling that followed, Margaret met her stepmother Marguerite for the first time. A decade after she had last laid eyes on her father, meeting his grieving widow and the sons in whose faces she could most likely perceive their shared lineage, may have emphasized to Margaret how distanced she was from her own family. Perhaps clinging to the familiar, the duchess spent time with her brother – it seems that the siblings laid down the foundation of a renewed friendship, as they continued to correspond on familiar terms, if infrequently, in the years that followed. Her private reaction to some of Edward's more peculiar behaviours during the marriage celebrations – including his decision to send the luxurious wedding gifts from his new father-in-law to Piers back in England – is impossible to ascertain, but the bond of their shared past may have eased their re-acquaintance, and the small Duchy of Brabant, for a time, kept a friend in the English king. Other guests at the wedding were more vocal in expressing a growing anxiety about the new king's capacity to rule effectively: on 31 January, a group of English barons in attendance at Boulogne signed a charter that, among vague promises to deliver the people from oppression, warned Edward, on pain of excommunication, of the need to preserve the honour of the Crown. Though couched in protestations of loyalty to the new king, the agreement was a coded message that he should moderate his relationship with Piers.[3]

When the wedding festivities had finally drawn to a close, Margaret and Jan joined a distinguished assortment of nobles who rode on poor winter roads to Wissant in a guard of honour to escort Edward and Isabella back to England for their joint coronation. Dozens of carts snaked north, carrying trunks full of the precious jewels and robes of kings, queens, princes, and dukes, not to mention the countless gold and silver vessels and yards of fine linens that comprised Princess Isabella's trousseau. After an uneventful sea journey, the small fleet docked at Dover on 7 February. For Margaret, the scene may have conjured memories of the welcome party she and her siblings had made nineteen years before – bumping along the road from Langley in their freshly cushioned carriage – when their parents landed at Dover after three years in Gascony. The homecoming must have been bittersweet, given the inescapable knowledge that there could be no reunion with those she had been closest to in her childhood, in particular Eleanora and Joanna, the two sisters who for many years had been her constant companions. Margaret may have been emotional as she caught sight of the white cliffs from her ship, and the familiar surroundings and the sound of English chatter from the dockworkers once she had disembarked were further reminders that she was home. Her brother rushed ashore without ceremony, but when Margaret stepped foot on her native soil once again, she was met by her surviving sisters, Mary and Elizabeth.

The nun and the countess had been summoned from their homes to be members of a select party of noble Englishwomen assigned to welcome Isabella, although the chance of a reunion with their sister Margaret may have enticed them to the port city in any event. Everyone hoped the new queen would form the same close bond with her husband's family as her predecessor had done, but Elizabeth seems to have taken particular care to befriend Isabella. Perhaps she did so out of loyalty to her brother, but she also knew intimately from her years in Holland the anxieties that accompanied living as consort in a foreign court, recognizing more intuitively than most the need the young queen would have for allies at court.[4]

As soon as Isabella arrived in England, it became clear to all that she would need friends, for, while the landing at Dover was intended as the first, grand introduction to her new life as Queen of England, she was upstaged from the start: on disembarking, her husband flew to Piers who stood waiting on shore, embracing and kissing him before the whole party, and utterly ignoring his bride, who was forced to present herself to the waiting English nobles unaccompanied. For Elizabeth, perhaps more than for any other witness, her brother's behaviour will have portended danger; Edward's reckless admiration for his friend was increasingly unconstrained, and increasingly reminiscent of Johan of Holland's unthinking, and ultimately disastrous, promotion of the 'traitor' Borsselen. If she felt anxious and personally embarrassed at the way her brother treated his young wife, she soon learned the situation was even worse than she might have guessed. Her husband Humphrey had been among the signatories of the Boulogne agreement and had begun to formally position himself against Piers. Humphrey's participation in this, and his subsequent efforts to chasten Edward into rethinking his partiality to Piers, is strong evidence of the nobility's extreme concern at the king's behaviour.

There is no way to know definitively what part Elizabeth played in her husband's plans to align with other lords against her brother's favourite, but she is likely to have at least supported Humphrey's position. Her experiences in Holland will have given her a unique awareness of the dangers inherent in a young ruler falling too closely under the influence of a favoured courtier, and she may well have voiced these concerns to Humphrey – particularly, perhaps, during the antagonistic aftermath of the tournament at Wallingford. Of her reaction to Piers being vested as Regent of England during her brother's time on the continent, we can surmise that, at the very least, it closely matched the perspective set down by the contemporary author of a *Life of Edward II*: 'What an astonishing thing, he who was lately an exile and outcast from England has now been made governor and keeper of the same land!' It is easy to imagine that Elizabeth and her two surviving sisters would have felt aghast to see such power in the hands of a man who had been so clearly distrusted by their father. Yet they also knew their personal interests – and those of their orphaned nieces and nephews – remained best-served with their brother as an ally, and hesitated to confront him directly and risk being cast out of the inner circle. It seemed much better to try to influence his behaviour from the position of loyal support, which is precisely how the Boulogne agreement was phrased. Unfortunately, the new king's unerring favouritism was not easily deterred.[5]

On the morning of 25 February, Margaret, Mary, and Elizabeth were once more inside the vast abbey church at Westminster. With them were Marguerite and their youngest half-siblings, their Clare nieces and nephew, and Joanna of Bar, as well as Isabella's French relatives and the assembled nobility of England, positioned at the front of crowds so thick that the very fabric of the church was strained: at some point during the day, a wall near the high altar collapsed under the pressure of the crowd, crushing a knightly spectator who had come to glimpse his king anointed and crowned. Outside, workmen had been building for weeks, constructing more than a dozen temporary dining halls among the palace courtyards and abbey green, where the crowds would feast after the ceremony. Forty ovens blazed while preparing courses of lampreys and beef, boar and fish, to be washed down by one thousand tuns of fine wine that had been imported from Bordeaux – red, white, and spiced – which would flow from a specially built fountain installed in the central courtyard.[6]

Inside, after more than a week of delays, the Bishop of Winchester stood before the great altar and shrine of Edward the Confessor, awaiting the arrival of a procession bearing the ancient royal regalia of England. Elizabeth's husband Humphrey was near the head of the parade, carrying the royal sceptre that signified the king's authority, while other magnates followed, parading the gilt spurs, royal rod, and ceremonial swords including *Curtana* – the sword that Gilbert de Clare had carried at Edward I's coronation, causing the king's brother such anguish that he skipped that ceremony. Other lords carried the robes that would be draped over Edward and Isabella as they were crowned. According to a contemporary account, Humphrey and his peers were dressed uniformly in robes of cloth-of-gold as they processed, declaring their status as leading lords of the realm. Elizabeth most likely also wore cloth-of-gold, in affirmation of her status. All was in order as the spectacle unfurled. However, when Piers Gaveston came into view, walking immediately in front of the king and queen dressed in purple silk peppered with pearls, 'so decorated [that] he more resembled the god Mars than a mortal', she and the whole assembly of nobles were mortified. Instantly, the abbey quivered with the collective rage of noblemen and -women, incensed at the unabashed impudence of the royal favourite to wear to the coronation a colour preserved by tradition exclusively for the king. Worse, as he approached the altar, onlookers saw that Piers – a Gascon of only middling nobility – carried the crown of England, the most sacred piece of royal regalia and the very symbol of monarchy itself, on a cushion.

When Edward and Isabella arrived before the high altar, flanked by the opulent tombs of his parents, the pair offered gold to the abbey as a gift of thanks, and the ceremony of kingship began. Already angered at Piers' brazen entrance, the assembled nobles were stunned to witness the recently exiled foreign favourite awarded the prized duty of fastening the new king's right spur (the left one was affixed by the bride's uncle, a prince of France). Their resentment swelled even further when, after the king had given his oath and been anointed and enthroned, with long lines of nobles kneeling to perform their homage, Piers grasped *Curtana*, before processing out of the church. It was an honour almost too great to bear for the nobles whose superior lineage and usual ceremonial precedence was being overlooked – at least one earl had to be restrained by his peers from challenging Piers inside the church itself – but further insult was heaped upon injury at the coronation banquet. The royal party processed to the great aisled hall of the palace, where, to mark his coronation, Edward stood on a dais and knighted several young noblemen, including his nephew, Gilbert de Clare. The feast should have followed imme-diately, but the kitchens were thrown into chaos by the scale of their task and purported mismanagement by Piers, who had been assigned to oversee the event, and the food was long-de-layed. As the guests grumbled from the hard wooden benches before still-empty trestle tables, they had ample time to cast their eyes over the rich new tapestries the king had ordered to hang from the walls, on which the royal arms of England were woven alongside those, not of his bride, but of Piers. The king was oblivious both to the anger of the magnates seated before him, and also to his new queen, whom he reportedly spent the feast ignoring while chatting merrily with Piers, to the consternation and rage of her watching uncles and brother. The guests ate late that night – the food arrived in the great hall cold and so poorly prepared as to have been basically inedible, long after sunset. When the nobles found time that evening and the next day to talk about the event, their almost uniform reaction was one of outrage. The French princes returned home aghast at the lack of courtesy shown to Isabella, and in a session of Parliament that began two days after the coronation, the English earls formulated a list of grievances against Piers that came to include a charge of treason, for alienating the king from his lords and rightful counsellors. Far from heeding the warning the earls had issued after his wedding in Boulogne, 'the mad folly of the King of England' gave Piers an ever-increasing and more dangerous level of influence; many of the most powerful lords decided in the days following the coronation that enough was enough.[7]

Margaret and Jan were at the English court at least as late as 5 March, two days after the king had called a Parliamentary recess, in an effort to buy time to address the charges his lords were making against Piers. They therefore witnessed not only the embarrassing and uncourtly behaviour of her brother – behaviour which must have shocked a couple as dedicated as they were to upholding normative chivalric virtues – but also the violence of the English nobles' reaction against it. In the days that followed, she said farewell to her three siblings, as well as the princely half-brothers she had just met, and departed back across the sea for Brabant. Though she lived for decades more, Margaret would never return to England, nor see any of her family again. Perhaps she was relieved to be set apart from the tumult that followed her brother's coronation. Certainly, she had access via diplomatic messengers to the anxiety and ever-present threat of civil war or deposition that characterized the English court during Edward's reign, and in 1311 her brother even imposed Piers Gaveston on Margaret and Jan's hospitality during one of his periods of exile. The problems in England during these years may have been among the factors that persuaded Jan in 1312 to enact the Charter of Kortenberg, in which he established a ruling council of nobles and townsmen for Brabant to monitor his rule – an early, and seemingly voluntary, limit on his powers. Although Margaret's name is not appended to the charter, her influence may have helped shape it, and she might have recognized in it a safeguard for Brabant, and for her own son and descendants against the difficulties faced by England under her brother. Perhaps she never went back home because she came to understand that the England of her youth – the court and culture of her father's reign – had been supplanted.

Mary also departed court in the weeks after the coronation, returning to her priory at Amesbury. After the consecutive deaths of her sister and father, she seems to have found solace from grief in the quiet, ordered life at Amesbury during this period, and only travelled to court to greet Isabella at Dover and for the coronation. Mary, like Margaret, was lucky in being able to step away from the politics of the English court at a time when civil war threatened. Their youngest sister was less fortunate; married to one of the leading English nobles, Elizabeth could not escape the outcome of their brother's poor judgment, though a period of residency in Humphrey's March lands in Wales suggests she tried. For her, the years that followed Edward's coronation must have been exceedingly painful, a sharp reminder of her time in Holland and that for royal women like her, family relationships were inextricably bound to high politics. Humphrey, too, became increasingly disillusioned, and by the autumn of 1310 refused to accompany the king on campaign to Scotland out of hatred for Piers – a remarkable act of defiance for the Constable of England. He was also among those earls who condemned Piers to death at Warwick two years later, threatening to permanently rupture Elizabeth's relationship with her brother. Her budding friendships with Joanna's daughters – Margaret, married to Piers, and Eleanor, whose husband was among Piers' rare defenders – were also compromised. And Marguerite, Elizabeth's closest friend, retired to the life of a dowager at Marlborough, among rumours that she was conspiring with the French king.

When Parliament gathered again near the end of April 1308, the English lords came armed for battle and demanded once more that Piers be banished. Edward's favourite had not helped himself by bestowing on each earl a nickname so boldly insulting it is hard to see how even the king did not occasionally take offence: Gilbert de Clare, the king's own nephew, was 'a cuckold's bird', a clear reference to the illicit liaison between his mother and Ralph de Monthermer a decade earlier. The fact that the king tolerated Piers casting such aspersions against his own sister – the sister who had risen to his defence in his time of greatest need – indicates the degree to which his influence was unchecked. Yet, even though his own honour as well as his mother's was being publicly impugned by Piers, young Gilbert de Clare, either restricted by his minority or anxious not to alienate his connection to the throne, struggled to oppose his uncle and brother-in-law directly, and declared himself neutral on the question of Piers' treason. Elizabeth's husband, Humphrey de Bohun, was less cowed – he was among those who openly called Piers a traitor and, by the spring of 1308, his wife must have longed for the stability and assurance that she had lost with her father. If she did, it was a sentiment that was widely shared.[8]

A number of popular songs lamenting the death of the old king survive from late 1307 and early 1308. 'Jerusalem, you have lost the flower of chivalry', opined one Norman-French song probably sung among the upper strata of society. The songs also record the hopeful expectation of the English people that his son might prove a worthy heir: 'The young Edward of England is anointed and crowned king / May God grant that he follow such counsel, that the country be governed, and so to keep the crown', and, in an English elegy:

> *Nou is Edward of Carnarvan*
> *King of Engelond al aplyht,*
> *Got lete him ner be worse man*
> *Then is fader, ne lasse of myth . . .*

Eight months into his reign, the English nobility were deeply concerned that young Edward was turning out to be an unworthy successor to his father – one who kept rash counsel and appeared potentially unfit to govern – and already his crown was in danger of being lost. A contemporary cleric wrote that 'very evil are the times in England now; and there are many who fear that worse times are still in store for us.'[9]

For Edward's surviving sisters, the early days of their brother's reign must have been a great disappointment and a grave concern. Whether as an English noblewoman, a foreign consort, or a nun, their positions as royal women of England had, so far, guaranteed them extraordinary lives. Their great wealth ensured they lived surrounded by material luxury that was nearly unthinkable to most of their contemporaries: they dined on prized meats and specially bred fish, exotic fruits and spices, and rich delicacies like almonds and sugar imported from the far ends of the known world; they were clothed in the finest linens, silks, and velvets – brilliantly coloured and shot through with gold thread or peppered with flashes of light reflecting off silver buttons; their heads, fingers, and waists were adorned with dazzling gemstones set into gleaming coronets, rings, and girdles. They ate in painted halls lined with warm tapestries and cushioned benches, and slept in feather beds, hung with thick curtains woven with pictures and heraldry; their chambers were brightly lit by large, glazed windows, and warmed by constantly roaring fires. They travelled often but comfortably, with new saddles on the finest riding horses, inside ornately decorated and cushioned carriages, and on barges and ships that offered the most lavish facilities available. They received educations from their mother, grandmother, and governesses to far outstrip their peers – perhaps even including their brother – and maintained libraries, kennels, stables, choirs, and minstrels to supply their love of literature,

music, and the hunt. For Mary, her status also provided her with
the luxury she prized above all: freedom of movement, a remarkable privilege for a woman who, at six, had been made to join
a religious order that advocated the strict enclosure of nuns. For
each of Edward's sisters, the ability to deploy intercession – to
request money or favours of the king and thereby offer patronage
to individuals and causes – throughout her father's reign, enabled
her to hold power even when far from the English court, whether
in Glamorgan, Brussels, Holland, or Bar.

Their status as daughters of the king provided Eleanora,
Joanna, Margaret, Mary, and Elizabeth the rare ability, as women
living in a deeply patriarchal society, to build and maintain an
influence that few of their contemporaries experienced and even
to realize a degree of self-determination in their lives. The ways
that each of his sisters sought to secure their brother's loyalty
in the final years of their father's reign – perhaps most especially
Joanna, who did not survive to see the ungracious way her
brother repaid her in allowing his favourite to besmirch her
name – suggests that these women realized how fully their
destinies were tied to his. These were not cynical gestures,
designed to convince Edward of a loyalty or love that was insin-
cere, but rather reminders of shared interests or experience forged
over decades: Elizabeth and her brother shared a passion for
music and prized dogs; Joanna felt an affinity to her brother
when he quarrelled with his father, whose ire she had also tasted;
Margaret sought to reconnect with a brother she barely knew,
as a peer and ally among the ruling families of Western Europe.
Mary, without the security of a powerful husband, had the most
to lose, but offered him what she could – the sanctuary of her
home at Amesbury. Above all, they shared with their brother
an indissoluble membership of the English royal family, which
linked their fates together. Undoubtedly, each of his sisters hoped

that their ability to intercede with a powerful king would continue once their brother wore the crown, securing their special position and the power and influence that flowed outwards from it. But, like so much else threatened by Edward's infatuation with Piers Gaveston and his naive reluctance to moderate his behaviour, the privileges his princess sisters had always enjoyed were endangered from the very start of his rule.

Epilogue

The reign of Edward II – most remembered for its gory, if probably apocryphal, end – lasted for twenty years. His record as a king and as husband to the French princess Isabella (who became known to posterity as the 'She-Wolf of France') has been examined by countless historians, some more sympathetically than others, but few have managed to avoid characterizing his kingship as a stark contrast to the reign of his father. Even contemporary commentators seem to have been fixed on the differences between the kings: persistent rumours that he was not really the old king's son dogged Edward of Caernarfon throughout the 1310s but, whether his perceived failings were connected to sexual relationships with successive, hated favourites – the question that has most obsessed writers – or otherwise, Edward's hold on power was clearly weaker than his father's had been. The comparative vulnerability of his position impacted those within his circle, including his sisters, whose influence rose or fell, depending on the king's own authority. Margaret's later years provide a good example of this impact: on Jan's death in 1312, their son was aged only twelve, and a regency was therefore instituted in Brabant. Although Margaret might have expected to act as regent herself – it was a common role for women in her position, and one she would have been well prepared for, having lived nearly two decades as consort – she played no formal role while her heir was under age, and nor did she assume a meaningful advisory role once her son began to rule, despite his youth and her trustworthy experience. Instead, Margaret's dowager period saw her living quietly and largely outside the sphere of influence around court, sidelined during the course of her brother's reign.

Mary and Elizabeth also saw their influence fade, in part because their brother's attention was normally focused on the advice of his favourites, and in part simply because they were less frequently at court. Mary continued to use her connection to the king when it benefitted Amesbury – in appeals to the Pope, or in disputes between the priory and the abbess of its motherhouse at Fontevraud. And, though she was less often at court, Mary still exercised the special freedoms of movement she had always enjoyed – once her estates had been confirmed by her brother, she continued to travel to her manors, including Swainston on the Isle of Wight, where she held a sizable house with a great hall brightened by large Gothic windows, that had been built in the thirteenth century by the Bishop of Winchester. Increasingly her energy, however, seems to have been expended in raising, educating, and safeguarding as much as she could the daughters of her sisters and nieces, including Elizabeth de Clare, Eleanor de Bohun, Joanna de Monthermer (who joined the priory at Amesbury as a fully professed nun), and Joanna Gaveston. The last of these died young while living at Amesbury, as did Mary's half-sister, Princess Eleanor, daughter of Queen Marguerite.[1]

In 1309, Elizabeth bore twin boys, followed in the next five years by three additional children, including Eleanor and a second daughter called Margaret. During the years of estrangement from her brother over Piers Gaveston, and the period when Humphrey was imprisoned after the English defeat at Bannockburn (when he fought Robert Bruce in single combat, but was forced to concede), her children may have provided Elizabeth – who seemed of all her sisters to most need to be surrounded by family – with a degree of comfort. She appears to have taken an active interest in her daughters' marriages, enlisting her stepmother and friend Marguerite to help secure favourable matches for them. She also provided them with exceptional educations, a fitting testimony to the lifelong impact of her own mother's memory: her daughter Margaret could read not only Latin but also Greek, and grew to be an enthusiastic collector of books. Finally reconciled with her brother three years after Piers' death, Elizabeth spent Christmas of 1315 with Edward and Isabella at Clipstone, and retired afterwards to Quendon in Essex to await the birth of her tenth child. There, on 5 May 1316, a daughter, named Isabella in honour of the queen, was born, but complications soon set in, and within days both mother and child were dead. Her husband buried her among his own ancestors at Walden Abbey. Though her death left many young children without a mother, Elizabeth was at least spared having to witness Humphrey's horrific death in battle while fighting against her brother's army at Boroughbridge in 1322, and the terrible years that followed.[2]

Margaret and Mary both lived to see the full tragedy of their brother's reign. Despite the many warnings from his counsellors, Edward's unchecked favouritism of his noble friends ultimately led to the tumultuous usurpation of his throne by his wife Isabella and her Marcher lord paramour, Roger Mortimer. Imprisoned under Isabella and Mortimer's orders, Edward was likely murdered at Berkeley Castle in September 1327. Three years later, his seventeen-year-old eldest son – in a manoeuvre redolent of Edward I's youthful daring – overthrew, captured and executed Mortimer, consigning Isabella to genteel retirement and gaining control of the throne he would hold for five decades. But far from the English court, Edward's surviving sisters were insulated from the most devastating consequences of their brother's mistakes. Mary lived out her years quietly, mostly at Amesbury, where she died in 1332 at the age of fifty-three, five years after her brother's death. Buried in the priory near her grandmother, a monument will have remembered the princess-nun, but it was lost with the destruction of the priory church during the Dissolution. Her sister Margaret was still alive at the age of fifty-eight in 1333, resident on her dower estate and uninvolved with the high politics of her son's or brother's courts, but perhaps close to her six young grandchildren. She most likely died soon after, as her name disappears from the historical record. She was buried next to Jan in the ducal chapel of the great collegiate church in Brussels, but her tomb, too, has been lost.

The next generation did not fare so well; their uncle's reign left the lives of Joanna's children utterly ravaged. Margaret de Clare, the wife of Piers Gaveston, endured the widespread hatred of her husband at court for five years, including during the two separate periods that he was exiled (during the latter of which she was heavily pregnant). Their only child, Joanna – named for her grandmother and sent to Amesbury to be raised by her great-aunt Mary – was six months old when her father was executed in 1312, by nobles including Humphrey de Bohun. Mother and daughter were forced to fall back on the king for support, but that also faded over time. Joanna's son Gilbert remained a loyal supporter of his uncle, often attempting a mediating role between the king and those opposed to Piers, but he died in battle at Bannockburn in 1314. According to one chronicler, Gilbert tried to dissuade the king from engaging the superior Scottish forces and, when Edward nevertheless insisted on fighting, he angrily and rashly flung himself into battle, unprotected by his men.

With the death of the childless Gilbert, the Clare estate was divided between his three sisters, which sparked an aggressive dispute between Eleanor's husband Hugh le Despenser – who had matured into the most bullying of the king's favourites – and her sisters. Hugh's avarice and intimidation led to a complete breakdown in the sisters' relationships: Margaret and Elizabeth de Clare were both held captive after they split from the king's party, and Elizabeth was forced to relinquish part of her estate to Eleanor and Hugh. But, although Eleanor spent most of her uncle's reign near the apex of power (some have even suggested that she may have had an adulterous and incestuous love affair with the king), she eventually suffered too; imprisoned for a time in the Tower of London, her unmarried daughters were forcibly veiled, and Hugh, as the king's final favourite, was condemned to a traitor's death by the invading forces of Queen Isabella. In 1330, Eleanor was forced to beg for royal permission to collect her husband's bones for burial near her father at Tewkesbury – his head from a spike on Tower Bridge, the rest taken, after quartering, to Bristol, Dover, York, and Newcastle. It is impossible not to wonder how different her children's lives might have turned out if Joanna, unafraid as she was to stand up to her father, had lived to stand against her brother.

If, having concluded the story of the five royal sisters at the court of Edward I – exceptional in their power, their education, and at times their bold action – we were to search for their legacy it might be found in the example their lives provided to some of their daughters, and above all to Joanna's youngest Clare daughter, Elizabeth. Although she was not yet twelve at the time of her mother's death, Elizabeth's life encapsulates the independence, the passion for learning, and the confident self-determination that characterized her mother and aunts.

Raised within Joanna's household and educated at Amesbury, Elizabeth's life began, like those of her sisters, with an early marriage to a young nobleman – but, following the deaths of her first husband and her brother, she determined to shape her own future. She copied her mother's example and defied her uncle, the king – who had hoped to betroth the widow-heiress to a favoured courtier – by eloping with a man of her choosing. She endured imprisonment under the orders of the king and was forced to concede parts of her estate, but emerged after the downfall of her enemies, a wealthy and powerful widow who outlived most of her generation. Clare Castle flourished under her management, supporting artisans and craftsmen, and cultivating gardens, stables, kennels, and menageries to rival the greatest in the kingdom. While her relationships with her Clare sisters suffered irreparably during their uncle's reign, she was able to support her Monthermer half-siblings well into the prosperous decades of Edward III's kingship, and also maintained a close friendship with her cousin Joanna of Bar, the spurned Countess of Surrey. However, Elizabeth's most lasting achievement was her foundation of Clare College in Cambridge, the earliest college endowed by a woman, and an example that would be emulated by countesses and queens in the centuries that followed. The foundation provided a memorial to commemorate the now-defunct Clare dynasty, but its purpose harks back to the legacy of exceptional learning Elizabeth inherited from the women who came before her. In a quiet corner of the hall in Clare College, a small shield showing the royal arms and a slim pane of glass listing her name are all that attests the part Joanna of Acre played in the college's establishment.

Beyond the enclosed walls of Cambridge, nothing today survives of the monuments that remembered Eleanora at Westminster, Joanna at Clare Priory, Margaret in Brussels, Mary at Amesbury, or Elizabeth at Walden. Nor do Joanna or any of her daughters through whom the great Clare estate was dispersed appear among the Earls of Gloucester that gaze across the centuries from the vivid stained glass at Tewkesbury. The sisters are not depicted on the great tomb chests at Westminster Abbey, where tourists still flock to remember their parents, as are the many children of Edward III and his queen, Philippa, on his tomb. Lacking such visual reminders, these women have been largely forgotten. But, by recovering their stories and showing how they used the pathways for wielding power and achieving influence and independence that were open to them, we may construct a different kind of monument to them – one that they were denied in their own era. It is time that these extraordinary women were remembered.

Acknowledgements

During the many years that this book existed only in my head, and in the several it has actually been in production, I have incurred an extraordinary number of debts. In the way that writing a book connects to all parts of one's life, the true list of those to whom I owe thanks would far outstrip the space allotted here.

My first thanks must go to my agent Ben Clark and his colleagues at Lucas Alexander Whitley, who saw a glimmer of promise in my desire to tell the story of some forgotten women from long ago and helped at a critical early stage to give structure to my aspiration. I am also incredibly indebted to the masterful Georgina Morley, who coaxed this still-raw idea into the book in your hands. She and her colleagues at Picador (in particular, Gillian Stern, Marissa Constantinou, and Chloe May, as well as the maps and design teams) have gently and persuasively, but (importantly) also thoroughly, advised, revised, and improved the argument and structure of the text, and made the book look as beautiful as some of the wondrous objects it describes.

The most significant among the debts I have incurred over many years to fellow historians are those owed to Nigel Saul, who taught me, among much else, how to understand the past through its material remains. His influence as a scholar, mentor, and friend has been essential to all of my historical research. Ever generous, he read much of this book in manuscript, as did Edward Wilson-Lee; any remaining errors are of course entirely my own. I am also grateful to the librarians and keepers of the manuscripts rooms at the British Library and Cambridge University Library, as well as the National Archives and the Victoria and Albert Museum. Thank you, too, to the Church of St Mary Magdalen, Bermondsey, for permission to include among the illustrations their splendid mazer.

The book and I have benefited enormously from the extraordinarily rich intellectual culture that I have been immensely privileged to inhabit in Cambridge, where over the years I have been encouraged, supported, and, above all, inspired in this endeavour by friends and colleagues including: Phil Allmendinger, Rosa Andujar, David Beckingham, Paul Binski, Cyprian Broodbank, Ambrogio Caiani, Julia Lovell, Rob Macfarlane, Joe Moshenska, Nicholas Rogers, David Runciman, and Patrick Zutshi.

The final thanks are to my family. To my parents, Bill and Wanda Lee (who will attest that my interest in princesses with power has been lifelong), for instilling in me the confidence to dream beyond my immediate horizons. This book is dedicated to them with love and gratitude. To Ben and Vivian Lee, for extremely generously buying the computer on which the book was written. To Gabriel and Ambrose Wilson-Lee, for bringing incalculable joy and humour into my life, and for curing me of a tendency to procrastinate. And to my husband, Edward Wilson-Lee, without whose unwavering support and encouragement, this – and all the rest – would be impossible.

Notes

INTRODUCTION

1 A note on naming: for ease of distinguishing between the queen known commonly as Eleanor of Castile and her eldest daughter, I have referred to the latter throughout as Eleanora, although the mother and daughter's names were, of course, identical – in Latin, Alianora; in French, Alianore. Similarly, in order to distinguish between the identically named Low Country husbands of Margaret and Elizabeth (Johannes in Latin, Jan in Dutch), I have referred to them throughout as Jan of Brabant and Johan of Holland.

I. CORONATION

1 For Wykes' description of the festivities surrounding Edward and Eleanor's coronation, see his chronicle in *Annales Monastici*, ed. H.R. Luard, iv (Kraus reprint, Wiesbaden, 1965), p. 259.
2 The extraordinary supply operation carried out to provide for the coronation feast can be glimpsed in the *Calendar of Close Rolls, 1272–79*, pp. 68–71.
3 Another contemporary account of the coronation, including the observation about the Cheapside conduit, can be found in *Croniques de London: depuis l'an 44 Hen. III jusqu'à l'an 17 Edw. III*, ed. G.J. Aungier (London, 1844), p. 13.
4 A list of those in attendance at the coronation is provided in Nicholas Trivet's *Annales sex regum Angliae, qui a comitibus Andegavensibus originem traxerunt, 1136–1307*, ed. Thomas Hog (London, 1845), p. 292. The account of hundreds of horses being released during the festivities is discussed by H.G. Richardson in his 'The Coronation of Edward I', *Bulletin of the Institute for Historical Research*, xv (1937–8), pp. 94–9.
5 A description of Guildford Castle, its layout, and principal features, can be found in *The History of the King's Works*, gen. ed. H.M. Colvin (London, 1963–75), ii: *The Middle Ages*, ed. R. Allen Brown, H.M. Colvin, A.J. Taylor, pp. 950–5. The wonderful survival of the Wardrobe Book for the children's household allows their lives during this period to be reconstructed fairly easily, including favourite treats.

It was edited by Hilda Johnstone as 'Wardrobe and Household of Henry, son of Edward I', *Bulletin of the John Rylands Library*, vii (1922–3), pp. 384–420. The original account rolls can still be found in the National Archives under E 101/350/18.

6   Among English ducal families between 1330 and 1479, some thirty-six per cent of boys and twenty-nine per cent of girls died before the age of five: Shulamith Shahar, *Childhood in the Middle Ages* (London, 1992), p. 35. The quotation attributed to a young Henry III appears in *Fœdera, conventiones, litteræ et cujuscunque generis Acta Publica*, ed. Thomas Rymer; (repr. London, 1816), ed. Adam Clarke, Frederic Holbrooke, John Caley (4 vols), i, p. 155.

7   See the notices of John's birth and death in the Annals of Winchester, within *Annales Monastici*, ed. Luard, ii (Kraus reprint, Nendeln, 1971), pp. 104, 111. Although the births of his elder sisters and his brother Henry were not included, those of sisters born in 1275 and 1277 were recorded by the annalist; their father's coronation in 1274 may have been a factor in this shift, as the birth of a child of the current king (regardless of gender) may have been considered noteworthy. For Edward's gifts to messengers bearing news of his grandchildren see *Calendar of Close Rolls*, 1288–96, pp. 169–70, and M.A.E. Green, *Lives of the Princesses, from the Norman Conquest* (London, 1850–7) 6 vols, iii, p. 42.

II. BETROTHAL

1   The King's Wardrobe Book containing an accounting of the necessary expenses for his household in the sixth year of his reign, from 20 November 1277–19 November 1278, is preserved as British Library Additional MS 36762.

2   For a full discussion on the diplomatic marriages of princesses in medieval England, including the roles played by their queenly mothers, see John Carmi Parsons, 'Mothers, Daughters, Marriage, Power: Some Plantagenet Evidence, 1150–1500', in *Medieval Queenship*, ed. John Carmi Parsons (Stroud, 1994), pp. 63–78. Henry III's 1254 statement on the importance of diplomatic marriage is preserved in *Fœdera*, i, p. 209.

3   The agreed terms of Margaret's marriage to Jan of Brabant can be found in *Fœdera*, i, pp. 550–4.

4   Edward's regular annual income totalled around 27,000 pounds throughout his reign, which was normally sufficient to supply his household and the general administration of England. This, however, needed to be supplemented to fund his many foreign wars, most

frequently by Italian lenders. On his death, King Edward had significant debts to his name, the resolution of which burdened his son's reign. See Marc Morris, *A Great and Terrible King: Edward I and the Forging of Britain* (London, 2008), p. xvi.

5 The details of Joanna's planned match with Hartman can be found in *Fœdera*, i, pp. 536, 545, 548, 554–7, 559, 563, 568.

6 John Carmi Parsons found a similar pattern of age at marriage and childbirth even among a broader study that also included English noblewomen: 'Mothers, Daughters,' pp. 65–7.

7 While visiting Bordeaux in early 1287, Eleanor bestowed a series of golden cloths to the local Dominican priory; these were presented to the high altar and to the tomb in the church of a daughter of the queen, the anniversary of whose death was celebrated in late May. No records indicate that Eleanor miscarried a pregnancy or had a still birth at this date, and nor do any of the queen's other children disappear from the historical record at this time. Eleanor's only previous visits to Bordeaux during May were to travel to England for the first time in 1255 or to return from Crusade in 1274. One of the three royal babies born on Crusade was a daughter who died at Acre in 1271, while the other two were healthy and still alive long after 1274. Either the king and queen brought back the body of their daughter who had died three years previously at Acre, and decided to bury her at Bordeaux rather than waiting to lay her to rest alongside her siblings at Westminster, or she bore a premature daughter in May 1255 who died immediately or shortly after birth. See entries from the Book of the Treasurer in *Records of the Wardrobe and Household, 1285–6*, ed. Benjamin F. Byerly and Catherine Ridder Byerly, 2 vols (London, 1977–86), ii, nos 1618–9.

8 The full text of Eleanora's letter can be found in *Fœdera*, i, p. 614.

9 That letter in 1290 appointed the same Anthony Bek to contract a marriage between the prince and Margaret, daughter of Eric, King of Norway, and the rightful Queen of Scotland: *Fœdera*, i, p. 737. The English hoped the proposed marriage would make Prince Edward the King of Scotland, effectively uniting England and Scotland when he succeeded his father, but Margaret died – reportedly of seasickness – just off the Orkney Islands, while travelling from Norway to Scotland a few months after the marriage was agreed.

10 On educating women in case they need to govern, and for the Barberino quotation, see Rowena Archer, '"How ladies . . . who live on their manors ought to manage their households and estates": Women as Landholders and Administrators in the Later Middle

Ages', *Woman is a Worthy Wight: Women in English Society c.1200–1500*, ed. P.J.P. Goldberg (Stroud, 1992), pp. 149–181 (151).

11 The king's letter directing his embassy to negotiate Eleanora's marriage, and the instruction for Italian bankers from Lucca and Piacenza to loan eight hundred pounds to the negotiators, de Vescy and Bek, repayable by the king, with two hundred further marks borrowed from an English merchant for the same purpose, are summarised in *Calendar of Patent Rolls*, 1281–92, pp. 10–11. The terms agreed for Eleanora's match are given in full in *Fœdera*, i, pp. 613–5.

12 For the letter declaring the shared objections of Eleanor of Castile and Eleanor of Provence to Eleanora's immediate transfer to the Aragonese court, see *Fœdera*, i, p. 593.

13 The chronicler Bartholomew of Norwich records that Prince Hartman was 'walking incautiously over the ice' when it gave way, but this seems to have been misinformation. For reference to the shipwreck in which he died, see British Library Cotton Nero C. v. fol. 204; Green, *Lives of the Princesses of England*, ii, p. 323. Hartman's brother Rudolf (who would ultimately succeed as Rudolf II), may already have been pledged informally to his eventual wife, the daughter of his father's greatest rival, Ottokar II of Bohemia, and therefore been unavailable to marry Joanna.

III. FAMILY

1 Years later, Joanna received a letter from Suger, one of the earliest Bishops of Cadiz, whom she may have known in Ponthieu, requesting her intercession on behalf of two Spaniards: see National Archives Special Collections 1/30/3. Edeline's husband, Philippe, joined Eleanor of Castile's household after the death of her mother, Jeanne de Dammartin. The couple remained in England within the royal household until Joanna's marriage in 1290: John Carmi Parsons, *The Court and Household of Eleanor of Castile in 1290: An Edition of British Library Additional Manuscript 35294 with Introduction and Notes* (Toronto, 1977), pp. 38–9. For Edward's letter instructing his servants to bring Joanna to England, see *Fœdera*, i, p. 559.

2 For Elizabeth's birth at Rhuddlan, see Green, *Lives of the Princesses*, iii, pp. 2–3. Joanna's solitary visit back to Rhuddlan the following year is described in ibid, ii, p. 324.

3 Joanna's father Edward had been the first royal child to maintain an independent household from a young age, and the king clearly felt the experience was useful in preparing him for adult life; as soon as he became king, he established a household for his then-heir Prince

Henry, and the unfortunate boy's younger sisters also benefitted from early opportunities to learn about the effective management of households: Johnstone, 'Household of Henry', p. 384.

4 Joanna's household is listed in Byerly and Byerly, *Wardrobe and Household*, i, no. 1714.

5 For the households of Eleanora and Margaret, see ibid, nos 1713, 1715; ii, no. 1948. Cecily de Cleware was granted the wood from six oaks in Windsor Forest, as a token of thanks from the king for acting as nurse to Margaret in June 1276: *Calendar of Close Rolls, 1272–79*, p. 296; for her service as Eleanora's nurse, see Johnstone, 'Household of Henry', pp. 389–90. A relative of Cecily's, John de Cleware, was serving as a valet in Eleanora's court in Bar as late as 1296, demonstrating the strength of Eleanora's loyalty to her early friends: *Book of Prests of the King's Wardrobe for 1294–5*, ed. E.B. Fryde (Oxford, 1962), p. 63.

6 For the association between Caernarfon, British Rome, and Constantine, see, for example, the Annals of Waverley, which conflated the Western Roman Emperor and general in command of British forces, Magnus Maximus, and his Welsh wife Elen, with the Emperor Constantius Cholrus (father of Constantine the Great), who died at York in 306, and his Byzantine wife, St Helena, discoverer of the True Cross. A Roman sarcophagus discovered at Caernarfon in 1283 was assumed on strength of local legend to belong to Maximus, though he, in fact, died in Italy. *Annales Monastici*, ed. Luard, ii, pp. 129–412. See 'The Dream of Maxen Wledig' in *Mabinogion Tales*, trans. Charlotte Guest, ed. Owen Edwards (Llanerch, 1991), pp. 64–76, especially pp. 65–7.

7 For the capture of the reputed crown of King Arthur and Alphonso's subsequent deposit of Welsh regalia at the shrine of Edward the Confessor, see *Annales Monastici*, ed. Luard, ii, 401; Matthew of Westminster, *Flores Historiarum*, ed. H.R. Luard (Kraus reprint, Nendeln, 1965) iii, p. 61 and n.

8 Sixteenth-century Welsh clergyman David Powel, in his *The historie of Cambria, now called Wales . . .*, trans. H. Lloyd (London, 1584), describes an apocryphal episode in which the Welsh lords declare they will only ever accept as their prince one born in Wales who speaks no English. King Edward secures their unwitting acceptance of his own heir when he produces the baby boy, born at Caernarfon and unable to speak anything at all: pp. 376–7.

9 *Annales Monastici*, ed. Luard, ii, 401.

10 The argument in this paragraph is indebted to John Carmi Parsons who has examined the role of an itinerant lifestyle in offering Edward

and Eleanor opportunities for performing their public role at sites across the country. He has determined that the queen's participation in the pageantry associated with royal entries into towns was perhaps as important as that of the king. See Parsons, *Court and Household*, p. 8; John Carmi Parsons, *Eleanor of Castile: Queen and Society in Thirteenth-Century England* (London, 1995), pp. 32–3.

11 Collette Bowie has suggested that rates of literacy among Anglo-Norman noblewomen may even have been higher than those of their husbands and brothers, who spent large portions of their time learning the arts of warfare: *The Daughters of Henry II and Eleanor of Aquitaine* (Turnhout, 2014), p. 60.

12 For the Siete Partidas, including their prescriptions related to female education, see Madaline W. Nichols, 'Las Siete Partidas', *California Law Review*, vol. 20.3 (1932), pp. 260–85 (268). Sara Cockerill discusses Alfonso's views on the education of princesses and its likely impact on Eleanor in her *Eleanor of Castile: The Shadow Queen* (Stroud, 2014), pp. 56–7. A contemporary treatise on the education of nobles in France, Vincent of Beauvais' *De Eruditione Filiorum Nobiliorum*, gives over its final ten chapters to the education of noble daughters, suggesting a curriculum including reading and writing as well as religious study, manners, and sewing skills: ed. A. Steiner (Cambridge, MA, 1938), pp. 172–219. A surviving copy of the *Life of St Edward the Confessor* dates from 1255 and may be Eleanor's own copy: Cambridge University Library Ee.3.59. See also Girart d'Amiens, *Der roman von Escanor, von Gerard von Amiens*, ed. Henri Victor Michelant (Tübingen, 1886).

13 Kim Philips discusses how elite young medieval English women not yet able to read by themselves were nevertheless normally part of 'textual communities', in which groups within a household would gather, listen to a text read aloud, and then discuss its moral and didactic teachings. See her *Medieval Maidens: Young Women and Gender in England, c. 1270–c. 1540* (Manchester, 2003), pp. 71–3. For the quotations from *The Parlement of the Three Ages*, see ed. M. Offord (London, 1967), lines 249–54.

14 See Eleanor's purchase of books of hours for reading practice in John Carmi Parsons, 'Of Queens, Courts, and Books: Reflections on the Literary Patronage of Thirteenth-Century Plantagenet Queens', in *The Cultural Patronage of Medieval Women*, ed. June Hall McCash (Athens, GA, 1996), pp. 175–201 (179).

15 See for Peter's purchase of writing tablets for Eleanora, Byerly and Byerly, *Wardrobe and Household*, i, no. 403. In 1291, Adam the queen's goldsmith purchased further 'tabliaus a liure' for Eleanora:

Parsons, *Eleanor of Castile*, p. 56. On the role of the queen in educating her daughters and promoting a literary upbringing, see Parsons, 'Of Queens, Courts, and Books'.

16 For the purchase of silks for Margaret's use, see Byerly and Byerly, *Wardrobe and Household, passim*; Green, *Lives of the Princesses*, ii, p. 365. For payments associated with the children hunting while their parents were abroad, see Parsons, *Eleanor of Castile*, p. 55; Byerly and Byerly, *Wardrobe and Household*, ii, Roll of the Expenses of the King's Children, which is National Archives, E 101/352/8. For Elizabeth's interest in polyphony, see her 1305 letter to her brother Prince Edward, in which she asked him to send a clerk from Windsor Castle to instruct the children of her own chapel choir in the new French art of choral polyphony: *Letters of Edward Prince of Wales, 1304–1305*, ed. H. Johnstone (Cambridge, 1931), p. 133.

17 The manuscript commissioned for Alphonso's marriage survives within the collection of the British Library as Additional MS 24686. It has been fully digitized and is able to be viewed online on the British Library's website. For Archbishop John Peckham's letter of condolence to Edward on Alphonso's death, see *Registrum Epistolarum Fratris Johannis Peckham* (Kraus reprint, Nendeln, 1965), iii, p. 819.

IV. VOWS

1 For a description of the priory church at Amesbury, see *A History of Wiltshire*, ed. R.B. Pugh and Elizabeth Crittall (London, 1957–2011), iii, p. 256. For an account of Mary's veiling, see William Dugdale, *Monasticon Anglicanum: a history of the abbies and other monasteries . . .*, new edn (Farnborough, 1970), ii, p. 334. The Worcester annalist does not record the names of the thirteen 'noble young daughters' who, he recorded, joined the Amesbury community alongside Mary: *Annales Monastici*, ed. Luard, iv, p. 491.

2 The letter from the abbess of Fontevrault to Eleanor is printed in *Fœdera*, i, p. 651. The Norman-French version of Nicholas Trivet's chronicle, which began with Genesis and continued down to the reign of Edward I, was dedicated to Mary and contains several sections relating to the life of the princess and her family; a separate (probably later) version was completed in Latin and dedicated to the Archbishop of Canterbury. Both have survived in multiple copies: see British Library Arundel MS 56, especially f. 75; Trivet, *Annales*.

3 For Eleanor of Provence's grief on losing her daughters, see *Annales Monastici*, ed. Luard, iv, p. 262.

4 The community of Amesbury was recorded during a visitation by John, sacrist of Fontevrault, in 1256. By 1318, it had grown to include 117 nuns: *History of Wiltshire*, iii, pp. 246, 249.

5 Seven other young aristocratic women were pledged to Amesbury at the same time as Eleanor of Brittany: BL Arundel MS 56, f. 75.

6 On the ages at which nuns could be professed, see Eileen Power, *Medieval English Nunneries, c. 1275–1535* (Cambridge, 1922), pp. 26–7; Marilyn Oliva, *The Convent and the Community in Late Medieval England: Female Monasteries in the Diocese of Norwich, 1350–1540* (Woodbridge, 1998), p. 45n. They detail how the fourteenth-century Bishop of Winchester William of Wykeham told the nuns of Romsey Abbey during a visitation that they could profess novitiates aged twelve and older, but also that the daughters of Guy Beauchamp, Earl of Warwick, seem to have joined houses at earlier ages. For the date of Mary's final vows, see John Carmi Parsons, 'The Year of Eleanor of Castile's Birth and Her Children by Edward I', *Mediaeval Studies* 46 (1984), pp. 245–65 (p. 264). For the dowries associated with the entrance of nuns to convents, see Oliva, *The Convent*, p. 48, who notes that the fee for male entrants was standardized throughout the late-medieval period at five pounds, likely comparable to entry fees for females. For the charter granting Melksham to Amesbury Priory, see *Calendar of Close Rolls*, 1288–96, p. 25. For the oaks and wines granted to Mary, see *Calendar of Patent Rolls*, 1281–92, p. 190.

7 Letters related to Eleanor of Provence's building works at Amesbury can be found in *Calendar of Close Rolls*, 1279–88, pp. 14, 96.

8 In 1222, the Council of Oxford specifically prohibited nuns from wearing silken wimples and belts embroidered with gold and silver thread, and declared the only jewellery they should wear was the ring that symbolized their vows. Throughout the following centuries, repeated injunctions were issued against the wearing of, among others, laced shoes, red dresses, expensive furs, long trains, ribboned headdresses, and open tunics fastened with brooches, as well as filed fingernails, fashionably plucked high foreheads, and locks of hair shaped with curling irons: Power, *Medieval English Nunneries*, pp. 303–5, 585–7. For Eleanora's sickness and the efforts made to comfort her, see Byerly and Byerly, *Wardrobe and Household*, i, nos 123, 163, 298, 332.

9 For the efforts made to enforce the enclosure of nuns in the late thirteenth century, see Power, *Medieval English Nunneries*, p. 348. The royal family's travelling, and Eleanora's purchase of a horse, can be found in Byerly and Byerly, *Wardrobe and Household*, i, nos 273, 300;

Green, *Lives of the Princesses*, ii, pp. 293–5. Eleanor's supplementary payments to Mary, twenty-five marks paid twice yearly, at Easter and Michaelmas, are printed in Byerly and Byerly, *Wardrobe and Household*, ii, nos 3111, 3124, 3128, 3141, 3149, 3165, 3177, 3192.

10   For a description of the rings, see Green, *Lives of the Princesses*, ii, pp. 409–10.

11   More on the court case in which Mary helped convince her father to side with the Abbess of Fontevrault over her fellow nuns of Amesbury can be found in *Calendar of Close Rolls*, 1288–96, p. 317; *History of Wiltshire*, iii, p. 248.

12   A manuscript from the convent of Nuneaton (Cambridge Fitzwilliam MS McClean 123) includes the *Chasteau d'Amours*, as well as a bestiary, apocryphal gospel, and apocalypse. On the popularity of the text in the late thirteenth century, see C. William Marx, *The Devil's Rights and the Redemption in the Literature of Medieval England* (Cambridge, 1995), Chapter 4.

V. GROWING UP

1   For the requests that Edward arbitrate on the rightful succession of Sicily, see *Fœdera*, i, pp. 626–7. For the papal injunction forbidding Edward's children from marrying into the royal house of Aragon, see ibid, p. 665.

2   For a description of the medieval palace, see David Neal, 'Excavations at the Palace of Kings Langley, Hertfordshire 1974–1976', *Medieval Archaeology* (1977), pp. 124–65 (125); Anthony Emery, *Greater Medieval Houses of England and Wales, 1300–1500* (Cambridge, 1996–2000) 2 vols, ii, p. 257; Hilda Johnstone, *Edward of Carnarvon, 1284–1307* (Manchester 1946), pp. 29–30.

3   On the military guard assigned to the children at Langley, see Johnstone, 'Household of Henry', p. 392.

4   Marie of Brittany had a governess while at Langley named Lady Marquessa, see Byerly and Byerly, *Wardrobe and Household*, ii, e.g. no. 1861. In 1292, Marie married the Count of Saint-Pol, a small province abutting Ponthieu. Her lasting affection for her English relatives is apparent: in 1297, though her father and husband were then at war with Edward, Marie joined the English king and three of his daughters for Christmas at Ghent. One of her own daughters, Marie of Châtillon, married the Earl of Pembroke, Aymer de Valence, and was a bosom-friend of Joanna's daughter Elizabeth de Burgh. Together, the two women founded Pembroke and Clare Colleges at Cambridge respectively, which survive today. Two rolls survive that

shed light on Christmas festivities at King's Langley during the years Edward and Eleanor were in Gascony: the Roll of Expenses for the King's Children (National Archives E 101/352/8), which offers a summation of all expenses from the household for 1286–9, and the Roll of the Great Wardrobe Expenses of the King's Children (National Archives E 101/352/16), which only survives for 1288–9. I have used the more detailed description of expenses in the latter document to flesh out the sparer account for Christmas in 1286 provided in the former. See Byerly and Byerly, *Wardrobe and Household*, ii, pp. 414–22.

5 See records of dresses being made for the eldest three princesses in 1289, Byerly and Byerly, ii, Roll of Necessary Expenses (which is National Archives E 101/352/14), *passim*. For foods consumed at the palace, see Neal, 'Excavations at the Palace of Kings Langley', p. 161.

6 Sir Eustace remained within the children's personal guard throughout their parents' time in Gascony: Byerly and Byerly, *Wardrobe and Household*, ii, nos 3400, 3411, 3423; Green, *Lives of the Princesses*, ii, pp. 298–9.

7 The king's order to restore to Eleanor of St Paul her estate is summarised in *Calendar of Close Rolls*, 1288–96, p. 27.

8 Edward's letter detailing his plans to move forward with Eleanora's marriage can be found in *Fœdera*, i, p. 678.

9 Legal separations, such as the one Gilbert and Alice de Lusignan experienced, were comparatively accessible in the later medieval period, with adultery and violence often given as the reason. Property including dowries might even be returned in these cases, but critically neither party was normally able to remarry. On marriage in the Middle Ages, see D. L. d'Avray, *Medieval Marriage: Symbolism and Society* (Oxford, 2005). For the terms of their divorce, see *Fœdera*, i, pp. 628, 654. For Gilbert's gift-giving to Joanna, see Green, *Lives of the Princesses*, ii, p. 328.

10 Ibid, p. 327.

11 On the way that the resistance practised by female saints might impact a medieval female reader, see Jocelyn Wogan-Browne, 'Saints' lives and the female reader', *Forum for Modern Language Studies*, 27 (1991), pp. 314–32.

12 See, for the purchase of silks for Margaret's use, Green, *Lives of the Princesses*, ii, p. 395. For a description of berceletts, see *Boucher's glossary of archaic and provincial words: a supplement to the dictionaries of the English language, particularly those of Dr. Johnson and Dr. Webster*, ed. Joseph Hunter and Joseph Stevenson (London, 1832–3).

13 For a description of Jan's seal, see Green, *Lives of the Princesses*, ii, pp. 378–9.
14 The terms agreeing Elizabeth's marriage to the son of the Count of Holland can be found in *Fœdera*, i, pp. 652, 658.
15 The preparations for the children's welcome party are listed in Johnstone, *Edward of Carnarvon*, p. 23 n1.

VI. UNION

1 See a description of this episode in Parsons, *Eleanor of Castile*, p. 40.
2 The letter confirming Joanna's permission to marry Gilbert is given in full in *Fœdera*, i, p. 721.
3 For the charters detailing the resettlement of the Clare estate, see *Calendar of Fine Rolls*, 1272–1307, pp. 274–5; *Calendar of Patent Rolls*, 1281–92, pp. 350–1, 359. See also K.B. McFarlane's consideration of the settlement of Joanna's marriage, and its differences with Elizabeth's subsequent union to the Earl of Hereford and Essex, in his 'Had Edward I a "Policy" towards the Earls?', *The Nobility of Later Medieval England: The Ford Lectures for 1953 and related studies* (Oxford, 1973), pp. 248–67 (especially pp. 260–1). The royal family had visited Amesbury the previous autumn, after their arrival back from Gascony. At that time, the prioress appealed to them for financial assistance, pressing that the welfare of their child was tied to that of the priory; the king responded with his grant in perpetuity of the manor of Melksham, a gift worth twenty-seven pounds per year: see above, Chapter 4, p. 58. Eleanor's gift to her eldest daughter is recorded in Parsons, *Court and Household*, p. 134.
4 For the 1290 Winchester tournament and its probable association with the surviving Round Table, see Martin Biddle, *King Arthur's Round Table: An Archaeological Investigation* (Woodbridge, 2000), Chapter 10.
5 For a description of the ritual blessing attending a second marriage – as was Gilbert's to Joanna – taken from the Sarum rite, dominant in late-medieval England, see d'Avray, *Medieval marriage*, pp. 152–5.
6 A description of Joanna's wedding feast appears in Green, *Lives of the Princesses*, ii, p. 330. The minstrels' presence is discussed in E.K. Chambers, *The Mediaeval Stage* (Oxford, 1903), ii, Appendix D.
7 For the status of Marcher lords and the quotation pertaining to the Clare lordship in Glamorgan, see R.R. Davies, *Lordship and Society in the March of Wales 1282–1400* (Oxford, 1978), especially p. 90. For Edward and Eleanor's anger on Joanna's early departure from London, see Parsons, *Court and Household*, p. 135. Gilbert's raid in Brecon is

mentioned in Michael Altschul, *A Baronial Family in Medieval England: The Clares, 1217–1314* (Baltimore, 1965), pp. 148–9.

8 For a clear and thorough explanation of the theories of 'wife-giving' and the 'exchange of women', and also how these are problematized in a medieval context, see Susan Crane, *The Performance of Self: Ritual, Clothing, and Identity During the Hundred Years War* (Philadelphia, 2002), pp. 28–32.

9 The king's instruction to his keeper at the Exchange is recorded in *Calendar of Close Rolls, 1288–96*, p. 89. Joanna's trousseau is described by Green in *Lives of the Princesses*, ii, pp. 334–5.

10 The queen's preparations for Margaret's wedding are detailed in Parsons, *Court and Household*, p. 109.

11 Joanna's presence at Clerkenwell is attested by a feast her husband hosted in her honour at their house there on 3 July. See Clive H. Knowles, 'Gilbert de Clare, seventh earl of Gloucester and sixth earl of Hereford', *Oxford Dictionary of National Biography*. For attendance at Margaret's wedding, see Bartholomew Cotton, *Historia Anglia*, ed. H.R. Luard (London, 1859), pp. 176–7; and Green, *Lives of the Princesses*, ii, 371–2.

12 Later regretting his violence, Edward paid the unnamed squire more than thirteen pounds in compensation, a significant sum: see Michael Prestwich, *Edward I* (London, 1988), p. 111.

13 Cotton, *Historia Anglia*, p. 174.

VII. THREE DEATHS

1 Edward's disappointment that Margaret was missing Mass is discussed in Green, *Lives of the Princesses*, ii, p. 373. The letter which Margaret sealed using her mother's seal can be read in *Fœdera*, i, p. 739.

2 The king's house at Clipstone was largely dismantled in the early modern period, most of its stone carted away for building projects elsewhere in Nottinghamshire, and its scant remains were long ago worn to ruin. For a description, see *History of the King's Works*, ed. Colvin, ii, pp. 918–21.

3 For the queen's final journey north and the commemorative programme that followed her death, see J. Hunter, 'On the Death of Eleanor of Castile, Consort of King Edward the First, and the Honours paid to her Memory', *Archaeologia* 29 (1842), pp. 167–91. Sara Cockerill offers a clear illustration of the queen's last year and decline in 1290; painstakingly reconstructing Eleanor's final journey northwards and demonstrating clearly the association between the itinerary north – and subsequent cortège south – with estates held

by the queen, in her *Eleanor of Castile: The Shadow Queen* (Stroud, 2014), Chapter 16.

4 As so often, frustratingly little can be gleaned from historical sources about how Edward's daughters perceived his expulsion of the Jewish population, but a few small glimmers hint at the potential that some of his children may have felt a greater sympathy than their father. Eleanora's intercession on behalf of the convert Eleanor of Saint Paul demonstrates at least an openness to using her influence to represent an ethnically Jewish woman. And in the decade that followed, Margaret's husband, Jan, once defended with arms the Jewish merchant population of Brussels from a mob of zealous locals intent on massacring them in the name of Christ.

5 Joanna and Gilbert's pledge to join the Crusade was noted by Bartholomew Cotton in his *Historia Anglia*, p. 177.

6 Eleanor of Provence's anxieties over the late-autumn travel of her young grandchildren are quoted in Johnstone, *Edward of Carnarvon*, p. 24; and listed in *List of ancient correspondence of the Chancery and Exchequer*, xvi, no. 170.

7 For Matthew Paris's shock at the use of carpets on the floor, see *Matthæi Parisiensis, monachi Sancti Albani, Chronica Majora*, ed. H.R. Luard, 7 vols, (Kraus reprint, Wiesbaden, 1964), v, pp. 513–4. The queen's wardrobe accounts record that she dispersed personal items to her children, but the list of these effects does not survive. The memory that the queen's crown was passed to her youngest daughter on this date is recorded in a catalogue of items owned by the princess following her own death: Parsons, *Court and Household*, p. 27.

8 On the process of embalming in thirteenth-century England, see Danielle Westerhof, *Death and the Noble Body in Medieval England* (Woodbridge, 2008), Chapter 4.

9 The crosses at Geddington, Hardingstone, and Waltham survive, with some restor-ations. The most famous, at Charing Cross near Trafalgar Square in London, is a Victorian reconstruction of the original, destroyed during the Civil War.

10 Edward's gift on learning the news of his first grandson is recorded in *Calendar of Close Rolls*, 1288–96, pp. 169–70. Gilbert's joy is noted in Wykes, *Annales Monastici*, ed. Luard, iv, p. 328.

VIII. ALLIANCE

1 The king's summons to Eleanora's wedding are discussed in Samuel Lyons, 'Copies of Writs Preserved among His Majesty's Records in the Tower . . .', *Archaeologia*, xv (1806), pp. 347–9.

2 See Cotton, *Historia Anglicana*, pp. 232–3.

3 For Eleanora's enlarged household in the aftermath of her mother's death, see Green, *Lives of the Princesses*, ii, 304.

4 See the order issued by Edward instructing his men to ensure the dower estate promised to Eleanora actually produced the expected income: *Calendar of Patent Rolls*, 1292–1301, p. 67.

5 For the travel of her youngest siblings to Eleanora's wedding, and of Mary and Jan's visits to Kennington, see Johnstone, *Edward of Carvarvon*, pp. 26, 28. Joanna's visit to Mortlake is discussed in Green, *Lives of the Princesses*, ii, p. 339. For Edward's letter confirming Mary's enlarged allowance, see *Fœdera*, i, p. 799.

6 Gilbert's anxiety over his child's health is noted in *List of ancient correspondence*, xxii, no. 156. For the children's household at Usk, see National Archives Special Collections 6/1247/25.

7 For the 1292 seizure and restoration of Glamorgan, see John E. Morris, *The Welsh Wars of Edward I: a contribution to mediaeval military history, based on original documents* (Oxford, 1901), p. 236.

8 Further details on the party that sailed for Ireland can be found in Altschul, *A Baronial Family*, p. 154; *Calendar of Patent Rolls*, 1292–1301, pp. 11, 19–28.

9 The king's order to the Keeper of the Forest of Dean is summarised in *Calendar of Close Rolls*, 1288–96, p. 302.

10 Surviving wardrobe entries record some of Eleanora's preparations for her move abroad. For example, an entry recording how her tailor Peter was reimbursed one hundred shillings in January for expenses he had incurred in making new robes for the princess, probably intended as part of her trousseau: *Book of Prests*, ed. Fryde, p. 133. For a list of those assigned to accompany Eleanora to Bar, see *Calendar of Patent Rolls*, 1292–1301, pp. 65–70. For the presentation of an English benefice to Theobald of Bar, see ibid, p. 66. For a letter describing the illnesses of Margaret and Prince Edward, see Green, *Lives of the Princesses*, ii, Appendix xvi.

11 For an account of the tournament and death of Duke John that follows Thielrode, see: Alphonse Wauters, *Le duc Jean Ier et le Brabant sous le règne de ce prince (1267–1294)* (Brussels, 1862), pp. 217–8. See also F. Christophe Butkens, *Trophées sacrés et profanes du Duche de Brabant*, 4 vols (The Hague, 1724), i, p. 331.

12 Ralph de Athelee is described as acting as chaplain to Margaret and Elizabeth in March 1295, suggesting that when Elizabeth visited court she joined the household of her older sister: *Book of Prests*, ed. Fryde, p. 36. Preparations for Margaret's departure can be found in ibid, pp. 92, 100, 111, 117, 134. For Jan's voyage to Brabant, see *Fœdera*, i, p. 802.

13 For the quotation, see Gottfried von Strassburg, *Tristan*, ed. A.T. Hatto (London, 2004), pp. 193–4.

14 The *Life of St Edward* which may have belonged to Eleanor is Cambridge University Library MS Ee.3.59. It has been fully digitized and is freely available to view on the library's website. The poem dedicated to Margaret was translated from the Middle Dutch by Green: *Lives of the Princesses*, ii, pp. 376–7.

15 The spokeswoman who approached Eleanor at St Albans was either struck dumb through nerves on meeting the queen or could not speak sufficient French; the letter the petitioners sent instead survives as National Archives Special Collections 1/11/90: see Parsons, *Eleanor of Castile*, p. 64; John Carmi Parsons, 'The Queen's Intercession in Thirteenth-Century England', in *Power of the Weak: Studies on Medieval Women* ed. Jennifer Carpenter and Sally Beth MacLean, pp. 148–77 (pp. 151–2).

16 The laundress Alice, who had served Eleanora, Joanna, and Margaret in 1285, was still employed as Margaret's laundress in 1295, when she was paid four-and-a-half pence per day; Roger, the duchess's tailor who repaired her dresses in September 1294, had held the same position in February 1286: *Book of Prests*, ed. Fryde, pp. 36, 92, 182; Byerly and Byerly, *Wardrobe and Household*, i, nos 1708, 1715. For Margaret's promotion of Alice de Neutembre, see *Calendar of Patent Rolls, 1292–1301*, p. 75. For the use of French at court in Brussels, see Wauters, *Le duc Jean Ier*, p. 391.

17 For examples of Margaret's intercession at the English court after her marriage on behalf of friends and Brabant, see *Calendar of Patent Rolls, 1292–1301*, pp. 150, 207, 229; *Calendar of Fine Rolls, 1272–1307*, p. 309.

18 On the nursery provision of Elizabeth and Prince Edward, see Johnstone, *Edward of Carnarvon*, Chapter 2. The poem praising the prince's riding is quoted at p. 13. On the siblings' interest in polyphony, see *Letters of Edward Prince of Wales*, ed. Johnstone, p. 133.

IX. LADIES OF WAR

1 For the 1294 preparations to sail to Gascony, see Prestwich, *Edward I*, p. 381.

2 For the Clares' experience of the uprising in Glamorgan, see Altschul, *A Baronial Family*, p. 154. For the lasting results of the uprising, see the description of the Glamorgan properties taken by the *inquisition post mortem* following Gilbert's death, which describes the castles and town as 'burnt': *Calendar of Inquisitions Post Mortem*, Edward I,

iii, no. 371. Kenfig was rebuilt early in the fourteenth century, but the castle at Llangynwyd (called an alternative name, Tyriatlh, in the inquisition) was never rebuilt after the 1294 rebellion.

3 On the Welsh Marches at this time, see Davies, *Lordship and Society*. For the value of the Clare estates, see ibid, p. 196, and for the quotation, p. 74.

4 For the Dunstable account, see *Annales Monastici*, ed. Luard, iii (Kraus reprint, Nendeln, 1972), p. 387.

5 For Gilbert's campaign to recapture Glamorgan, see Altschul, *A Baronial Family*, pp. 154–5. Edward's confiscation of Glamorgan in 1294 is discussed in Davies, *Lordship and Society*, pp. 90–1.

6 Joanna's confirmation of Gilbert's alienation of estates is preserved in *Calendar of Patent Rolls, 1292–1301*, p. 140. For Elizabeth's birth, see Frances A. Underhill, *For Her Good Estate: The life of Elizabeth de Burgh* (Basingstoke, 1999), p. 5. The letter reinstating their estate to Gilbert and Joanna is summarized in *Calendar of Patent Rolls, 1292–1301*, p. 154.

7 For the renewed plans surrounding a marriage between Elizabeth and Johan, see *Fœdera*, i, p. 841. For Edward's pledge to pay Brabant to support his war effort against France, see ibid, pp. 808, 820.

8 For references to messages sent between Edward and Bar, see the king's wardrobe accounts for 20 November 1296–20 November 1297, which is preserved as British Library Additional MS 7965, ff. 34v, 55, 113.

9 For the passage from Christine de Pisan, see *The Treasure of the City of Ladies, or the Book of the Three Virtues*, ed. Sarah Lawson (Harmondsworth, 1985), p. 129.

10 The French perspective on Henri's campaign is recorded in *Grandes Chroniques de France: selon que elles sont conservée en l'église de Saint-Denis de France*, ed. M. Paulin Paris (Paris, 1836–8), v, pp. 119–20. The quotation from Pisan can be found in *Treasure of the City of Ladies*, p. 129.

11 Edward's letter requesting help for Henri is preserved in *Fœdera*, i, p. 867.

12 Edward calls Henri 'a noble man and our dear son' in a letter of 1297: *Foedera*, i, p. 871.

X. UNCONSTRAINED

1 For Gilbert's death, see Altschul, *A Baronial Family*, p. 155 and n.

2 I am grateful to Nigel Saul for pointing out the location within Tewkesbury Abbey of the Clare burials, and the source for this

information. For a ground plan showing the burials, see *Tewkesbury Abbey: History, Art and Architecture*, ed. R.K. Morris and R. Shoesmith (Almeley, 2003) p. 162.

3 Edward's order to take the Clare estate into custody after Gilbert's death appears in *Calendar of Fine Rolls*, 1272–1307, p. 368.

4 For a fuller discussion of the ways in which elite widows might rise above the patriarchal system in medieval England, see Linda E. Mitchell, *Portraits of Medieval Women: Family, Marriage, and Politics in England 1225–1350* (New York, 2003), especially Chapter 9.

5 For the reasons why widows might remarry, see Chrétien de Troyes, *Yvain, or The Knight with the Lion*, trans. Ruth Harwood Cline (Athens, GA, 1975), p. 59. On second marriages, see d'Avray, *Medieval Marriage*, p. 143.

6 See Linda E. Mitchell 'Noble Widowhood in the Thirteenth Century: Three Generations of Mortimer Widows, 1246–1334', in *Upon My Husband's Death: Widows in the Literature and Histories of Medieval Europe*, ed. Louise Mirrer (Ann Arbor, 1992), pp. 169–92.

7 For agreements around Gilbert's debts, see *Calendar of Patent Rolls*, 1292–1301, p. 183; Green, *Lives of the Princesses*, ii, p. 341.

8 For vows spoken during the ceremony of homage, see Frederick Pollock and Frederic William Maitland, *The history of English law before the time of Edward I* (Cambridge, 1895), pp. 180–3.

9 On the shift in thinking around women performing homage, see ibid, p. 186.

10 The order to restore Joanna's estate is summarized in *Calendar of Close Rolls*, 1288–96, p. 470. Joanna's appointment of a representative for her Irish estates can be found in *Calendar of Patent Rolls*, 1292–1302, p. 179. The whole estate at Gilbert's death is described in depth in *Calendar of Inquisitions Post Mortem*, Edward I, iii, no. 371; and see p. 237 for the granting of Thaxted to Alice de Lusignan. For the early fourteenth-century valuation of the estate, see Davies, *Lordship and Society*, p. 196.

11 Edward's instruction to his tax collectors regarding Joanna's estate is described in *Calendar of Close Rolls*, 1288–96, p. 471.

12 For the letter assigning the children to Bristol Castle, see ibid, p. 471.

13 For the custody of Owain ap Dafydd at Bristol, see ibid, p. 298.

XI. ACQUIESCENCE AND INSUBORDINATION

1 For the celebrations surrounding Elizabeth's wedding and the gifts exchanged by the family, see Green, *Lives of the Princesses*, ii, pp. 382, 384; iii, pp. 13–5.

2 For Bartholomew Cotton's description of the event, see his *Historia Anglia*, p. 316.

3 On the treaty negotiated between Holland and Brabant at Elizabeth's wedding, see *Foedera*, i, p. 852.

4 Margaret's trousseau is discussed in detail in Green, *Lives of the Princesses*, ii, pp. 383–4; see also BL Add MS 7965, ff. 15, 16, 16v, 134, 135v. On the expected cost of a princess's trousseau, see Edward's deathbed provision for the dowry of his youngest daughter, Eleanor (by Margaret of France), which included funds to support a trousseau worth more than three thousand pounds; this sum was probably estimated on his experience by that date of having provided trousseaux for four older daughters: *Calendar of Patent Rolls, 1302–7*, p. 460. The fleet is described within 'Willelmi Monaschi & Procuratoris Egmondani Chronicon ab Ann. DC XLVII usque at Ann. MCCCXXXIII' printed in Antonius Matthaeus *Veteris aevi analecta, seu, Vetera monumenta hactenus nondum visa . . .*, 2nd edn, 5 vols (Hagæ-Comitum, 1738), ii, p. 541. For Margaret's English servant who remained with her, see Thomas de Caumvill, who in July 1297 received permission to remain with Margaret for one year: *Calendar of Patent Rolls, 1292–1301*, p. 295. The other members of Margaret's entourage are listed in ibid, pp. 226–8.

5 For the wardrobe entry ordering the replacement of stones in Elizabeth's crown, see BL Add MS 7965, f. 15v. For the men sent to confirm the value of Elizabeth's dower, see *Calendar of Patent Rolls, 1292–1302*, p. 229.

6 Edward's parting gift to Margaret is recorded in the king's wardrobe book for 20 November 1300–20 November 1301, preserved as British Library Additional MS 7596, f. 15v.

7 Edward's order to confiscate Joanna's properties is described in *Calendar of Close Rolls, 1296–1302*, p. 12. For Edward's instruction dispatching his confessor to seek out Joanna, see BL Add MS 7965, 9v.

8 For the order confiscating the property of the bailiff of Tonbridge, see *Calendar of Fine Rolls, 1272–1307*, p. 383.

9 Edward's correspondence with Amadeus regarding the latter's request to marry Joanna can be read in *Foedera*, i, pp. 853–6, 861.

10 For a contemporary response by an unknown chronicler to Joanna's marriage to Ralph, see *Opus Chronicorum*, part of the *Chronica Monasterii S Albani*, ed. Henry Thomas Riley, iii (Kraus reprint, Nendeln, 1972), p. 27. For Rishanger's reaction, see William Rishanger, *Chronica et Annales*, part of the *Chronica Monasterii S Albani*, ed. Henry Thomas Riley, ii (Kraus reprint, Millwood, NY, 1983) p. 416.

11 For Matthew Paris's description of the events leading up to the
   marriage of Eleanor and Simon de Montfort, see *Chronica Majora*,
   ed. Luard, iii, pp. 470–1, 475, 487, 566–7.
12 For the arrival of Joanna's children at court, see BL Add MS 7965,
   f. 33.
13 For Joanna's maintenance grant, see *Calendar of Close Rolls*, 1296–
   1302, p. 30. For Edward's men travelling into Joanna's Welsh
   dominion to hear complaints directly from her tenants, see *Calendar
   of Patent Rolls*, 1292–1302, p. 249, and for the significance of this,
   see Davies, *Lordship and Society*, pp. 268–9. For Edward's grant of
   income from Joanna's estates to his men, see *Calendar of Patent
   Rolls*, 1292–1302, p. 292. Anthony Bek's guidance that Edward accept
   Joanna's remarriage is recorded in *The Chronicle of Walter of
   Guisborough*, ed. H. Rothwell (London, 1957), p. 259.
14 Joanna's speech is preserved in *Opus Chronicorum*, ed. Riley,
   p. 27.
15 For a discussion of Capellanus' views on marriage and social status,
   see Peter Coss, *The Lady in Medieval England, 1000–1500* (Stroud,
   1998), p. 150.
16 The restoration of Joanna's estate is described in *Calendar of Fine
   Rolls*, 1272–1307, pp. 389–90.

XII. CRISIS

1 For the items Elizabeth took to Holland, see BL Add MS 7965, ff. 22,
   23, 28, 142.
2 For Elizabeth's travel and entertainment, see BL Add MS 7965, ff.
   27v, 52. For Elizabeth and Mary's commissioning of Mass for Eleanor
   of Castile, see Green, *Lives of the Princesses*, ii, p. 420.
3 For a description of the fleet that sailed with Elizabeth, see Bryce
   and Mary Lyon, 'The Logistics for Edward I's ill-fated campaign in
   Flanders (1297–8)', in *Handelingen der Maatschappij voor
   Geschiedenis en Oudheidkunde te Gent*, 55 (2001), pp. 77–92;
   Bryce Lyon, 'The Failed Flemish Campaign of Edward I in 1297: A
   case study of efficient logistics and inadequate military planning',
   in *Handelingen der Maatschappij voor Geschiedenis en
   Oudheidkunde te Gent*, 59 (2005), pp. 31–42; Prestwich, *Edward I*,
   Chapter 16, *passim*.
4 Margaret's gift to her father is recorded in BL Add MS 7965, f. 57,
   while the offerings made by the king and his daughter can be found
   at f. 10.
5 Joanna likely delivered her daughter Mary Monthermer at Windsor

Castle, where her father directed the houses in the outer bailey for the use of her and Ralph in September: *Calendar of Close Rolls, 1296–1302*, p. 63. Her father's gift on news of the birth appears in ibid, p. 72.

6 For the foods provided for Elizabeth and her father, see BL Add MS 7596, f. 28.

7 Eleanora's gift to her father is noted in BL Add MS 7596, f. 57v. Edward's contribution to Henri's ransom is discussed by Green in *Lives of the Princesses*, ii, p. 312. Marie's gifts to Edward in Ghent are recorded in BL Add MS 7966, f. 148.

8 Eleanora's gifts to her father are recorded in Green, *Lives of the Princesses*, ii, pp. 312–3; BL Add MS 7966, f. 148.

9 Margaret's intercessory efforts while in Ghent are described in Green, *Lives of the Princesses*, ii, p. 388.

10 The chaos at court in Ghent is described by Green, at ibid, pp. 313–4, and 314 n1.

11 For Edward's delight at seeing Brussels, see ibid, pp. 388–9, and 389 n1.

12 Green discusses the episode in which Edward pays off Mary's substantial debts to Martin in *Lives of the Princesses*, ii, p. 421.

13 For the notice of Eleanora's death, see the Hagnaby chronicle: British Library Cotton MS Vespasian B XI, f. 46.

14 Eleanora's monument at Westminster is described in John Stow and John Strype, *A Survey of the Cities of London and Westminster: containing the original, antiquity, increase, modern estate and government of those cities . . . in six books* (London, 1720), vi, p. 14. Katherine and Joanna, born around 1261 and 1265 respectively, were both dead before John's birth in 1266. In addition to those whose burials are listed at Westminster, at least one other sibling died abroad, the girl born to Eleanor of Castile during her first year in residence at Acre, one year before Joanna's birth in the same city. Her burial location is unknown. An unnamed daughter is also thought to have been born to Eleanor in her first year of marriage, buried at Bordeaux.

15 Elizabeth's role in the Borselen episode is recounted in Matthaeus Vossius, *Annales Hollandiae Zelandiaeque . . .* (Amsterdam, 1680), p. 199; Antoine-Marie Cerisier, *Tableau de l'histoire general des province-unies* (Utrecht, 1777–84), i, p. 358. The quotation appears in Cerisier.

16 Green discusses the Borselen episode and its aftermath for Elizabeth, including her elevated position, in *Lives of the Princesses*, iii, p. 27. For the attendance of English servants on Elizabeth after Johan's

death, see *Foedera*, i, p. 918; *Calendar of Close Rolls*, 1296–1302, pp. 382–3. Vossius describes Elizabeth's departure for England in his *Annales Hollandiae*, p. 204.

XIII. HOMECOMING

1 Messages to and from Brabant are attested in the king's wardrobe book for the twenty-eighth year of Edward's reign, preserved as British Library Additional MS 35291, f. 71v; BL Add MS 7966, ff. 66, 66v, 69.

2 For the description of Ralph at Caerlaverock, see *The Siege of Carlaverock*, ed. Nicholas Harris Nicolas (London, 1828), pp. 48–9. For the feast at Westminster where Joanna presided, see Green, *Lives of the Princesses*, ii, p. 349.

3 For Edward's anxiety on Margaret's early delivery, see *The Chronicle of Pierre de Langtoft, in French verse, from the earliest period to the death of Edward I*, ed. Thomas Wright, 2 vols, (Kraus reprint, Wiesbaden, 1964), ii, pp. 324–5. A full account of the baby's birth can be found in K. Staniland, 'Welcome, Royal Babe! The Birth of Thomas of Brotherton in 1300', *Costume* (1985), pp. 1–13. For Robert Mannyng of Brunne's effusive compliment of Marguerite, see John Carmi Parsons, 'Margaret of France (1279–1318)', in *Historical Dictionary of Late Medieval England, 1272–1485*, ed. Ronald H. Fritze and William B. Robison (Westport, CT, 2002), p. 337. An example of Marguerite and Elizabeth joining together to intercede with the king is recorded in *Calendar of Patent Rolls, 1301–7*, p. 38.

4 For Prince Edward's introduction to Piers Gaveston, see Johnstone, *Edward of Carnarvon*, p. 54.

5 For the royal gifts to the messenger who brought news of Margaret's successful delivery, see John Topham, *Liber quotidianus contrarotulatoris garderobae. Anno regni regis Edwardi primi vicesimo octavo . . .* (London, 1787), pp. 170, 182. For Margaret's diplomacy, see *Calendar of Patent Rolls*, 1292–1301, pp. 557–8; *Calendar of Close Rolls*, 1296–1302, p. 474.

6 The Masses said for Johan's anniversary are recorded in Topham, *Liber quotidianus*, p. 43; as are the necessary payments associated with Elizabeth's trip to Kirkby Fleetham, at p. 75. (Cf. Green, *Lives of the Princesses*, iii, p. 32, in which in a rare error, Green records Elizabeth having travelled to Kirkletham on the east coast, rather than Kirkby Fleetham ['Kirkebifletham' in the wardrobe book], on her way to Ripon.) Payment for Elizabeth's new gown is noted at

BL Add MS 7966, f. 34v. For Elizabeth's intercession on behalf of her deceased mother's associates, see *Calendar of Patent Rolls*, 1301–7, p. 36.

7   The purchase and transport of items for Elizabeth to wear appear throughout BL Add MS 7966, including at, e.g., ff. 31, 31v, 32, 32v. For the Christmas entertainments and gifts at Northampton, see ibid, ff. 66v, 67.

8   For Elizabeth's journey to Hailes, see BL Add MS 7966, f. 35. Her intercessory efforts are detailed in *Calendar of Patent Rolls*, 1292–1301, pp. 589, 590. For Lady de Saux's departure, see Green, *Lives of the Princesses*, iii, p. 35. For the ongoing efforts to obtain Elizabeth's dower, see *Calendar of Patent Rolls*, 1292–1301, p. 587; *Calendar of Close Rolls*, 1296–1302, p. 442.

9   For the order requesting Gilbert de Clare join the royal household, see *Calendar of Patent Rolls*, 1292–1301, p. 606.

10 For the restoration of Tonbridge, see *Calendar of Close Rolls*, 1296–1302, p. 473.

XIV. COMPANIONSHIP

1   Green surmises Elizabeth had known Humphrey since her childhood: *Lives of the Princesses*, iii, p. 36.

2   For the terms governing Humphrey's estate upon his marriage to Elizabeth, see *Calendar of Patent Rolls*, 1301–7, p. 96. Perhaps in order to avoid Elizabeth having the same freedoms regarding the Bohun estate that Joanna had enjoyed and exploited with the Clare estate, Humphrey's estate – in the event his marriage with Elizabeth proved childless and he predeceased his wife – would default to his usual heirs, rather than to Elizabeth: see McFarlane, 'Had Edward I a "Policy"', p. 261. For a description of Elizabeth's bridal crown, see Green, *Lives of the Princesses*, iii, p. 38–9.

3   For the 1302 tax associated with Joanna's first wedding, see Prestwich, *Edward I*, p. 529.

4   Edward's purchase of armour for his eldest grandson is noted in Green, *Lives of the Princesses*, ii, p. 353 n6.

5   Green details the installation of the royal women at Tynemouth, at ibid, p. 353.

6   For this episode, see *Calendar of Patent Rolls*, 1301–7, p. 50.

7   See for Elizabeth's post-partum gift giving, and the breaking of the minstrel's instrument, Green, *Lives of the Princesses*, iii, pp. 39–40. The anniversary of Joanna de Mereworth's death on 13 August is recorded (as are those of Elizabeth's mother, grandmother, and sisters

who predeceased her) in the calendar affixed to Elizabeth's psalter, BL
Add MS 24686, 8v.

8 For Ralph's good standing with his father-in-law by this date, see
Green, *Lives of the Princesses*, ii, p. 352.

9 Margaret's letter to her father is transcribed within Green, *Lives
of the Princesses*, ii, p. 392. For further detail surrounding this
episode, see *Calendar of Close Rolls*, 1302–7, pp. 4, 6, 17, 22,
40, 110.

10 Sara Cockerill dicusses how Eleanor of Castile's decision to travel
with Edward on campaign was likely influenced by the choice of her
own mother, Jeanne de Dammartin, to accompany her husband,
Ferdinand III of Castile, on his military campaigns in her *Eleanor of
Castile*, p. 49. Elizabeth's household during this period is detailed in
Green, *Lives of the Princesses*, iii, p. 41 n1.

11 Joanna's intercession at Jedburgh is recorded in *Calendar of Patent
Rolls*, 1301–7, p. 254. For Elizabeth's equipment at Knaresborough,
see Green, *Lives of the Princesses*, iii, pp. 41–2.

12 For Aveline's death, see Trivet, *Annales sex regum*, p. 294; see also
Margaret Howell, *Eleanor of Provence: Queenship in Thirteenth-
Century England* (Oxford, 2001), p. 246. On medieval childbirth and
fear, see Roberta Gilchrist, *Medieval Life: Archaeology and the Life
Course* (Cambridge, 2013), Chapter 4.

13 For the Westminster Girdle, see J. Perkins, *Westminster Abbey, its
Worship and Ornaments* (London, 1938–52), ii, p. 57.

14 On the use of the Westminster Girdle, see *Women of the English
Nobility and Gentry: 1066–1500*, ed. Jennifer Ward (Manchester,
1995), pp. 68–9.

15 King Edward only gave forty marks to the messenger who brought
the news from Knaresborough, about one-third of what he gifted to
the messenger who had delivered the news of the successful birth of
little Jan III of Brabant, and only one-quarter of the gift he gave on
learning of the birth of Gilbert de Clare: *Calendar of Patent Rolls*,
1301–7, p. 176; Green, *Lives of the Princesses*, iii, p. 42.

Much confusion has surrounded the birth dates of Elizabeth's
children. Strong evidence for Humphrey's birth and death can be
found in the surviving accounts of Elizabeth's household from
November 1303 to November 1304, which detail the September loan
of the Girdle of the Virgin at Knaresborough and her October
purification, as well as the funeral proceedings for baby Humphrey in
October and November of that year: *Women of the English Nobility
and Gentry*, ed. Ward, pp. 68–9.

For the date of Humphrey's death, see the Bohun manuscript

genealogy, which gives 10 September 1304: Dugdale, *Monasticon Anglicanum*, vi, p. 135.

16 A manuscript genealogy associated with Llanthony Priory recounts the pedigree of the Bohun family (founders of the priory); of Margaret, it records only that she 'died young': Dugdale, *Monasticon Anglicanum*, vi, p. 135. For the effects of Katherine's death on her parents, see *Chronica Majora*, v, pp. 632, 643.

17 Edward's role in caring for his grandchildren in Bar is made clear in a letter of October 1302, in which he wrote to the nobles of Bar to ratify the list of guardians by whose hands the county would be governed until his grandson and namesake, Count Edward, reached his majority: *Calendar of Patent Rolls, 1301–7*, p. 66.

18 The monument is described in *The History and Antiquities of the Abbey Church of St Peter: Westminster*, ed. W.E. Brayley (London, 1818–23), ii, pp. 182–3.

XV. OPULENCE

1 For Edward's requirement that Mary remain in England, see *Calendar of Patent Rolls, 1301–7*, p. 327.

2 For the king's allowances made to Mary, see ibid, pp. 262, 269, 280.

3 For enhancements to Mary's income and provision for her chamber, see ibid, pp. 52, 325, 342; *Calendar of Close Rolls, 1302–7*, pp. 416–7.

4 Mary's furnishings, jewels, and foods are mentioned in Green, *Lives of the Princesses*, ii, pp. 422, 424, 429.

5 For Mary's appointment to visit the other English houses within the order of Fontevrault, see ibid, p. 424.

6 Green details Mary's expenditure while on pilgrimage or travelling to court in ibid, pp. 423, 427.

7 For Prince Edward's gambling, see Johnstone, *Edward of Carnarvon*, p. 86. For Mary's gambling loss of borrowed money, see Green, *Lives of the Princesses*, ii, p. 434.

8 For Eleanor's furnishings and foods, see Cockerill, *Eleanor of Castile*, pp. 230–3; Parsons, *Eleanor of Castile*, pp. 51–4. Matthew Paris's criticism of the queen's chambers appears in his *Chronica Majora*, v, pp. 513–4. See also Paul Binski, *The Painted Chamber at Westminster* (London, 1986).

9 See surviving copies of the work: BL Arundel MS 56; Trivet, *Annales sex regum*.

10 For a description of Clare Castle, see David Hatton, *Clare, Suffolk, an account of historical features of the town, its Priory and its Parish Church* (Clare, 1994), i, pp. 28–9.

11 For Margaret's role in building the castle, see Green, *Lives of the Princesses*, ii, pp. 389–90.

12 Prince Edward's letters to his sister are preserved in *Letters of Edward Prince of Wales*, ed. Johnstone, pp. 116, 133. For the prince's love of music, see Johnstone, *Edward of Carnarvon*, pp. 64–5. For the king's livery worn by Elizabeth's household, see Green, *Lives of the Princesses*, iii, p. 48.

13 For the marriage between John de Warenne and Joanna of Bar, see *Calendar of Close Rolls*, 1302–7, p. 321.

14 On chansons des nonnes, and for the quotation, see Lisa Colton, 'The Articulation of Virginity in the Medieval "Chanson de nonne"', *Journal of the Royal Musical Association*, 133, no. 2 (2008), pp. 159–88 (184). On the theme of nuns breaking their vows of chastity or even becoming apostate, see Power, *Medieval English Nunneries*, Chapter 11, and for the scandal at Amesbury, p. 445; for Bale's comment on the nuns of St Radegund's, see *The Biographical Dictionary; Or, Complete Historic Library: Containing the Lives of the Most Celebrated Personages of Great Britain and Ireland, Whether Admirals, Generals, Poets, Statesmen, Philosophers, Or Divines* (London, 1780), p. 31.

15 For the date of John de Bohun's birth, see *Calendar of Close Rolls*, 1327–30, p. 26. Cf. G.E.C. Cokayne, *The Complete Peerage of England, Scotland, Ireland, Great Britain and the United Kindom* (London, 1887–9), vi, p. 470, which gives his birth date in 1306. For the ongoing efforts at claiming Elizabeth's dower during this period, see *Calendar of Patent Rolls*, 1301–7, pp. 13, 63, 102, 111, 130, 215, 330.

16 For Edward's forgiving of Joanna's debts, see Altshul, *A Baronial Family*, pp. 158–9; *Calendar of Patent Rolls*, 1301–7, p. 308.

XVI. THE STORM APPROACHES

1 For Higden's description of Prince Edward, see *Polychronicon Ranulphi Higden, monachi Cestrensis*, ed. J.R. Lumby, 9 vols, (Kraus reprint, Wiesbaden, 1964), viii, p. 298.

2 For the prince's letters on this occasion, see *Letters of Edward Prince of Wales*, ed. Johnstone, pp. 60–1, p. 74.

3 For correspondence related to his sisters' efforts to support Prince Edward in his argument with their father, see ibid, pp. 70, 73 (the Gilbert de Clare mentioned in this letter was a cousin of Joanna's first husband and should not be confused with her son of the same name); Green, *Lives of the Princesses*, iii, p. 46 and appendix III.

Queen Marguerite's intercession is recorded in *Calendar of Close Rolls, 1302–7*, p. 342.

4 For Joanna's new year's gift from her father, see Green, *Lives of the Princesses*, ii, p. 354.

5 For the Earl of Atholl's execution, see Prestwich, *Edward I*, p. 508.

6 For the weavers' revolt, see Green, *Lives of the Princesses*, ii, p. 397.

7 For the capture and subsequent treatment of the Scottish ladies, see Johnstone, *Edward of Carnarvon*, pp. 114–5; Prestwich, *Edward I*, pp. 508–9.

8 For the women's period of residency at Winchester, see Green, *Lives of the Princesses*, iii, p. 48. For Joanna of Bar's travel to England to marry and the king's efforts to secure her brother's future, see *Calendar of Patent Rolls, 1301–7*, p. 386; *Calendar of Close Rolls, 1302–7*, pp. 321, 436–7, 443–4.

9 For the king's grants and gifts to Eleanor de Clare, see Green, *Lives of the Princesses*, ii, p. 353 n6; *Calendar of Close Rolls, 1302–7*, p. 443.

10 For Marguerite's delivery date, and her presence at the Feast of the Swans three weeks later, see John Carmi Parsons, 'Margaret [Margaret of France]', *Oxford Dictionary of National Biography*. For the attendance of Joanna's children at the Feast, see Green, *Lives of the Princesses*, ii, p. 353 n6. On the 1306 tax raised, see Prestwich, *Edward I*, pp. 529–30. For contemporary descriptions of the ceremony and its preparations, see Paris, *Flores Historiarum*, iii, pp. 131–2; see also the *Annales Londonienses* in *Chronicles of the Reigns of Edward I and Edward II*, ed. William Stubbs, (Kraus reprint, Nendeln, 1965), i, p. 146; *Chronicle of Langtoft*, pp. 368–9; *Chronicle of Walter of Guisborough*, pp. 367–8. See also Johnstone, *Edward of Carnarvon*, p. 108.

11 For a description of a knighting ceremony and its rituals, see Maurice Keen, *Chivalry* (New Haven, 1984), pp. 64–5.

12 For a list of some of the minstrels present, including Poveret, who sang at Joanna's first wedding sixteen years earlier, see Chambers, *The Mediaeval Stage*, Appendix D.

13 For Edward's grants to his children by Margaret, see *Calendar of Patent Rolls, 1302–7*, p. 460.

14 For Mary's pilgrimage, see Green, *Lives of the Princesses*, ii, pp. 426–7. For the capture of Lochmaben, see Johnstone, *Edward of Carnarvon*, p. 112.

XVII: DEATH RETURNS

1 For Edward's final illness, see Prestwich, *Edward I*, p. 556. On the desertion of men including Humphrey de Bohun, see *Calendar of*

Fine Rolls, 1272–1307, pp. 543–4; Johnstone, *Edward of Carnarvon*, pp. 115–6. For Marguerite's intercession on the deserters' behalf, see *Calendar of Close Rolls, 1302–7*, pp. 481–2. The king's frustration at the slow pace of progress is recorded, ibid, p. 524.

2 Guisborough's account of the king's anger at his son can be found in *Chronicle of Walter of Guisborough*, pp. 382–3. Gaveston's payoff is recorded in *Foedera*, i, p. 1010.

3 For notice of Joanna's death, see Paris, *Flores Historiarum*, iii, p. 329. For the date, see the calendar of the Alphonso Psalter, BL MS Add 24686, f. 6v. The minstrel she sent to Cumbria is noted in the account of the king's Treasurer for 1306–7, preserved as British Library Additional MS 22923, f. 14v. Joanna and Ralph's search for additional funds can be seen in *Calendar of Close Rolls, 1302–7*, pp. 495–6.

4 The king's orders on behalf of Joanna's soul are recorded in *Foedera*, i, pp. 1013, 1016. See also Green, *Lives of the Princesses*, ii, p. 355.

5 For Joanna's burial at Stoke Clare, see Dugdale, *Monasticon Anglicanum*, vi, pp. 1599–1600.

6 For Edward's order to send men from Glamorgan to fight in Scotland, see *Calendar of Patent Rolls, 1301–7*, p. 526.

7 For Edward's grant of manors from the Clare estate to Mary, see ibid, p. 530. See for the grant to Ralph, ibid, p. 534.

8 For an account of Mary and Marguerite's journey, see Green, *Lives of the Princesses*, ii, p. 430.

XVIII. ANOTHER CORONATION

1 For the installation of Gaveston as Regent see *Foedera, conventiones, literæ, et cujuscunque generis acta publica*, 3rd edn (London, 1744) i, pt 4, p. 106.

2 For Edward's efforts to help secure Elizabeth's dower, and the reconfirmation of both her and Mary's lands, see ibid, pp. 95, 97, 99. For the tournament at Wallingford, see *Vita Edwardi Secundi: The Life of Edward the Second*, ed. Wendy R. Childs (Oxford, 2005), pp. 6–7.

3 For Margaret and Edward's renewed relationship, see Green, *Lives of the Princesses*, ii, p. 395.

4 For the list of those women summoned to welcome Isabella at Dover, see *Foedera*, 3rd edn, i, pt 4, p. 110.

5 A contemporary account of nobles' reaction to Piers' investment as Regent can be found in *Vita Edwardi Secundi*, ed. Childs, pp. 8–9.

6 For a contemporary account of the coronation, see *Annales Paulini* in *Chronicles of the Reigns of Edward I and Edward II*, i, ed. Stubbs, i, pp. 258–62; see also *Foedera*, i pt 2, 3rd edn, p. 92.

7   The quotation can be found in Paris, *Flores Historiarum*, iii, p. 229. On the centrality of clothing to medieval ritual performance, see Gilchrist, *Medieval Life*, Chapter 3.

8   For Gaveston's nicknaming of Gilbert de Clare, see *Chronicles of the Mayor and Sheriffs of London, A.D. 1188 to A.D. 1274*, ed. Henry Thomas Riley (London 1863), p. 250 and nl. Some of the other insulting nicknames bestowed on noblemen by Piers Gaveston are recorded in *Historia Anglicana*, ed. Henry Thomas Riley, 2 vols, (Kraus reprint, Wiesbaden, 1965), i, 115. For the increasing resistance to Piers, see *Gesta Edwardi de Carnarvan auctore canonico Bridlingtoniensi* in *Chronicles of the Reigns of Edward I and Edward II*, ii, ed. William Stubbs (Kraus reprint, Wiesbaden, 1965), p. 33.

9   The songs are preserved in Cambridge University Library MS Gg.1.1 f. 489; and in a miscellany of secular and religious lyrics (the 'Harley Lyrics') preserved in British Library Harley MS 2253, f. 73. For the cleric's view, see ed. F.C. Hingeston-Randolph, *The Register of Walter de Stapledon, Bishop of Exeter 1307–1326* (London, 1892), pp. 11–2.

EPILOGUE

1   For Mary's time at Swainston, see Green, *Lives of the Princesses*, ii, p. 433.

2   For the ongoing relationship between Elizabeth and Marguerite, see the terms agreeing the wedding of Margaret de Bohun and Hugh de Courtenay, heir to the Earl of Devon, in which the dowager queen was named first among the party: *Women of the English Nobility and Gentry*, ed. Ward, pp. 29–30. The reuse of names – as in Elizabeth's second Humphrey and second Margaret – after the infant deaths of children was a common practice in medieval England. The births of her sons and some of her daughters are recorded in manuscripts associated with Walden Abbey, transcribed in Dugdale, *Monasticon Anglicanum*, iv, 139–40.

Select Bibliography

MANUSCRIPT AND ARCHIVAL SOURCES

British Library:
  Additional MS 7965
  Additional MS 7966
  Additional MS 22923
  Additional MS 24686
  Additional MS 35291
  Additional MS 36762
  Arundel MS 56
  Cotton Nero C. v.
  Cotton Vespasian B XI
  Harley MS 2253
Cambridge Fitzwilliam Museum MS McClean 123
Cambridge University Library:
  Ee.3.59
  Gg.1.1
National Archives:
  Special Collections 1/30/3
  Special Collections 6/1247/25
  E 101/350/18

PRINTED PRIMARY SOURCES

Annales Londoniensis, contained within *Chronicles of the Reigns of Edward I and Edward II,*
ed. William Stubbs (Kraus reprint, Nendeln, 1965).
Annales Paulini, contained within *Chronicles of the Reigns of Edward I and Edward II*, ed. William Stubbs, i (Kraus reprint, Nendeln, 1965).
'Annals of Dunstable Priory', contained within *Annales Monastici*, ed. H.R. Luard, iii (Kraus reprint, Nendeln, 1972).
'Annals of the Monastery of Osney', contained within *Annales Monastici*, ed. H.R. Luard, iv (Kraus reprint, Wiesbaden, 1965).
'Annals of Waverley', contained within *Annales Monastici*, ed. H.R. Luard, ii (Kraus reprint, Nendeln, 1971).

'Annals of Winchester', contained within *Annales Monastici*, ed. H.R. Luard, ii (Kraus reprint, Nendeln, 1971).

'Annals of the Priory of Worcester', contained within *Annales Monastici*, ed. H.R. Luard, iv (Kraus reprint, Wiesbaden, 1965).

Byerly, Benjamin F. and Catherine Ridder Byerly eds., *Records of the Wardrobe and Household, 1285–6* (London, 1977–86).

Calendar of Close Rolls

Calendar of Fine Rolls

Calendar of Inquisitions Post Mortem

Calendar of Patent Rolls

Chrétien de Troyes, *Yvain, or The Knight with the Lion*, trans. Ruth Harwood Cline (Athens, GA, 1975).

Cotton, Bartholomew, *Historia Anglia*, ed. H.R. Luard (London, 1859).

Croniques de London: depuis l'an 44 Hen. III jusqu'à l'an Edw. III, ed. G.J. Aungier (London, 1844).

Edward of Caernarfon, *Letters of Edward Prince of Wales, 1304–1305*, ed. H. Johnstone (Cambridge, 1931).

Froissart, Jean, *Chroniques*, 4 vols (Paris, 1869–1966).

Gesta Edwardi de Carnarvan auctore canonico Bridlingtoniensi, contained within *Chronica Monasterii S. Albani*, ed. Henry Thomas Riley, ii (Kraus reprint, Wiesbaden, 1965).

Girart d'Amiens, *Der roman von Escanor, von Gerard von Amiens*, ed. Henri Victor Michelant (Tübingen, 1886).

Grandes Chroniques de France: selon que elles sont conservées en l'Eglise de Saint-Denis de France, ed. M. Paulin Paris (Paris, 1836–8).

Grosseteste, Robert, *Robert Grosseteste's Chasteau d'Amour: to which are added La Vie de Sainte Maire egyptienne and an English version of the Chasteau d'Amour*, ed. M.Cooke (London, 1852).

Higden, Ranulf, *Polychronicon Ranulphi Higden, monachi Cestrensis*, ed. J.R. Lumby, 9 vols (Kraus reprint, Wiesbaden, 1964).

Hingeston-Randolph, F.C., ed., *The Register of Walter de Stapledon, Bishop of Exeter 1307–1326* (London, 1892).

Johnstone, Hilda, 'Wardrobe and Household of Henry, son of Edward I', *Bulletin of the John Rylands Library*, vii (1922–3).

Langtoft, Peter, *The Chronicle of Pierre de Langtoft, in French verse, from the earliest period to the death of Edward I*, ed. Thomas Wright, 2 vols (Kraus reprint, Wiesbaden, 1964).

List of ancient correspondence of the Chancery and Exchequer.

Lorris, Guillaume de, and Jean de Meun, *The Romance of the Rose*, trans. and ed. Frances Horgan (Oxford, 1994).

Matthaeus, Antonius, ed., *Veteris aevi analecta, seu, Vetera monumenta hactenus nondum visa . . .*, 2nd edn, 5 vols (Hagæ-Comitum, 1738).

Matthew Paris, *Matthæi Parisiensis, monachi Sancti Albani, Chronica Majora*, ed. H.R. Luard, 7 vols (Kraus reprint, Wiesbaden, 1964).

—, *Flores Historiarum*, ed. H.R. Luard (Kraus reprint, Nendeln, 1965).

Opus Chronicorum, contained within *Chronica Monasterii S. Albani*, ed. Henry Thomas Riley, iii (Kraus reprint, Nendeln, 1972).

The Parlement of the Three Ages, ed. M. Offord (London, 1967).

Parsons, John Carmi, *The Court and Household of Eleanor of Castile in 1290: An Edition of British Library Additional Manuscript 35294 with Introduction and Notes* (Toronto, 1977).

Peckham, John, *Registrum Epistolarum Fratris Johannis Peckham* (Kraus reprint, Nendeln, 1965).

Pisan, Christine, *The Treasure of the City of Ladies, or the Book of the Three Virtues*, ed. Sarah Lawson (Harmondsworth, 1985).

Rishanger, William, *Chronica et Annales*, contained within *Chronica Monasterii S. Albani*, ed.Henry Thomas Riley, ii (Kraus reprint, Millwood, NY, 1983).

Rymer, Thomas, ed., *Foedera, conventiones, literæ, et cujuscunque generis acta publica*, 3rd edn (London, 1744).

—, *Fœdera, conventiones, litteræ et cujuscunque generis Acta Publica* (repr. London, 1816).

Trivet, Nicholas, *Annales sex regum Angliae, qui a comitibus Andegavensibus originem traxerunt, 1136-1307* (London, 1845).

Vincent of Beauvais, *De Eruditione Filiorum Nobiliorum*, ed. A. Steiner (Cambridge, MA, 1938).

Vita Edwardi Secundi: The Life of Edward the Second, ed. Wendy R. Childs (Oxford, 2005).

Von Strassburg, Gottfried, *Tristan*, ed. A.T. Hatto (London, 2004).

Vossius, Matthaeus, *Annales Hollandiae Zelandiaeque . . .* (Amsterdam, 1680).

Walsingham, Thomas, *Historia Anglicana*, contained within *Chronica Monasterii S. Albani*, ed. Henry Thomas Riley, 2 vols (Kraus reprint, Wiesbaden, 1965).

Walter of Guisborough, *The Chronicle of Walter of Guisborough*, ed. H. Rothwell (London, 1957).

Wykes, Thomas, *The Chronicle of Thomas Wykes*, contained within *Annales Monastici*, ed. H.R. Luard, iv (Kraus reprint, Wiesbaden, 1965)

SECONDARY SOURCES

Adams, Jenny, and Nancy M. Bradbury, ed., *Medieval Women and Their Objects* (Ann Arbor, 2017).

Select Bibliography

Alexander, Jonathan, and Paul Binski, ed., *Age of Chivalry: Art in Plantagenet England, 1200-1400* (London, 1987).

Altschul, Michael, *A Baronial Family in Medieval England: The Clares, 1271–1314* (Baltimore, 1965).

Biddle, Martin, *King Arthur's Round Table: An Archaeological Investigation* (Woodbridge, 2000).

Binski, Paul, *The Painted Chamber at Westminster* (London, 1986).

—, *Westminster Abbey and the Plantagenets: Kingship and the Representation of Power, 1200–1400* (New Haven, 1995).

The Biographical Dictionary; Or, Complete Historic Library: Containing the Lives of the Most Celebrated Personages of Great Britain and Ireland, Whether Admirals, Generals, Poets, Statesmen, Philosophers, Or Divines (London, 1780).

Boucher's glossary of archaic and provincial words: a supplement to the dictionaries of the English language, particularly those of Dr. Johnson and Dr. Webster, ed. Joseph Hunter and Joseph Stevenson (London, 1832–3).

Bowie, Collette, *The Daughters of Henry II and Eleanor of Aquitaine* (Turnhout, 2014).

Brayley, W.E., ed., *The History and Antiquities of the Abbey Church of St Peter: Westminster* (London, 1818–23).

Brooke, Christopher N.L., *The Medieval Idea of Marriage* (Oxford, 1989).

Brown, Andrew D., *Popular Piety in Late Medieval England: the Diocese of Salisbury, 1250–1550* (Oxford, 1995).

Butkens, F. Christophe, *Trophées tant sacrés que profanes du duché de Brabant*, 4 vols (The Hague, 1724).

Bynum, Caroline Walker, *Holy Feast and Holy Fast: The Religious Significance of Food to Medieval Women* (London, 1988).

Carpenter, Jennifer, and Sally Beth Maclean, ed., *Power of the Weak: Studies on Medieval Women* (Urbana, 1995).

Cerisier, Antoine-Marie, *Tableau de l'histoire general des province-unies* (Utrecht, 1777–84).

Chambers, E.K., *The Mediaeval Stage* (Oxford, 1903).

Clanchy, M.T., *From Memory to Written Record: England, 1066-1307* (London, 1987).

Cockayne, G.E.C., *The Complete Peerage of England, Scotland, Ireland, Great Britain, and the United Kingdom* (London, 1887–9).

Cockerill, Sara, *Eleanor of Castile: The Shadow Queen* (Stroud, 2014).

Colton, Lisa, 'The Articulation of Virginity in the Medieval "Chanson de nonne"', *Journal of the Royal Musical Association*, 133, no. 2 (2008), pp. 159–88.

Colvin, H.M., gen. ed., *The History of the King's Works* (London, 1963–75).

Cook, J.H., *Medieval Chantries and Chantry Chapels* (London, 1963).

Coss, Peter, *The Knight in Medieval England 1000-1400* (Stroud, 1993).

—, *The Lady in Medieval England, 1000-1500* (Stroud, 1998).

Crane, Susan, *The Performance of Self: Ritual, Clothing, and Identity During the Hundred Years War* (Philadelphia, 2002).

Davies, R.R., *Lordship and Society in the March of Wales 1282–1400* (Oxford, 1978).

d'Avray, D.L., *Medieval Marriage: Symbolism and Society* (Oxford, 2005).

Donald, Moira and Linda Hurcombe, ed., *Gender and Material Culture in Historical Perspectives* (Basingstoke, 2000).

Dugdale, William, *The Baronage of England* . . . (London, 1676).

—, *Monasticon Anglicanum: a history of the abbies and other monasteries* . . . new edn (Farnborough, 1970).

Duggan, Anne J., ed., *Queens and Queenship in Medieval Europe* (Woodbridge, 1997).

Dyer, Christopher, *Everyday Life in Medieval England* (Hambledon, 1994).

Eales, R., and S. Tyas, ed., *Family and Dynasty in Late-Medieval England: Proceedings of the 1997 Harlaxton Symposium* (Donington, 2003).

Edwards, Owen, ed., 'The Dream of Maxen Wledig', in *Mabinogion Tales*, trans. Charlotte Guest (Llanerch, 1991), pp. 64–76.

Emery, Anthony, *Greater Medieval Houses of England and Wales, 1300–1500* (Cambridge, 1996–2000).

Erler, Mary, and Maryanne Kowaleski, *Women and Power in the Middle Ages* (Athens, GA, 1988).

Fritze, Ronald H., and William B. Robison, ed., *Historical Dictionary of Late Medieval England, 1272–1485* (Westport, CT, 2002).

Fryde, E.B., ed., *Book of Prests of the King's Wardrobe for 1294–5* (Oxford, 1962).

Gee, Loveday Lewis, *Women, Art and Patronage from Henry III to Edward III, 1216-1377* (Woodbridge, 2002).

Gilchrist, Roberta, *Gender and Material Culture: The Archaeology of Religious Women* (London, 1994).

—, *Medieval Life: Archaeology and the Life Course* (Cambridge, 2013).

Given-Wilson, Chris, *The English Nobility in the Late Middle Ages* (London, 1987).

Goldberg, P.J.P, ed., *Woman is a Worthy Wight: Women in English Society c.1200–1500* (Stroud, 1992).

Green, M.A.E., *Lives of the Princesses of England, from the Norman Conquest* (London, 1850-7), 6 vols.

Haskell, Francis, *History and its Images: Art and the Interpretation of the Past*, 3rd edn (New Haven, 1995).

Hatton, David, *Clare, Suffolk, an account of historical features of the town, its Priory and its Parish Church* (Clare, 1994).

Hilton, Lisa, *Queens Consort: England's Medieval Queens* (London, 2008).

Howell, Margaret, *Eleanor of Provence: Queenship in Thirteenth-century England* (Oxford, 2001).

Hunter, J., 'On the Death of Eleanor of Castile, Consort of King Edward the First, and the Honours paid to her Memory', *Archaeologia* 29 (1842), pp. 167–91.

Johnstone, Hilda, *Edward of Carnarvon, 1284–1307* (Manchester, 1946).

Kantorowicz, Ernst H., *The King's Two Bodies: A Study in Mediaeval Political Theology* (Princeton, 1997).

Keen, Maurice, *Chivalry* (New Haven, 1984).

Lewis, Katherine J., Nöel James Menuge and Kim Phelps, ed., *Young Medieval Women* (Stroud, 1999).

Leyser, Henrietta, *Medieval Women: A Social History of Women in England 450–1500* (London, 1995).

Lodge, John, *The Peerage of Ireland* (Dublin, 1754).

Loomis, Roger Sherman, 'Edward I, Arthurian enthusiast', *Speculum*, 28 (1953) pp. 114–27.

Lyon, Bryce and Mary, 'The Logistics for Edward I's ill-fated campaign in Flanders (1297–8)', in *Handelingen der Maatschappij voor Geschiedenis en Oudheidkunde te Gent*, 55 (2001), pp. 77–92.

Lyon, Bryce, 'The Failed Flemish Campaign of Edward I in 1297: A case study of efficient logistics and inadequate military spending', in *Handelingen der Maatschappij voor Geschiedenis en Oudheidkunde te Gent*, 59 (2005), pp. 31–42.

Lyons, Samuel, 'Copies of Writs Preserved among His Majesty's Records in the Tower . . .', *Archaeologia*, xv (1806), pp. 347–9.

Marx, C. William, *The Devil's Rights and the Redemption in the Literature of Medieval England* (Cambridge, 1995).

Mate, Mavis E., *Women in Medieval English Society* (Cambridge, 1999).

McCash, June Hall, ed., *The Cultural Patronage of Medieval Women* (Athens, GA, 1996).

McFarlane, K.B., *The Nobility of Later Medieval England: The Ford Lectures for 1953 and related studies* (Oxford, 1973).

Mirrer, Louise, ed., *Upon My Husband's Death: Widows in the Literature and Histories of Medieval Europe* (Ann Arbor, 1992).

Mitchell, Linda E., *Portraits of Medieval Women: Family, Marriage, and Politics in England 1225–1350* (New York, 2003).

Moor, C., *Knights of Edward I*, 5 vols (London, 1929–32).

Morris, John E., *The Welsh Wars of Edward I: a contribution to mediaeval military history, based on original documents* (Oxford, 1901).

Morris, Marc, *A Great and Terrible King: Edward I and the Forging of Britain* (London, 2008).

Morris, R.K., and R. Shoesmith, *Tewkesbury Abbey: History, Art and Architecture* (Almeley, 2003).

Neal, David, 'Excavations at the Palace of Kings Langley, Hertfordshire 1974–1976', *Medieval Archaeology* (1977), pp. 125–65.

Nichols, Madaline W., 'Las Siete Partidas', *California Law Review*, vol 20.3 (1992), pp. 260–85.

Nicolas, Nicholas Harris, ed., *The Siege of Carlaverock* (London, 1828).

Oliva, Marilyn, *The Convent and the Community in Late Medieval England: Female Monasteries in the Diocese of Norwich, 1350–1540* (Woodbridge, 1998).

Orme, Nicholas, *From Childhood to Chivalry: The education of English kings and aristocracy 1066–1530* (London, 1984).

Ormrod, W.M., ed., *England in the Thirteenth Century: Proceedings of the 1984 Harlaxton Symposium* (Woodbridge, 1985).

Oxford Dictionary of National Biography.

Parsons, John Carmi, 'The Year of Eleanor of Castile's Birth and Her Children by Edward I', *Mediaeval Studies* 46 (1984), pp. 245–65.

—, ed., *Medieval Queenship* (Stroud, 1994).

—, *Eleanor of Castile: Queen and Society in Thirteenth-Century England* (London, 1995).

Perkins, J., *Westminster Abbey, its Worship and Ornaments* (London, 1938–52).

Philips, Kim, *Medieval Maidens: Young Women and Gender in England, c.1270–c.1540* (Manchester, 2003).

Pollock, Frederick, and Frederic William Maitland, *The history of English law before the time of Edward I* (Cambridge, 1895).

Powel, David, *The historie of Cambria, now called Wales* . . . , trans. H. Lloyd (London, 1584).

Power, Eileen, *Medieval English Nunneries, c.1275–1535* (Cambridge, 1922).

—, *Medieval Women*, ed. M.M. Postan (Cambridge, 1975).

Prestwich, Michael, *Edward I* (London, 1988).

Pugh, R.B., and Elizabeth Crittall, eds., *A History of Wiltshire* (London, 1957–2011).

Renn, D.F., *Norman Castles in Britain*, 2nd edn (London, 1973).

Richardson, H.G., 'The Coronation of Edward I', *Bulletin of the Institute for Historical Research*, xv (1937–8).

Roffey, Simon, *The Medieval Chantry Chapel: An Archaeology* (Woodbridge, 2007).

Rogers, Nicholas, ed., *England in the Fourteenth Century: Proceedings of the 1991 Harlaxton Symposium* (Stamford, 1993).

Saul, Nigel, *For Honour and Fame: Chivalry in England, 1066–1500* (London, 2011).

Scott, Margaret, *A Visual History of Costume: The Fourteenth & Fifteenth Centuries* (London, 1986).

Shahar, Shulamith, *Childhood in the Middle Ages* (London, 1992).

Sherborne, J.W., and V.J. Scattergood, *English Court Culture of the Later Middle Ages* (London, 1983).

Skinner, Patricia, and Elisabeth van Houts, ed., *Medieval Writings on Secular Women* (London, 2011).

Staniland, K., 'Welcome, Royal Babe! The Birth of Thomas of Brotherton in 1300', *Costume* (1985), pp. 1–13.

Stow, John, and John Strype, *A Survey of the Cities of London and Westminster: containing the original, antiquity, increase, modern estate and government of those cities . . . in six books* (London, 1720).

Strickland, Agnes, *Lives of the Queens of England from the Norman Conquest*, 12 vols (London, 1841).

Topham, John, *Liber quotidianus contrarotulatoris garderobae. Anno regni regis Edwardi primi vicesimo octavo* (London, 1787).

Underhill, Frances A., *For Her Good Estate: The life of Elizabeth de Burgh* (Basingstoke, 1999).

Wagner, Anthony, *Heralds and Heraldry in the Middle Ages: An Inquiry into the Growth of the Armorial Function of Heralds* (London, 1939).

Ward, Jennifer C., *English Noblewomen in the Later Middle Ages* (London, 1992).

—, ed., *Women of the English Nobility and Gentry: 1066–1500* (Manchester, 1995).

Warner, Marina, *Alone of All Her Sex: The Myth and the Cult of the Virgin Mary* (London, 1976).

Wauters, Alphonse, *Le duc Jean Ier et le Brabant sous le règne de ce prince (1267–1294)* (Brussels, 1862).

Westerhof, Danielle, *Death and the Noble Body in Medieval England* (Woodbridge, 2008).

Wogan-Browne, Jocelyn, 'Saints' lives and the female reader', *Forum for Modern Language Studies*, 27 (1991), pp. 314–32.

Woolgar, C.M., *The Great Household in Medieval England* (New Haven, 1999).

—, D. Serjeantson and T. Waldron, ed., *Food in medieval England: diet and nutrition* (Oxford, 2006).

Index